ENGLISH HERITAGE

ENGLISH HERITAGE

Lord Montagu of Beaulieu

Edited by P.H. Reed

WITH PHOTOGRAPHS BY

JORGE LEWINSKI
& MAYOTTE MAGNUS

English # Heritage

Macdonald
Queen Anne Press

A *Queen Anne Press* BOOK

First published in Great Britain in 1987 by
Queen Anne Press, a division of
Macdonald & Co (Publishers) Ltd
3rd Floor
Greater London House
Hampstead Road
London NW1 7QX

A BPCC plc Company

Title page: Dunstanburgh Castle, Northumberland

Maps by Ellen Moorcraft
Aerial photography by Aerofilms
Photographs of Eynsford Castle and Old Sarum by courtesy of English Heritage
Glossary illustrations by Annie Owen

British Library Cataloguing in Publication Data

English Heritage
    English heritage.
    1. Historic buildings——England——Guide-
    books.   2. England——Description and
    travel——1971- ——Guide-books
    I. Title   II. Montagu of Beaulieu, Edward
    Douglas-Scott-Montagu, *Baron*   III. Reed,
    Patricia Harbottle
    914.2'04858   DA660

    ISBN 0-356-12773-7

Typeset by Leaper & Gard Ltd, Bristol
Printed and bound in Spain

CONTENTS

INTRODUCTION
A FUTURE FOR OUR PAST

The Work of
English Heritage

In 1984 the Government created a new body to care for England's great inheritance of historic buildings and ancient monuments. It is aptly named English Heritage. It assumed the responsibilities acquired by successive bodies since 1882, when the Act for the Better Protection of Ancient Monuments first acknowledged the nation's duty to preserve the best of our man–made environment as a historical record for the future.

The tasks of English Heritage are wide ranging. They include the scheduling of ancient monuments, listing of buildings and registration of gardens, so that historic properties are legally protected from alteration or demolition. We give grant aid to historic properties, whether owned by a Local Authority, the National Trust or privately, enabling them to maintain and preserve their buildings. Funds are provided for rescue archaeology, so that crucial excavations can take place before roads or buildings are developed on historically important sites. Faced with the various threats of urban development, modern farming and road building, our job is to ensure that alteration, demolition, or, perhaps more pernicious gradual abuse, are identified and curbed.

This book, however, is concerned with the best-known aspect of the work of English Heritage. We are directly responsible for the maintenance, the public opening and display of nearly 400 properties. They include some of England's most famous historic sites — Stonehenge, Hadrian's Wall, Dover Castle, Rievaulx Abbey, and Osborne House, to name a few. Others are less well known, but often no less fascinating; they range in time from prehistoric burial chambers and Roman forts, through medieval castles, abbeys and coastal fortifications, to historic houses and gardens and industrial buildings. We are proud to have been entrusted with such treasures, and to share them with many thousands of visitors each year.

One of the specific tasks given to English Heritage was to improve the public's understanding and enjoyment of the properties in its care. To this end, we aim to publicise, present and interpret these properties, making them attractive, exciting and enlightening for visitors of all ages. This involves the erection of explanatory displays and exhibitions, the provision of amenities, the training of our staff and the selling of publications and souvenirs. Then there is the organisation of events, concerts and historical re-enactments, designed to put flesh on the bare bones of history.

The key element in our plan for involving every man, woman and child in our important work is the English Heritage Membership Scheme, which has already enrolled nearly 100,000 members. It provides free admission to all English Heritage properties, and also to some royal palaces such as the Tower of London and Hampton Court, as well as half-price entry to many monuments in Wales and Scotland. Members receive a comprehensive guidebook and map to all the properties in our care, a quarterly newsletter and privileged prices for certain publications and products. There is even a special section for junior members known as KEEP.

All members are encouraged to help in a variety of ways: by spreading the word and recruiting others; by promoting responsible public attitudes towards the preservation of our heritage; and, specifically, by offering local support to individual properties. Several sites now have a Friends Group who organise concerts and other events to help to bring our properties to life and to provide an added amenity for the neighbourhood. In short, membership of English Heritage provides an opportunity for everybody to make a valuable personal contribution to a worthwhile task.

English Heritage is still young, but our influence is increasing all the time. The built inheritance of England is a unique national asset, to be shared with

everyone but cared for by professionals for the benefit of future generations.

This book is a comprehensive record of all the properties in our care — almost 400 in all — from the lesser known sites to our most famous monument — Stonehenge in Wiltshire. I hope that these magnificent photographs and the exciting variety of the properties described will encourage you to visit the sites and monuments themselves and see at first hand our fascinating heritage.

ABOVE: The Little Drawing Room, Audley End, Essex

OPPOSITE: Uffington White Horse, Oxfordshire

NORTHUMBRIA

AND THE LAKES

Cleveland · Cumbria
Durham · Hadrian's Wall
Northumberland
Tyne and Wear

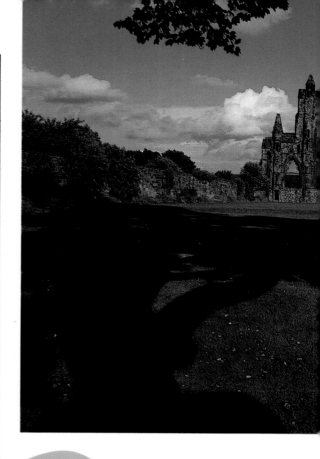

Berwick Castle
Berwick-on-Tweed
Berwick Ramparts
Berwick Barracks
Norham Castle
Lindisfarne Priory
Etal Castle

Heddon-on-the-Wall
Benwell Vallum Crossing
Benwell Roman Temple
Denton Hall Turret and West Denton

Dunstanburgh Castle

Edlingham Castle
Warkworth Castle and Hermitage
Brinkburn Priory

NORTHUMBERLAND

Black Middens Bastle House

Belsay Hall, Castle and Gardens
Aydon Castle
Newcastle-upon-Tyne
TYNE AND WEAR
Tynemouth Castle and Priory
Lanercost Priory
Prudhoe Castle
St Paul's Monastery
Hylton Castle

Carlisle Castle
Wetheral Priory Gatehouse
Finchale Priory

CUMBRIA
DURHAM

Penrith Castle
Auckland Castle Deer House
Mayburgh Earthwork
Brougham Castle
Arthur's Round Table
Countess Pillar
Guisborough Priory
Clifton Hall
Barnard Castle
Middlesbrough
CLEVELAND
Castlerigg Stone Circle
Bowes Castle
Piercebridge Roman Bridge
Shap Abbey
Egglestone Abbey
Brough Castle
Ravenglass Roman Bath House
Ambleside Roman Fort
Hardknott Roman Fort
Kendal
Stott Park Bobbin Mill

Furness Abbey
Bow Bridge
Barrow-in-Furness
Piel Castle

coincided with the Anglo-Scottish wars in which their founder's descendant played a major role. Later it recovered and at the Dissolution Guisborough was the fourth richest monastery in Yorkshire. The site was leased to one of the Royal Commissioners in charge of the Dissolution of the Monasteries, Dr Legh, and the buildings were systematically dismantled soon after. Dr Legh was careful to act according to the law, for it was one of the conditions of the sale or lease of former monastic property that the new owners demolish the church and major buildings within a fixed period of time, if the Commissioners had not already done so. Some new owners avoided this by converting the monastic buildings into dwellings, and it is often these that have come down to us. The parish church of St Nicholas contains the splendid Brus cenotaph, an early sixteenth-century chest tomb that formerly stood in the priory church.

OPPOSITE: Guisborough Priory

BELOW: Ambleside Roman Fort

Guisborough Priory

CLEVELAND

The east end of Guisborough Priory stands like a triumphal arch in the landscape, an outstanding example of Gothic architecture in the Decorated style. The priory was founded for Augustinian canons *c.* 1119 by Robert de Brus, the most powerful of the Norman barons in the north-east. He and his descendants were buried here, including Robert de Brus IV, father of the fourteenth-century Scottish King, Robert Bruce. The priory was a particularly well-endowed foundation. No sooner had the original buildings been completed in the twelfth century than it was decided to rebuild them; the little gatehouse to the north-east of the church dates from this rebuilding, begun late twelfth century. The work was almost complete in 1289 when disaster struck. A plumber was working on the south transept, soldering the cracks in the lead roof; his young assistants failed to douse the red-hot coals properly when they went for their meal, and a strong south wind ignited the roof beams. Molten lead poured down into the church which was largely destroyed. The west end that we see today was all that survived, and here traces of the fire can still be seen. Such were the resources of the priory however that a third building campaign commenced almost at once. The fourteenth century was a difficult period for the priory, for the rebuilding

Ambleside Roman Fort

CUMBRIA

Visible remains of the Roman fort of Galava are scanty. However, no one can deny the beauty of its position at the head of Lake Windermere, set between the trees and reeds that fringe the shore. This tranquil setting is in complete contrast with the dramatic location of *Hardknott*, the next fort defending the Roman road which ran from *Ravenglass* on the west coast via Ambleside to *Brough*. Excavations have revealed two forts at Ambleside. The first was of timber erected *c.* AD 90, which was rebuilt in stone on a slightly different site *c.* AD 120-30 and occupied well into the fourth century.

Arthur's Round Table
CUMBRIA

This mysteriously flat circular earthwork, 300 feet in diameter, is surrounded by a ditch. It is a Neolithic henge, a ceremonial site, and probably contained a timber or stone structure which has long since disappeared. There is only one entrance now on the south side, but in the seventeenth century a north entrance marked by two standing stones still existed. Arthur's Round Table stands rather prosaically at the junction of the A6 and the B6262, overshadowed by twentieth-century housing. There must be a connection between it and the far more attractively-sited henge at *Mayburgh*, a quarter of a mile to the west; but roads and later buildings have obscured it. Both date from 2000-1000 BC.

Brough Castle
CUMBRIA

The ruins of Brough Castle lie beside the Swindale Beck, a palimpsest of British history astride one of the great Prehistoric trade routes, connecting Ireland with North Europe via Carlisle and York. Known as the Stainmore Road, it crosses the Pennines via Brough, and the strategic importance of the site was quickly recognised by the Romans who built the fort of Verterae here. This fort provides part of the earthwork for the castle we see today, which stands in the northern third of the three-acre site. The plan comprises the keep set in the northwest angle of the fort (on the site of the Roman barracks), with the curtain walls following the line of the fort on the north side, returned for a short distance in the north-east corner, the circular south-east tower linked to the keep by a curtain wall pierced by remains of the gatehouse on this south front. The castle was begun by William Rufus soon after 1092 when Carlisle, Cumberland and Westmorland became part of Norman England. A little herringbone masonry survives from this period, but in 1172 the castle was destroyed by William the Lion of Scotland. Not long after it was recaptured by the English, and Henry II rebuilt the castle which he gave to Roger de Vipont, ancestor of the great Northern family of Clifford. Henry's keep largely survives, but later buildings were destroyed by fire at Christmas, 1521. The castle was in ruins until rebuilt by the redoubtable Anne,

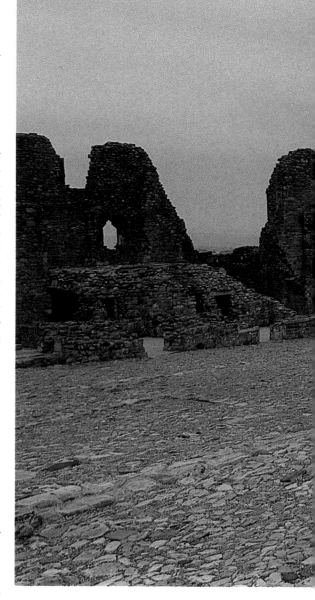

Countess of Clifford 1659-62. 'The repairer of the breach, the restorer of paths to dwell in,' as she described herself in the words of Isaiah. The southeast tower remains from her period, set on the foundations of the *c.*1300 tower, and known as the Clifford Tower. Unfortunately it was only a few years before the castle was again burnt out, and in the eighteenth century its owners stripped it for building materials.

Brougham:
Countess Pillar
CUMBRIA

This unusal little monument is a charming idea. It was erected by Anne, Countess of Clifford, in 1656 to commemorate the last time that she saw her

Arthur's Round Table

mother, some forty years before. Lady Anne was born in 1590 and it might generally be said that until she was about fifty, everything seemed to go wrong for her. However, in the last forty years of her life matters were transformed. She gained the estates that were rightfully hers and set about restoring her castles with such energy that even Cromwell felt it best to leave her alone. Needless to say she was devoted to her mother and was also inordinately proud of her family connections. It was through her father, George Clifford, Earl of Cumberland, that she finally inherited the Clifford estates. One of Queen Elizabeth's favourite courtiers, he was a man of great charm and courage whose many interests did not include family life. As well as restoring six castles and at least one church, his daughter erected a monument to the poet Spenser in Westminster Abbey and wrote her autobiography — a modern edition of which has been edited by Vita Sackville-West. Lady Anne lies buried at Appleby beside the splendid tomb that she erected for her mother; her own has no effigy but displays a family tree of twenty-four shields.

Brougham Castle
CUMBRIA

On the south banks of the River Eamont lie the remains of Brougham Castle, one of those restored by Anne, Countess of Clifford. The castle was begun in the early thirteenth century by Roger de Vipont who erected the keep. In the following century his descendants, the Cliffords, added the curtain walls, rebuilt the Tower of the League and added a first floor hall and chapel. Lady Anne restored the castle and died here in 1676. She spent her old age living in feudal splendour as accompanied by a small court, she travelled around her various castles, spending some time at each. A housekeeper looked after Brougham when the castle was unoccupied and it is known that two shillings and sixpence a week board wages were paid, with threepence a week for the housekeeper's cat. (Cats had to earn their living in those days.) The Countess's descendants preferred a more sedentary life and they resided at Appleby, partly demolishing Brougham in 1691 for building materials. The castle has a small display of tombstones from the cemetery of the Roman fort of Brocavum (not in the care of English Heritage), the remains of which lie to the south-east of the castle. The fort guarded the river crossing on the important road from Carlisle to the south.

ABOVE: Brougham Castle

RIGHT: Carlisle Castle,
prisoners' carvings in the keep

Castlerigg Stone Circle

Carlisle Castle

CUMBRIA

Carlisle Castle, begun in 1092 by William Rufus, has been the scene of many sieges and skirmishes and has frequently changed hands, most recently in 1745 when it was taken by Bonnie Prince Charlie and then, in quick succession, by the Hanoverians. It has a grim and forbidding appearance and still retains a military presence — a museum of the Kings Own Royal Border Regiment. The outer bailey contains nineteenth-century and twentieth-century barracks and buildings. Thus the castle has frequently been remodelled and in the nineteenth century much was demolished. The main features surviving today are the inner and outer gatehouses and curtain walls enclosing the inner and outer baileys, and the keep. The latter is twelfth century, the upper storey altered in the sixteenth century to take artillery — hence the solid embrasures which give it rather a squat appearance. The Elizabethan buttresses on the north side of the inner bailey curtain wall are very impressive, however. It was to Carlisle that the 28-year-old Mary Queen of Scots fled in May 1568, after her defeat at the Battle of Langside. Her refuge at Carlisle turned out to be a prison, and after a couple of months she began her series of journeyings further south which were to end on the scaffold in 1586. The rooms where she lodged were destroyed in the nineteenth century but there is evidence of the many other prisoners who have been confined here in the form of a fascinating collection of wall carvings, or graffiti.

Carlisle Castle

Castlerigg Stone Circle

CUMBRIA

This may be one of the earliest stone circles Britain, and it certainly has one of the most beautiful settings. Of the thirty-eight stones all but five are still standing, enclosing an area 110 feet in diameter. Inside the circle is an unexplained rectangle of stones, not found in any other stone circle. Castlerigg was probably erected c.2000 BC, at the beginning of a period in the Neolithic age which was distinguished by the building of many ceremonial sites such as henges, stone circles and stone avenues. We can only guess at their functions.

Clifton Hall

CUMBRIA

The dour remains of a tower of *c.*1500 survive at the north end of Clifton village beside the A6. This inhospitable stone structure was one of the latest parts of a larger complex of buildings, to which it was linked by the three doorways to be seen at ground floor level. It was designed to be quickly and easily defensible, a necessity in this troubled area. Here only the floor joists remain inside, visible from a viewing platform on the first floor. Clifton can claim to be the site of the last battle fought on English soil. In 1745 Bonnie Prince Charlie and his army had penetrated as far south into England as Manchester and Derby, but had failed to find the support anticipated. As winter drew on they retired north, with the Duke of Cumberland in pursuit. At Clifton an advance guard of Cumberland's Dragoons encountered a group of Highlanders and fierce skirmishes took place. Cumberland's forces were effectively checked and the Scots withdrew across the border. The following year saw their victory at Falkirk, followed by disaster at Culloden.

Furness Abbey

CUMBRIA

RIGHT: Clifton Hall

ABOVE RIGHT: Furness Abbey, the chapter house

OPPOSITE: Furness Abbey from the south

The warm and mellow local sandstone, the beauty of the landscape and the happy survival of much of this wealthy abbey, makes Furness one of the finest monastic sites in England. The abbey was founded for the Savignac order *c.*1123 by Stephen, later King of England, and it was very well endowed. Not only did the abbey own the rich agricultural land of the Furness peninsula but it also had coal and iron deposits, and in the sixteenth century coal was being used as fuel at the abbey. This wealth is reflected in the quality of the buildings and their continual enlargement and rebuilding. The Savignacs had joined the Cistercian order in 1147 and at the Dissolution, Furness was the second richest house of that order after Fountains. The transepts and quire of the abby church stand almost to full height and the presbytery contains a very fine fifteenth-century canopied four-seat sedilia with piscina and towel recess included. The west tower of *c.*1500 was built after unsuccessful attempts to build a crossing tower and it partly lies inside the nave. The cloister was a rectangle rather than the usual square and one of its finest features are five round-headed arches, the first and third forming book cupboard openings flanking the entrance to the chapter house. This aisled building has a vaulted vestibule and the rear wall stands almost to full height. The infirmary range beyond the dormitory rebuilt in the early fourteenth century is unusually large and has a vaulted chapel adjoining. Apart from caring for the sick and aged monks, monastic infirmaries also housed the monks who were undergoing the most common form of medieval preventive medicine, bloodletting. This was very popular and took place four times each year, entitling a monk to special food, exemption from arduous duties and a relaxation of the strict rules limiting conversation. The foundations of the interesting mid thirteenth-century octagonal kitchen stand close by.

Hardknott Roman Fort

CUMBRIA

A superb setting near the head of the steep and tortuous Eskdale Pass makes Hardknott one of the most dramatic Roman sites in Britain. There are stunning views down the valleys. The fort defences were partially rebuilt in the 1930s and the entire circuit of walls can be seen standing eight to ten feet high in places. Foundations of the headquarter's building with part of the granaries and commander's building can be seen. (The barracks and other buildings would have been of timber.) Remains of the bath house can be seen outside the fort to the south, while to the east the parade ground can be identified. This is the finest example in Britain and the creation of a large flat area in this terrain was no mean feat. Hardknott, or Mediobogdum, was founded in the reign of Hadrian and formed part of the chain of forts that culminated at *Ravenglass* on the Cumbrian coast. The fort was garrisoned by the 4th Cohort of Dalmations, from Yugoslavia, who must have felt quite at home in this mountainous terrain. Occupation probably did not last beyond the second century. Despite the waterlogged nature of the ground, Mediobogdum means 'in the middle of a bend' (of the River Esk). The road through the pass is very steep and narrow with hairpin bends, and extreme care should be exercised. The fort is about half a mile from the carpark.

ABOVE: Hardknott Roman Fort

RIGHT: Lanercost Priory, the tomb of Sir Thomas Dacre in the south transept

Lanercost Priory

CUMBRIA

Worship has continued in part of the priory church at Lanercost ever since the twelfth century, when Robert de Vaux founded a house for Augustinian canons here in the lovely valley of the River Irthing. The church was completed around 1220 and buildings were laid out around the cloister to the south. In the late thirteenth century and early fourteenth century the canons suffered much from the border warfare between England and Scotland. During the 1290s the claustral buildings were burnt out twice within three years by the Scots, and in 1306 Edward I was taken ill while staying here. He and his retinue had to be accommodated for nearly six months, which was a great strain on the priory's resources. The buildings where he stayed were converted into a dwelling at the time of the Dissolution by Sir Thomas Dacre, whose descendants continued to live here until the eighteenth century. The north aisle of the church remained in use as the parish church, and in the mid eighteenth century the nave was also reclaimed for parish worship. A wall was built at the crossing and some fine stained-glass windows designed by Burne-Jones for Morris and Co were later added. The imposing east end of the church rises to full height, though roofless, and it contains some interesting tombs of the Vaux and Dacre families. There is the massive sixteenth cen-

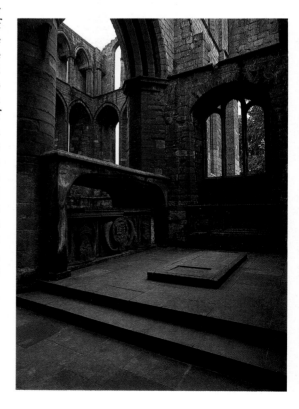

tury chest tomb of Sir Thomas Dacre, strongly carved with heraldic achievements, and a touching little nineteenth century monument with a life-size effigy of the infant Elizabeth Dacre Howard. Of the claustral buildings, the west range contains the ruins of the prior's house at the southern end, while the buildings nearer the church continue as a dwelling and are not accessible to the public. Adjoining at right angles are the remains of the refectory set over the cellarium where the priory's food and produce were stored. The cellarium, with its stone roof of ribbed vaults, is an impressive room that now houses a collection of carved stones recovered both from the priory and from nearby *Hadrian's Wall*. There is little to be seen of the refectory, or of the buildings that stood on the east side of the cloister. Although not in the care of English Heritage, the range of medieval buildings that flank the approach to the church contribute much to the beautiful setting of this fine building.

Mayburgh Earthwork

CUMBRIA

Mayburgh, with its single standing stone, is like a magic circle set beside the River Eamont. This circular earthwork, with banks eight to fifteen feet high, encloses a one-and-a-half acre site. In the eighteenth century two pairs of standing stones marked the entrance on the east side, facing towards *Arthur's Round Table*, while there were four other stones in the centre of the earthwork. This Neolithic henge dates from 2500–1700 BC.

ABOVE: the Priory church seen from the south-east
RIGHT: Mayburgh Earthwork, the standing stone

Penrith Castle

CUMBRIA

Set in a park on the edge of the town, opposite the railway station, are the red sandstone remains of Penrith Castle. The castle was begun *c.*1399 by William Strickland, later Bishop of Carlisle, who erected a large square castle with four ranges of buildings set around an open courtyard. It was altered in the 1470s by Richard, Duke of Glouces-ter, when he became Warden of the Western Marches. Towers projected to the east and north, the latter adjoining the gatehouse. The south wall is the best preserved, and the north-east tower stands, but all the interior walls have gone. After the Civil War the castle was largely dismantled by the Parlia-mentarians.

Piel Castle, Piel Island

CUMBRIA

Built by the abbot of *Furness Abbey*, Piel is a roman-tic ruin accessible only by boat. Also known as Pile of Foudray, Piel or Foudray Island guards the entrance to the bay at Barrow in Furness, which is formed by the 'island' of Walney to the west. The castle was built *c.*1327, on the site of earlier fortifi-cations, after the disastrous Scottish raids of 1316 and 1323, when the abbey lands on their fertile peninsula suffered severe damage. The castle is constructed of boulders from the beach with red sandstone dressings. The keep is square, divided internally into two rectangular blocks by a corridor that opens into the gatehouse on the north front. There is evidence of a spiral stair in the north-west corner and a chapel extension in the south-east. Some fireplaces remain and window openings can be seen in the eight foot thick walls. The east wall and the east ends of the north and south walls have disappeared. There are quite substantial remains of the inner bailey curtain walls and towers, while the outer bailey survives only to the north and west. Perhaps the most exciting event in the castle's history was when the pretender to the English throne, Lambert Simnel, landed here in 1487 with his army from Ireland, en route to their defeat at Stoke Field. Otherwise life has been peaceful. Piel Island is uninhabited, apart from a public house, and is accessible by ferry from Roa Island, linked to the mainland by a causeway.

Ravenglass Roman Bath House

CUMBRIA

The walls of the bath house at Ravenglass are remarkably well preserved and are among the most complete standing Roman remains in Britain. The bath house served the fort of Glannoventa which covered a three-and-a-half acre site to the south-west. Nothing can be seen of the fort now for the area is thickly wooded and bisected by the Furness railway line. It was built *c.*AD 130 to protect the Roman naval base here, and was occupied until *c.*AD 400. The bath house, as usual, stood outside the fort and owes its preservation to inclusion into a medieval building which has since disappeared. Known locally as Walls Castle, traces of coloured plaster remain on some of the bath house walls, whilst door and window openings can be identified. The site was excavated in the 1880s but the layout of the rooms has not been precisely determined.

OPPOSITE: Piel Castle

ABOVE: Penrith Castle looking north-west

BELOW: Ravenglass Roman Bath House

Shap Abbey

CUMBRIA

The Premonstratensian canons liked to build their monasteries in isolated locations, and Shap must surely be one of the most remote. Some years snow falls on Shap Fell in October and does not melt until June. However the site was already of importance in Prehistoric times. When first colonised in the late twelfth century it was known as Hepp, a heap, because of the remains of the Prehistoric avenue of stones nearby. Hepp became Hiap, and by 1300, Shap. (The Shap Stones were largely destroyed in the eighteenth century.) All the abbey's records have been lost so little is known of its history. The impressive west tower is the most important part of the abbey to survive; this was erected *c.*1500–10 after attempts to build a crossing tower had failed. Similar problems were encountered at *Furness*. The foundations of the church and the claustral buildings have been excavated and can easily be identified. One notable feature is the rare survival of processional circles marked out on the floor of the nave. In common with other monastic orders, the canons would walk in procession on Sundays and feast days around the abbey buildings. Organised by the precentor and his assistant the sub-cantor, they carried banners and sometimes holy relics, chanting as they walked, and sprinkled holy water in the buildings round the cloister and in the church. From the presbytery they moved along the transept, through the east door into the cloister. Then back through the west door from the cloister and into the nave where they stood in double file on the positions marked on the floor. At Shap there were eighteen places marked, ten of which have survived. Finally the canons filed

though the two doorways in the roodscreen and through the pulpitium, back into the quire. There were some variations between the orders. At Canterbury until the late eighteenth century, the positions were scratched on the floor, but these were lost when the floor was relaid, as happened in other churches. Of the claustral buildings at Shap, the east range is the best preserved. It appears to have been built as one large T-shaped room, divided by thin stone walls to form the sacristy, chapter house, parlour and warming house. It is a daunting thought that, according to the monastic rule, merely the infirmary and warming house were heated, the latter from September to Easter only.

Stott Park Bobbin Mill

CUMBRIA

Stott Park Bobbin Mill is great fun. It is unique among English Heritage properties in that it is a working industrial museum and visitors are shown around by past employees of the mill, which closed in 1971. Their enthusiasm for this little known industry is quite contagious. The forests of the Lake District with their ample supply of water power were the main ingredients for the bobbin-making industry which grew up in the late eighteenth century as a by-product of the industrial production of textiles. Stott Park was built in 1835 and it is typical of the many hundreds of mills in the area which have since disappeared. Cotton bobbins, wire bobbins, handles, toggles for duffel coats, spout bobbins for drain pipes, and a whole variety of wooden items that could be turned out on a lathe were mass produced. (All are items that are now

BELOW: Shap Abbey, the church tower seen from the site of the chapter house

BELOW RIGHT: Stott Park Bobbin Mill: the polishing barrels, the final stage in the bobbin-making process

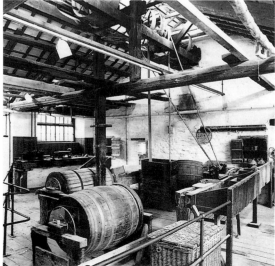

produced in plastic.) The transformation, carried out under one roof, of a tree trunk into the finished item ready for sale is fascinating, and visitors are shown the whole process. The original water wheel was replaced by turbines and then a steam engine in the late nineteenth century. In 1941 two electric motors were installed. Otherwise the mill continued to operate as it had done in the nineteenth century right down to the day it closed, for lathes are remarkably flexible pieces of machinery. When the market for one item collapsed, the cutting edges on the lathe were rearranged and a new item was created. The motto at Stott Park seemed to be, 'If you can make it in wood, we can make it on our lathes.' Standing ankle-deep in wood shavings and mesmerised by the continuous movement of the flapping belts slanting in all directions, the visitor is almost deafened by the noise — step back into the nineteenth century at Stott Park.

Wetheral Priory Gatehouse

CUMBRIA

The fifteenth-century gatehouse is all that remains of the Benedictine priory founded 1106-12 by Ranulph de Meschines. At the Dissolution the priory was sold, stripped of buildings materials, and left to decay. A farm now stands on the site of the cloisters. The gatehouse alone survived because it served as the vicarage for the parish church. The design is a simple rectangular block, crenellated with a tunnel-vaulted entrance; though larger than many gatehouses, being three storey instead of two. Possibly the janitor had a room here. It was his job to make sure that the gate was kept locked when it should be, for example during Chapter, for all monasteries were enclosed by high walls and access was only through the gates. Wetheral had the distinction of being one of the few places where a criminal could claim the right of sanctuary for crimes committed outside the bounds of the priory. This privilege was conferred by Henry I soon after the priory was founded. It is not known how many people took advantage of this, nor how it affected the life of the priory. There must have been a fair number of 'grithmen' as they were known, for in 1342 Edward III offered a free pardon to all criminals who had obtained 'grith', or peace, at Wetheral, Beverley, Ripon and Tynemouth, on condition that they would go out and fight the Scots. In theory any church was a place of sanctuary, but it depended on custom and chance, or Divine Providence, whether

the pursuers recognised it as such. Lord Lovell, for instance, successfully claimed sanctuary at Colchester after the Battle of Bosworth. In the parish church there are inscriptions to the last two priors at Wetheral, and the church also contains a life-size monument by Nollekens to Lady Maria Howard, who died at the age of twenty-three in 1789. She reclines, supported by a draped figure representing Religion, her lifeless infant in her lap.

Wetheral Priory Gatehouse

Auckland Castle Deer House

DURHAM

This charming building was erected in the 1760s at the behest of the Bishop of Durham, so that the deer in his parkland at Bishop Auckland would have somewhere to shelter and obtain food in cold weather. There was also a room for 'deer viewing', provided in the little tower. The design was probably supplied by the amateur architect Sir Thomas Robinson of Rokeby, who had also designed Claydon House, Bucks (National Trust). Whereas Claydon has rococo and chinoiserie decoration, the deer house is in the Gothic style, eminently suitable for the august Bishop Trevor for whom it was designed. Sir Thomas also designed Trevor Gate at Auckland Castle in a similar style. The deer house belongs to that delightful group of buildings which can not be classed as follies, for they have functions, but functions that many would dismiss as folly; like the Thunder House that Lutyens designed for Gertrude Jekyll, where she could enjoy the summer thunderstorms over the Surrey hills.

Bowes Castle

DURHAM

The ruins of Henry II's tower keep, begun c.1170 and completed 1187, stand in the north-west corner of the Roman fort of Lavatrae, both guarding the Stainmore Pass. The Roman road through the pass connected Carlisle and the Scottish Lowlands with the fertile vale of York. The Roman fort was begun by Agricola c.AD 78. Square in plan, it enclosed an area of about three-and-three-quarter acres with an earthen rampart faced with timber; this was replaced by stone in the second century. Today the south and west ramparts are the best preserved. The parish church occupies the north-east corner, and a couple of inscribed stones recovered from the fort are preserved here. In the north-west angle stands the Norman castle keep. It is unusual in that it seems to have been built as a keep only, without any ancillary buildings. A ditch was added to protect the keep on the south and west sides while the Roman ditch to the north was redug. The entrance was at first-floor level on the east front, via a forebuilding that has now disappeared. Rectangular in plan, the massive walls of the castle keep are strengthened by angle and pilaster buttresses, and there were a number of little chambers set within the thickness of the walls. In the south-east corner was a spiral stair, and in the south-west a garderobe block.

ABOVE: Auckland Castle Deer House

RIGHT: Egglestone Abbey, the south transept of the abbey church and reredorter to the north

Egglestone Abbey

DURHAM

Monasteries were usually located beside a river for water and drainage, and here, in a bend of the Rivers Tees, are the remains of the Premonstratensian abbey of St Mary and St John the Baptist, founded *c*.1198. The east and west ends of the aisleless church and part of the south transept survive, plus the north-east corner of the cloister range, which was rebuilt as a house after the Dissolution of the Monasteries. The Premonstratensians were a reformed group of the Augustinian canons who lived the communal life of the monastery, but who served as priests where needed, so they were often absent from the monastery. They liked to build in isolated locations which is why a disproportionate number of their ruined houses have survived. Despite being an abbey, the foundation was very poorly endowed. At the beginning of the thirteenth century there was a suggestion that it should be reduced to priory status, an idea that was abandoned, but it was always short of money and in the fourteenth century suffered from the attentions of the marauding Scottish armies. Between 1195-1225

the buildings were planned out around the cloister to the north of the church, and from this period dates the fine doorway in the north-west corner, designed as the processional door into the nave. Building then began on the east end of the church, which dates from *c*.1250, progressing to the south transept some twenty-five years later and finally to the nave around 1300. Here the financial problems of the canons are revealed, for they could no longer afford a nave as long as had originally been intended. Thus the nave never extended as far as the processional doorway; an almost cruciform plan church was the result, and a fine doorway that leads nowhere. In the nave can be seen various tomb slabs and a chest tomb to Sir Ralph Bowes of Streatlam, died 1482. The cloister, with remains of the canons' dormitory and adjoining reredorter (latrine block) survive, and on the north side the refectory over the warming house, all of which were converted into a dwelling *c*.1548. Window openings and a fireplace remain from this period. Later the property became labourers' cottages, and a source of building materials and garden ornaments for the neighbourhood. Various pieces of carved stonework have since been reinstated. To the north-east of the abbey is a medieval packhorse bridge for travellers to and from Barnard Castle.

Bowes Castle and the Church of St Giles

Barnard Castle

DURHAM

Dramatically sited to command a crossing of the River Tees, Barnard Castle encloses an area of six-and-a-half acres and is one of the largest castles in the country. The earthworks date possibly from the 1090s, much of the curtain walls from *c.*1125–40, and the inner ward or bailey from *c.*1230–40. For much of the twelfth century the castle was held by Bernard Baliol and his son, also called Bernard, so their name became attached to the castle and to the town that grew up beside it. Their descendants included the founder of Balliol College, Oxford, and John Baliol, King of Scotland, 1292–96. In 1216 the castle withstood a siege by Alexander of Scotland, but after the fourteenth century it ceased to be of great importance. During the Rising of the North the castle was garrisoned for Queen Elizabeth against the rebel earls by Sir George Bowes of Streatlam. He surrendered after an eleven-day siege, but his resistance had been enough to check the spread of the revolt, which collapsed soon after. Sir George's tomb can be seen nearby at *Egglestone Abbey*. In the 1620s Sir Henry Vane purchased the castle in order to obtain building materials for his castle at Raby. However, there are still extensive remains to be seen, including the earthworks of the four wards. The Town Ward through which the visitor enters, via the north gate, retains its curtain wall and Brackenbury's Tower. A deep rock-hewn ditch separates the Inner Ward, where remains of towers and the early fourteenth-century Great Hall with Great Chamber survive. The climax of the castle is the Round Tower, from where splendid views of the surrounding countryside are to be had.

Barnard Castle seen from the Town Ward

Finchale Priory

DURHAM

The extensive remains of the priory lie in a loop of the River Wear, a site first occupied by one of the more colourful English saints, St Godric. He originated probably from East Anglia, and after undertaking a pilgrimage to Rome at the age of twenty became a pirate. However, he later undertook further pilgrimages, including visits to both Jerusalem and Compostella, and he finally settled down as a hermit at Finchale around 1115. Here he died at the age of 107 in 1170. His tomb attracted pilgrims and a cell of Durham was established here, which became formalised in 1237 as a Benedictine priory, dependent on Durham. There are architectural fragments from each period, but the majority are thirteenth century with later alterations. The church originally had north and south aisles to the nave and quire, but these were demolished in 1364

and the arcades blocked. The upper courses of masonry have gone, but the crowns of the arches to the arcades remain, giving the church ruins their distinctive outline. The early fourteenth-century refectory has a good vaulted undercroft, and the remains of the prior's house are unusually extensive. This reflects the particular interest of Finchale since it was used as a holiday home for monks from Durham from the fourteenth century. Statutes of 1408 explain the arrangements: the number of permanent residents was fixed at five, four monks and the prior, with an additional four monks on leave from Durham, who would stay for three-week periods. During the fourteenth century holidays became an accepted feature of monastic life, and also included visits home to friends and relations. However, no other monastic settlement is known to have filled the precise function of Finchale. The idea of monastic holidays is very far removed from the concepts of early monasticism, but in the 500-odd years down to the Dissolution of the Monasteries there were of necessity many changes both in the monastic Rules and in their interpretation.

Finchale Priory from the east, looking across the site of the first monastic buildings to the priory church with the prior's lodgings to the south

HADRIAN'S WALL

The remains of this outstanding piece of Roman military engineering, unparalleled in Europe, are to be found amidst some spectacular countryside. Eighty Roman miles long (seventy-three modern miles), the Wall ran from coast to coast making use of a great outcrop of limestone, the Whin Sill, in the centre. This provides the most dramatic scenery and the best preserved sections of the Wall. The remains at the east and west extremities are disappointing but there are museums at both Newcastle and Carlisle which contain much interesting material. The Museum of Antiquities at the University of Newcastle is particularly good, for as well as many finds and reconstructions, it contains a scale model of the entire length of the Wall which gives an excellent overview and makes the surviving remains more readily comprehensible.

The Wall was begun in AD 122, after a visit by the Emperor Hadrian, as part of his policy of consolidating the boundaries of his Empire. Some twenty years previously the two Roman roads running north had been linked east-west by the Stanegate military road. This connected Dere Street at *Corbridge* with Carlisle to the west and a number of forts were built along the way. It was now decided to place a defensive wall north of this chain of communication and after the Wall was partly built a decision was reached to incorporate forts into the Wall itself. Various other changes took place during construction and the Wall was repaired on a number of occasions. As planned, the Wall was masonry from the new bridge at Newcastle to the River Irthing at Willowford, thereafter it was a turf rampart. (A reconstruction of

this section of the Wall in the twentieth century has been destroyed in ten years — by rabbits, but there were no rabbits in Roman Britain.) Building the wall was divided between groups of soldiers, some for the Wall and others for the turrets and milecastles, and the latter finished well in advance. Originally planned to be ten feet wide and twenty feet high including the parapet, the later parts of the wall were reduced to eight feet wide and the turf sections rebuilt in stone. Every Roman mile there was a milecastle with gateway, now numbered from the east, and between were two turrets, a third of a mile apart, which are lettered a and b with the number of the milecastle adjoining to the east. The design of the seventeen forts varied slightly depending on whether originally they were for cavalry or infantry. *Chesters* was a cavalry fort, for instance, whereas *Housesteads* was infantry. By AD 128, the Wall was largely complete and the garrison numbered about 9,500 men.

Mention should also be made of the vallum ditch which is today often more conspicuous than the Wall in places. This was added when the forts were in place and it separated the civilian population to the south from the military zone of the Wall and the road that ran beside it. The vallum was a ten foot deep ditch, thirty feet wide with ramparts on either side. By the end of the second century the · civilian population was no longer excluded from the military road and the vallum was sometimes filled in. On the north side of the wall a ditch enhanced its defences.

It seems strange, but no sooner had Hadrian died in AD 138 than his successor's expansionist policy led to the abandonment of the Wall. The frontier was pushed north and defined by the earthen ramparts of the Antonine Wall of which parts may still be seen. The Romans quickly found that they had over-extended themselves and they refortified Hadrian's Wall c.AD 158, permanently abandoning the Antonine Wall twenty years later. Hadrian's Wall is believed to have been garrisoned as late as AD 400.

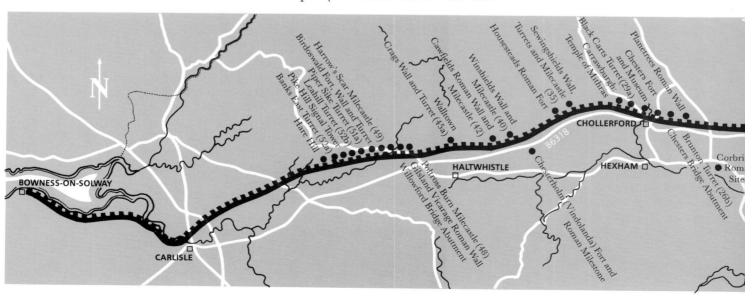

Benwell Vallum Crossing

HADRIAN'S WALL

There is little left to enjoy of the Benwell Vallum Crossing. However, it is the only surviving example of the causeway crossings over the vallum ditch, which stood to the south of every fort. A gateway spanned the crossing, a model of which can be seen in the Museum of Antiquities at Newcastle.

Benwell Roman Temple

HADRIAN'S WALL

The foundations of this little Romano-Celtic shrine can be seen here with facsimiles of the two altars discovered *in situ* when the site was excavated in 1862. The cult shrine had been destroyed at the end of the second century and not rebuilt. It stood about 200 yards east of the fort of Condercum, between the vallum and the Wall, and from the dedications on the altars it is thought to have been erected *c.*177–80 on an existing site. Thus it was only in use for about thirty years. The shrine was rectangular, eighteen feet by ten feet internally, with altars flanking the south apse that contained a larger-than-life-size statue of the god Antenociticus. Apart from an invocation to him at *Chesters Fort* he is unknown, and his name is an enigma. The head of the statue can be seen in the Museum of Antiquities, Newcastle. While the statue belongs to the Greco-Roman tradition, it has definite Celtic features including a torque about the neck, symbol of magic powers, and the thick strands of hair that divide over the god's forehead like the antlers of a young stag.

Denton Hall Turret (7b) and West Denton

HADRIAN'S WALL

This is the first section of Wall in the care of English Heritage, located on an island of grass between a major and minor road. The foundations of the Wall turret can be seen with evidence of the stairway and pivot hole of the door. Roman doors were pivoted rather than hinged. There were two turrets between each milecastle which contained access to the rampart walk with a lookout post on the probably flat roof. To the east, at West Denton, can be seen the foundations of a piece of the Wall, uncherished in the midst of an industrial estate.

ABOVE: Denton Hall Turret

LEFT: Benwell Roman Temple

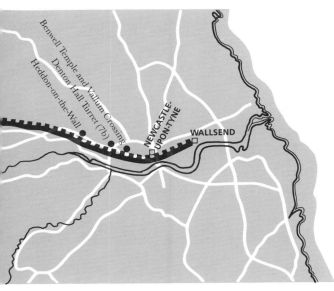

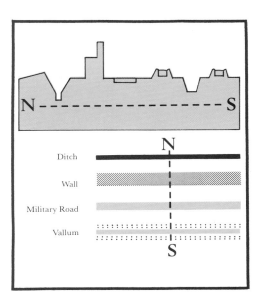

Corbridge Roman Site

HADRIAN'S WALL

The remains at Corbridge are extensive, including the foundations of some fine granaries, and subsidence has been created intriguing undulations of masonry in the southern half of the site, like ridges in the sand when the tide has ebbed. Only a fraction of this very large settlement is exposed. Corbridge (Corstopitum), at the junction of Dere Street with the Stanegate, was one of the earliest Roman forts in the area and around AD 80 a cavalry regiment was based here. The site commanded one of the best crossings of the River Tyne, although the river has since changed its shape and this important relationship is no longer very apparent. Once Hadrian's Wall was built Corbridge was abandoned for about fifteen years but it was reoccupied AD 139 and soon became the main supply base for the Scottish campaigns and a leave centre for the troops. A sizeable, multi-racial settlement grew up here, including Greeks, and others from the furthest corners of the Empire. Around AD 160 it ceased to be primarily a military base and there were ambitious plans to lay it out with all the amenities of a Roman town, although a military presence remained until the end of the Roman period. These plans were abandoned *c.*180 but the famous Corbridge lion is part of the fountain and aqueduct dating from this

Heddon-on-the-Wall

HADRIAN'S WALL

TOP: Corbridge Roman Site, the granaries

BELOW: The Corbridge Lion

RIGHT: Heddon Wall with the foundations of a medieval kiln

Here is a 280-yard stretch of the Wall foundations. This is best approached from the east on the B6528 where it snakes up the hill in anticipation of greater things. The foundations of a medieval kiln that was built out of the Wall can also be seen.

period, as are the granaries. The latter are the best preserved examples in Britain. They rest on small pillars to allow air to circulate (not to be confused with the pilae of a hypocaust) and had louvred wooden sides and a pitched roof.

Corbridge held a year's supply of grain in camp and this was the staple element of the soldiers' diet; rice, potatoes and pasta were unknown, as was the army canteen. The soldiers had to do their own cooking: they were divided into sections of eight men who drew a daily ration of five bushels of corn. This they then had to grind into flour and turn into loaves to be baked in the camp ovens to make the day's supply of bread. There is a modern museum on site containing finds since 1906. The most spectacular find, the Corbridge Lanyx, a fourth century silver dish discovered in 1731 can be seen in facsimile. Among the other exhibits is a tombstone inscribed simply to 'Ertola, properly called Vellibia, (who) lived most happily 4 years and 60 days'.

Planetrees Roman Wall

HADRIAN'S WALL

From *Heddon* to *Sewingshields* the B6318 runs mainly on top of the Wall, between the vallum and the ditch that stood on the north side of the Wall. Good sections of both are visible from the road. This is the famous military road built by General Wade after the '45 Rebellion. The Young Pretender's forces had been advancing down the west coast and General Wade in Newcastle found that the lack of a decent east-west road meant that he was unable to get his artillery across to Carlisle, which consequently fell to the rebels. Stone from the Wall was used to build the road. The section at Planetrees, just before *Brunton Turret*, is fenced off beside the road.

Brunton Turret (26b)

HADRIAN'S WALL

Here is one of the best preserved turrets, about seven foot high with about seventy yards of wall running down towards the River Tyne, set against a backdrop of trees. This is the most westerly section of the wall with broad foundations — the west side is ten foot wide but to the east it has narrowed to eight feet. The site is close to the carpark.

ABOVE: Planetrees Roman Wall

LEFT: Brunton Turret

of Cilurnum, the best-preserved example of a Roman cavalry fort to be seen anywhere in Britain. The site is noted for the fine bath house on the banks of the Tyne, as well as for the very interesting museum and for the foundations of various buildings. The fort was erected over the site of a wall turret (27a), as at *Birdoswald*, during the latter part of Hadrian's reign. Remains of the headquarter's building with its vaulted strongroom are visible, as is the commandant's house with adjoining bath house and part of the barracks. Outside the fort on the banks of the Tyne lie the ruins of the bath house with its distinctive arched recesses. These were probably lockers in the changing rooms. How pleasant it must have been for the soldiers to steam away the raw Northumbria cold from their bones, and remember briefly what it was like to be warm again. Little excavation has been carried out at Chesters during the twentieth century and most of the work here was done during the last century by the Clayton family who erected the museum. This houses a splendid collection of Roman sculpture, massed row upon row in the late nineteenth century tradition, and gathered from many different sites along the Wall. They include altars, tombstones and architectural fragments and the famous

Chesters Bridge Abutment

HADRIAN'S WALL

Here are the remains of the east abutment to the bridge that carried Hadrian's Wall across the River Tyne. The course of the river has altered slightly and the west abutment now lies on the river bed, visible at low water. The bridge had masonry piers with a timber superstructure, about 190 feet long and 20 feet wide, and a model can be seen in the museum at *Chesters*, which lies on the opposite bank. The construction is impressive: iron clamps and ties run in with lead fastening the blocks of ashlar masonry, and the location is most attractive. Excavations in the nineteenth century threw up an embankment around the site which is now lined with trees. Looking across the river, the bath house at Chesters can be seen. The crossing is now down river at Chollerford Bridge and Chesters Bridge Abutment is about a twenty-minute walk from the road. There is a good-luck phallic symbol carved on the north side of the bridge abutment.

ABOVE: Chesters Bridge Abutment

BELOW Statue of Juno, Chesters Fort Museum

Chesters Fort and Museum

HADRIAN'S WALL

The word 'chesters' was used by the Anglo-Saxons to describe any site with old stone buildings and here it has been attached to the Roman cavalry fort

headless statue of Juno standing on the back of a cow, also damaged, can be seen here. The pottery, including some charming incense burners, is of interest, as are the collections of iron tools and other artefacts.

Cawfields Roman Wall and Milecastle (42)
HADRIAN'S WALL

Another dramatic section of Wall — the land drops steeply away and the vallum ditch can be identified running in straight stretches along the valley to the south. At the west end of almost three quarters of a mile of Wall stands Cawfields Milecastle, built on a considerable slope, with the masonry of the south gate still standing six feet high. Close by a carpark and picnic area have been created out of a land-scaped, disused quarry.

Cawfields Roman Wall

Black Carts Turret (29a)
HADRIAN'S WALL

Set in a field on the north side of the road are the foundations of a turret and a 500-yard length of wall. The vallum is noticeable on the south side of the road. About a mile further on the road mounts the brow of the hill at Limestone Corner and a great panorama of landscape and Wall stretches away to the horizon.

Sewingshields Wall, Turrets and Milecastle (35)
HADRIAN'S WALL

Two miles of Roman wall set in spectacular scenery. Part of the Wall and Milecastle 35 have been excavated and consolidated.

LEFT: Black Carts Turret

Carrawburgh: Temple of Mithras

HADRIAN'S WALL

Here are the remains of the little Mithratic temple that stood outside the fort at Brocolitia. (The fort has not been excavated and it is not in the care of English Heritage.) Mithras was a Persian deity, popular with soldiers, whose followers were initiated into different stages of knowledge with the promise of happiness to come in life after death. Facsimiles of the altars found in the temple are preserved on the site, whilst the originals are to be seen in the Museum of Antiquities at Newcastle. One dedicated to Mithras is particularly interesting for the pierced stonework around the deity's head show that a light was set inside the altar, creating the effect of a flickering halo to the god. The little temple had windowless stone walls and a steeply pitched thatched roof. Entering the temple through

an annexe, the worshippers (men only) would have found themselves in a dark, smokey room, the air heavy with the smell of the Mediterranean pine cones that were burnt in honour of the god. A dramatic relief on the end wall depicted Mithras slaying the bull from whose life-blood creation came. Below, the altar of the god welcomed worshippers with its flickering light and in the half-light the painted face of the god with his golden halo must have seemed quite tangible. Statues of the two acolytes who always accompanied him stood nearby. Votive altars and statues lined the central pathway while the worshippers stood in the tiny aisles on either side. The ceremonials were closely guarded secrets but they probably involved animal sacrifices and initiation trials of various kinds. The temple was built c.AD 205 and was extended on three occasions before it was destroyed in the early fourth century, probably by Christians. There is a life-size reconstruction of the interior at the Museum of Antiquities at Newcastle.

RIGHT: Temple of Mithras, Carrawburgh

FAR RIGHT: Chesterholm (Vindolanda) looking south across the mansio to the replica turrets

OPPOSITE ABOVE: Housesteads Roman Fort, the north granary

OPPOSITE BELOW: the Wall at Winshields Crag

Chesterholm (Vindolanda) Fort and Roman Milestone

HADRIAN'S WALL

The fort lies on the Stanegate, the main road that ran along the south side of the Wall, in a landscape that seems pleasantly hospitable after the drama of *Sewingshields* and *Housesteads*. A Roman milestone still survives to the east of the fort where the Stanegate crosses Bradley Burn, one of only two that can still be seen in their original location. There was a fort here from c.AD 80, in the early days of the occupation before the Wall was built, but what survives today dates mainly from c.AD 300 with later alterations. A large civilian settlement grew up beside the three-and-a-half acre fort. An active programme of excavations has been underway here since 1970, when the Vindolanda Trust took over the administration of the site. (They levy a charge for admission with a reduction for English Heritage members.) Remains of various buildings including a mansio, or guest house, and a bath house can be seen. Two very interesting full-size replicas have been constructed, one of the stone wall with a stone turret and another of the turf wall with a timber turret. Standing on the west side of the replica wall one gets a good idea of how imposing it must have appeared when intact. The museum contains some reconstructions of Roman interiors and displays items discovered on site, including a remarkable number of wood and leather items that have been preserved in the water-logged soil. Perhaps the most fascinating discovery has been the writing tablets covering a range of everyday topics that include invitations to a birthday party and correspondence concerning a soldier's missing socks.

Housesteads Roman Fort

HADRIAN'S WALL

Spectacular scenery and a wealth of remains make this the most popular of the Hadrian's Wall sites. The infantry fort covers five acres and there was a large civilian settlement adjoining to the south, laid out on a series of terraces. Founded during Hadrian's reign, the fort was destroyed more than once and eventually civilians moved into the fort also. At what date the fort was finally abandoned is not known, but it ended violently. The remains of walls and gateways can be seen, also granaries, the commandant's house, barrack blocks and the latrine. The latter is in a fine state of preservation and it is the best surviving example in Britain. (It is interesting to compare it with the monastic arrangements in a reredorter.) The latrine is set in the south-east corner of the fort, near one of the corner turrets which still preserves the fine lead-lined water tank that collected water from the gutter round the turret roof. Inside the rectangular latrine block wooden seats were set over a deep sewer that ran along each wall, fronted by a little gutter of fresh running water. Here the sponges were washed out, the Roman equivalent of toilet-paper, each soldier having his own personal sponge attached to a short stick. There were also two wash hand basins. Rain water was probably used to flush the sewers but it is not known exactly how the water supply and drainage worked at Housesteads. There does not seem to have been a well, but with the third-century garrison numbering a thousand men, the arrangements must have been quite complex. Other features of interest include evidence of a Mithraeum, and there is a small site museum. This is an excellent location for walking along the Wall, in either direction, with tremendous views all around. The carpark is half a mile below the site.

Winshields Wall and Milecastle (40)

HADRIAN'S WALL

This is one of the most spectacular sections of the Wall, including its highest point at Winshields Crag. The carpark is a short walk to the east at Steel Rigg.

Walltown Crags Walls and Turret (45a)
HADRIAN'S WALL

This is one of the best-preserved sections of the Wall, snaking across the landscape. Turret 45a was a lone signal station here before the Wall was built, later incorporated into it. The carpark is 100 yards or so from the Wall.

Gilsland Vicarage Roman Wall
HADRIAN'S WALL

Two hundred and twenty yards of Wall survive in the garden of a private house. The wall is eight foot wide on a ten foot foundation. This is the beginning of the 'Narrow Wall', but the foundations had already been laid for the 'Broad Wall' when the orders were changed.

ABOVE: the Wall at Gilsland Vicarage

RIGHT: Walltown Crags turret

OPPOSITE: the Wall at Walltown Crags

Poltross Burn Milecastle (48)

HADRIAN'S WALL

Another well-preserved milecastle just south of Gilsland, where the Poltross Burn joins the River Irthing. The burn tumbles down a little cascade and the ruins are quite impressive. It was here that the remains of a flight of steps that led to the rampart walk enabled archaeologists to calculate the height of the Wall at fifteen feet, with another five feet for the parapet.

Piper Sike Turret (51a)

HADRIAN'S WALL

Only the foundations of the turret survive beside the road. By examining the masonry it is possible to see the butt joint with the Wall, for this turret was originally constructed for the turf wall.

Willowford Bridge Abutment

HADRIAN'S WALL

Here are the remains of the bridge across the River Irthing at the end of a fine stretch of Wall. The river has since altered its course, leaving the whole site of the bridge on the east bank. The remains of one pier can be seen, the eastern one of three, and a close examination of the masonry may enable visitors to detect evidence of two rebuildings of the original bridge.

ABOVE: Poltross Burn Milecastle

RIGHT: Piper Sike Turret

FAR RIGHT: the wall near Willowford Bridge

Birdoswald Fort

HADRIAN'S WALL

From the west bank of the River Irthing the Wall was originally constructed of turf, later rebuilt in stone. The turrets and forts were always of stone but the milecastles were also originally built of turf. Birdoswald was built as a cavalry fort on the site of one of the turrets (49a) that then became an infantry fort when the Wall was rebuilt. The alteration in planning that this change entailed has resulted in the unique survival of a section of the 'turf wall'. This is most readily identified from the OS Hadrian's Wall Map. At NGR NY 596 658, near a barn at Appletree, a section through the turf wall can be seen, with the alternating bands of dark and light soil created by the piled turves — a detour only recommended for the most devoted. Birdoswald (Camboglanna) enjoys a fine site with views across the River Irthing from its south-west corner. The fort has not yet been excavated but works are planned for the period 1987–1992. Remains of the masonry Wall lie beside the road, just before the turn-off to the fort.

Harrow's Scar Milecastle (49)

HADRIAN'S WALL

ABOVE: Turret 49b near Birdoswald Fort

Harrow's Scar Milecastle stands on a spur of land overlooking the River Irthing and the former bridge, at the east end of a long stretch of Wall running to *Birdoswald Fort* and beyond. The west bank of the river was probably not as steep in Roman times as it is today. Since it is no longer possible to cross the river at this point, visitors must return via *Gilsland* and cross by Mumpshall Bridge. Once on the west bank, the road looks down on the Wall which runs below through a pleasant wooded valley. The road then takes a sharp left-hand down to cross the site of the Wall which strides away into the distance.

Leahill Turret (51b)

HADRIAN'S WALL

The foundations of another turret beside the road.

Pike Hill Signal Tower
HADRIAN'S WALL

Set on the south side of the road are the remains of this signal tower. It is easy to miss and is not marked on the OS map. However, it is quite interesting as visitors can climb up into the south corner of the tower which is all that remains, for the road runs straight through the site of the tower, following the line of the Wall. The slight kink in the road here indicates the unusual relationship of the tower to the Wall. The square structure stood at an angle and the Wall joined the north-west corner about ten feet north of the south-east continuation. This was part of a long-range signalling system, preceding the building of the Wall.

RIGHT: Pike Hill Signal Tower

BELOW: Banks East Turret

BOTTOM: the Wall at Hare Hill

Banks East Turret (52a)
HADRIAN'S WALL

A good example of a turret with adjoining stretches of Wall and a fine sweep of landscape away to the south. The walls stand to about six feet high and there is a carpark adjoining. This marked the end of the first stage of rebuilding of the turf wall in stone. It was not until the late second century that the Wall was completed in stone as far west as Bowness-on-Solway.

Hare Hill
HADRIAN'S WALL

The countryside becomes much gentler now and the road winds down beside Banks Burn to rejoin the River Irthing. Much of the stone from this section of the Wall went to build Lanercost Priory. The Hare Hill section of the Wall lies at the end of a private road, sixteen courses of masonry high.

Aydon Castle

NORTHUMBERLAND

This is an important example of a fortified manor house of the late thirteenth century with a first-floor hall approached by an external stone stair. The evolution of the building can be readily appreciated as it grew into an L-plan with the kitchen wing over the stables in the early fourteenth century. The courtyard was then enclosed and soon after an outer wall was built, creating an outer courtyard. In 1315 the house was captured and ransacked by a band of marauding Scotsmen. Two years later a similar disaster occurred, but this time the robbers were English. The owners, the de Reymes family, removed to another of their properties and the house was let to tenants. Thus it survived largely unaltered until the seventeenth century when it was converted into a farmhouse. Some later alterations have since been removed and there are no internal fittings to distract the visitor from the development of this interesting structure.

The inner courtyard and entrance to the hall at Aydon Castle

Belsay Hall, Castle and Gardens

NORTHUMBERLAND

This is one of the finest English Heritage properties. It consists of a ruined tower house of the fourteenth century with a sixteenth-century range adjoining that was largely rebuilt in the nineteenth century. Behind these ruins are the remains of an eighteenth-century model farm, and this is only the beginning. To the east lies one of the finest neo-Classical houses in Europe, built 1806-15 by Sir Charles Monk. He acted as his own architect and the building is more successful as a residence than the almost contemporary *Grange*. The interior of the house is accessible and it retains much of its original austere decoration, for example in the library. Between the two groups of buildings lie fine gardens, particularly the Quarry Gardens from where the stone for the new Belsay was excavated. It is full of romantic chasms and there are other more formal gardens nearby. The evolution of the estate from a fortified dwelling to mansion of European importance forms the subject of an excellent exhibition on site.

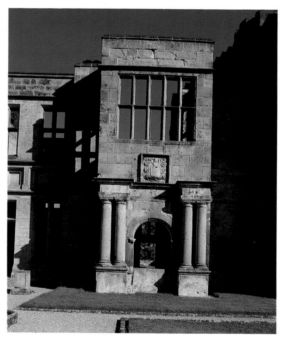

LEFT: the pillar hall

ABOVE: Belsay Hall from the park

BELOW: the sixteenth-century porch at Belsay Castle

Berwick-Upon-Tweed Castle

NORTHUMBERLAND

Berwick-upon-Tweed Castle was largely destroyed in the 1840s when the railway station was built. Gazing at Stephenson's majestic Royal Border Bridge across the Tweed, the railway viaduct of 1847, one almost does not mind. However, remains of the west wall of Edward I's castle continued down to the river's edge as a stepped wall still remain, set in a public park. Berwick was a Royal Scottish burgh when the castle was first built in the twelfth century but it was captured by Edward I and rebuilt. The town changed hands many times thereafter and for many years it was a free town, maintaining its independence from either side.

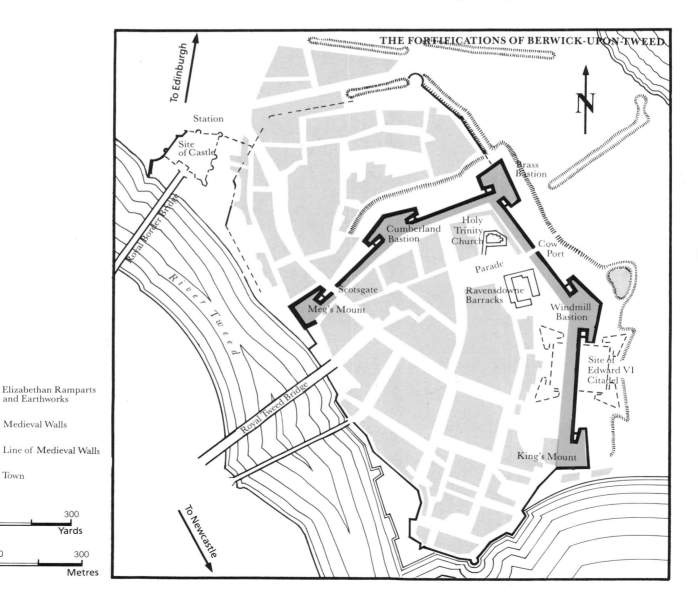

THE FORTIFICATIONS OF BERWICK-UPON-TWEED

To Edinburgh

Station

Site of Castle

Royal Border Bridge

River Tweed

Royal Tweed Bridge

To Newcastle

Brass Bastion

Cumberland Bastion

Holy Trinity Church

Cow Port

Parade

Ravensdowne Barracks

Windmill Bastion

Site of Edward VI Citadel

Scotsgate

Meg's Mount

King's Mount

N

Elizabethan Ramparts and Earthworks

Medieval Walls

Line of Medieval Walls

Town

0   100   300
Yards

0   100   300
Metres

Berwick-Upon-Tweed Ramparts

NORTHUMBERLAND

The defences at Berwick are the outstanding example of sixteenth century town fortifications, strengthened in the mid seventeenth century, and surviving almost in their entirety. They were the costliest government undertaking of Queen Elizabeth I's reign. Work began under Henry VIII and the outlines of a fort with arrowhead bastions planned by his son, Edward VI, but never built, can be detected. (The plan was identical to that intended on St Mary's in the Scilly Isles, but never completed, known as *Harry's Walls*.) Under the direction of Sir Richard Lee, work began in 1558 to a new design, making use of angled bastions. These were raised with earthwork gun platforms during the Protectorate. Visitors can walk the circuit of the ramparts and there are fine views down the coast. This is the best place in England to get to grips with the finer points of artillery defences on the bastion principle; normally their functions are not easily appreciable at ground level and are better understood from plans.

OPPOSITE: Berwick-upon-Tweed Castle from the north-west

LEFT: looking east along the ramparts from Cumberland Bastion to Brass Bastion

Berwick-Upon-Tweed: Ravensdowne Barracks

NORTHUMBERLAND

The Ravensdowne Barracks are one of the first purpose-built barracks in England, dating from 1717-21 and possible built by Andrew Jelf under the supervision of Sir John Vanbrugh. There are three ranges placed around the parade ground, the north side closed with a handsome gateway. The Clock Block now houses the Borough Museum and Art Gallery and the first floor contains part of the Burrell Collection. This is a surprising place to find a Daubigny and a Degas. The east range contains the Museum of the Kings Own Scottish Borderers, who still occupy part of the barracks, and the remainder is given over to the English Heritage exhibition 'By Beat of Drum'. This traces the history of the British infantry from 1660 to 1880 and makes full use of life-size reconstructions. It is full of interesting information and one leaves feeling deeply grateful for not having been a member of the British infantry in the eighteenth century. To the north of the barracks stands Holy Trinity Church, one of the very few churches in England built during the Protectorate. Erected 1648-52, it is little altered, apart from the addition of two small turrets in the nineteenth century and the rebuilding of the chancel.

ABOVE: *The Clock Block, Ravensdowne Barracks*

ABOVE RIGHT: *Black Middens Bastle House*

Black Middens Bastle House

NORTHUMBERLAND

Set in the Tarset valley amidst excellent walking country, Black Middens is a good example of a sixteenth-century bastle house. This type of farmhouse was peculiar to the lawless Border regions, thus the emphasis is on defence. These two-storey farmhouses were sometimes built in groups, generally within shouting distance of each other, and had first floor living accommodation over stabling for animals. This was not permanent stabling, rather it was for protection against marauding bands of cattle rustlers that plagued the area. Usually the ground floor had a stone vault to give greater security to the upper floor, but at Black Middens there was a timber floor and now only a roofless shell survives.

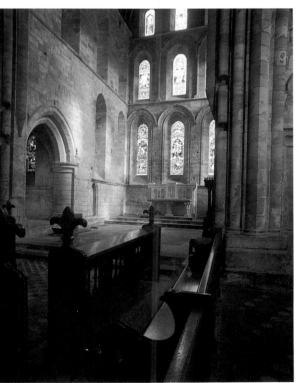

Brinkburn Priory

NORTHUMBERLAND

The twelfth-century church of the Augustinian canons at Brinkburn was preserved at the Dissolution of the Monasteries through its use as a parish church, though by 1858 it was in ruins prior to an extensive restoration by Thomas Austin. Thus the church is now roofed and furnished, and unlike *Lanercost*, the eastern end is also included. The church has only one aisle, the northern one, entered by a fine late Norman porch with a thirteenth century gable. It is interesting to see the vaulted chapels of the transepts, the foundations of which are so frequently seen in ruined monastic churches but which so rarely survive intact. Little or nothing of the claustral buildings survive and a pleasing nineteenth-century house with Gothick windows stands south-west of the church. The priory was founded *c.* 1130 and its situation by a bend in the River Coquet was frequently praised and painted by eighteenth and nineteenth-century visitors, though the favourite view of the church, seen from the west, is no longer possible because this land is not in the care of English Heritage. The ten-minute walk from the carpark down the sloping river valley passes some gnarled and ancient trees which frame the first and finest view of the church.

ABOVE: Brinkburn Priory from the south-east

LEFT: the chancel of the Priory church

tower. The outer bailey between the gatehouse keep and the sea covers an extensive area and it is thought that the castle was intended primarily as a refuge, rather than as a permanent residence, or as part of the border defences. The castle was begun in 1313 by Thomas, Earl of Lancaster, an opponent of Edward II, and altered by John of Gaunt *c.* 1380. His son, Henry Bolingbroke, became Henry IV and the castle was thus a crown possession. During the Wars of the Roses it was a Lancastrian stronghold and its condition today is largely the result of damage sustained under siege which was never repaired.

Edlingham Castle

NORTHUMBERLAND

South-west of Alnwick the road descends the steep heather-covered sides of the valley and there below on the valley floor is Edlingham. A fine railway viaduct completes the view and the castle is an intriguing ruin. The tower house is the best-preserved part, split open with one wall leaning at a crazy angle. Built in the fourteenth century, it is square with angle buttresses that finish as little turrets and a stair turret on the courtyard front. There was one room on each floor. Enough evidence survives to show that the hall, set over a vaulted stone undercroft, had a quatripartite stone-vaulted roof and a fine chimney piece. This must have been a sumptuous little room. The tower house is the most recent addition to the castle and the foundations of earlier buildings around the cobbled courtyard can be seen, though not readily identified. The fact that the small church nearby is largely Norman indicates that the site of the castle was probably occupied in the twelfth century. The church is well worth a visit.

Dunstanburgh Castle

NORTHUMBERLAND

ABOVE: Lilburn Tower, Dunstanburgh Castle

RIGHT: Edlingham Castle

This is an excellent castle, standing on a rocky promontory above the sea, surrounded by flat sands and a treeless, uninhabited landscape. It can only be reached on foot and it is hard to decide whether the walk from Embleton (two miles), or from Craster (one-and-a-half miles), is the more enjoyable. Ruins of the great twin-towered gatehouse keep survive, with remains of the curtain walls and postern

Etal Castle

NORTHUMBERLAND

Etal, the early home of the Manners family, now the Dukes of Rutland, consists of a ruined fourteenth-century gatehouse and keep, standing at the end of the village street. There are slight earthworks and the site has no natural defensive properties, so its appearance comes as a slight surprise. The curtain wall has gone on three sides, but the gatehouse and keep remain. Both rise to nearly full height and the latter is three storeys over a vaulted stone undercroft. It is rectangular in plan and unadorned, as befits a stern Border castle. The gatehouse has square towers flanking the gateway and a ground floor room with a stone-ribbed vault for the gatekeeper. The castle was besieged and captured by the Scots on their way to Flodden Field in 1513.

Lindisfarne Priory

NORTHUMBERLAND

The ruins of this famous Benedictine Priory on Holy Island stand on the site of the religious house founded by St Aidan in 635, less than forty years after St Augustine had landed in Kent. Aidan and his disciples and successors, the most famous of whom was St Cuthbert, undertook the conversion of pagan Northumbria, and the Lindisfarne Gospels, now in the British Museum, are a memorial of the piety and culture of this heroic community. Lindisfarne became the seat of the bishopric of Northumbria until 875 when it was destroyed by the Danes. The island has been frequently attacked throughout the ages and nothing remains of the early church. The ruins of the Benedictine priory, founded in 1082, are part of the village, with the romantic outlines of the castle at the eastern end of the island often glimpsed between the broken masonry. The remains of the twelfth-century priory church are extensive, including the west end, the arcaded nave, and transepts — with one of the ribs of the crossing vault defying time and gravity to link the transepts. Foundations of the claustral buildings can be identified, and evidence of the fortification of the site in the fourteenth century. The island can be reached by the causeway at low tide, and the tide timetables are displayed at either end of the road.

LEFT: *Etal Castle gatehouse with the keep beyond*

RIGHT: *looking west from the foundations of the apsidal chancel to the crossing and beyond, Lindisfarne Priory church*

Norham Castle

NORTHUMBERLAND

When, in the early fourteenth century, the beloved of Sir William Marmion bade him prove his love by seeking out the most dangerous place in Britain to use the helmet with the golden crest that she had given him, he did not hesitate. He took horse at once for Norham. This key border fortress belonging to the bishops of Durham was frequently besieged by the Scots — the siege of 1318 was famous as was that in 1513 when it was sacked on the eve of Flodden Field. The ruins of the castle, which was founded in 1121 and frequently rebuilt, are interesting and not too tiring. The rectangular twelfth-century keep with remains of a vaulted stone basement are imposing and a sixteenth-century curtain wall encloses the inner bailey on the foundations of the earlier wall. Foundations of the Great Hall can be seen and the inner moat is still a formidable obstacle. The walls of the outer bailey with remains of the towers are again mostly sixteenth-century on earlier foundations. The castle dominates the village below to the west, while on the north side, concealed behind the trees, there is a sheer drop down to the River Tweed.

Prudhoe Castle

NORTHUMBERLAND

The remains of this important medieval castle controlling the centre of the Tyne valley are most impressive. It was built in the twelfth century for the Umfravilles and was restored in the early nineteenth century when a farmhouse and stables were built within the bailey. Medieval earthworks enhance the natural defensive properties of the site and the curtain walls are well preserved, as high as twenty-six feet in places. Above them rises the keep. It is rare to find a gatehouse and barbican together in such good condition as at Prudhoe, and visitors trudging up the narrow, corridor-like barbican with the gatehouse towering above them get a real feeling that they are entering a medieval castle. In the Middle Ages only the lowly and godly walked, and to a knight on horseback the gradient would not have been apparent, only the fine views through the openings in the barbican walls. An exhibition on the castles of Northumbria is housed in the nineteenth-century farmhouse.

TOP: Prudhoe Castle from the south

ABOVE: the keep at Norham seen from the West Gate

Warkworth Castle and Hermitage

NORTHUMBERLAND

An object lesson in castle development, Warkworth stands in a position of great natural strength and beauty. It was founded in the late eleventh century as a motte and bailey castle and was enlarged in each of the following centuries, culminating in the magnificent keep rebuilt by the Percys to a unique cruciform plan in the fifteenth century. This was later adapted by Salvin as a residence for the Dowager Duchess of Northumberland in the nineteenth century, but the rest of the castle remains ruined. The bailey, lying on the south side of the keep, is divided by the foundations of the collegiate church of *c.*1400. The remains of the single-aisled Great Hall lie on the west side of the bailey with the Lion Tower as the hall porch. This fourteenth-century structure bears the arms of the Percys who acquired the castle in 1332. On the south (entrance) front is the fine late thirteenth-century gatehouse with polygonal turrets. During the Middle Ages the castle was frequently besieged, and again in the Civil War, though by the seventeenth century Alnwick had become the principal residence of the family. About a mile away up river the delightful Hermitage can be seen. For once this is a genuine medieval hermitage: a fourteenth-century chapel hewn out of the living rock with accommodation for the hermit. He also had a little garden on the riverbank. Various legends are attached to this romantic spot, which can only be reached by boat or on foot. The most popular tale is that there were two brothers contending for the hand of the same lady, each being unaware of the other's identity. A fight ensued and one slew the other, fatally wounding the lady who had tried to intervene. The survivor thereupon became a hermit. Documentary evidence is lacking, however, and on a summer's afternoon, drifting past the hermitage in a boat, one feels that the life of a hermit here would have appealed to many, without the inducements of expiating fratricide.

ABOVE: Warkworth Castle keep from the south

(west) breaks forward with four crenellated turrets, partly adorned with statues as at Alnwick — here nineteenth-century reconstructions. The windows are also the work of the 1860s, inserted by Mr Briggs the owner to replace the sash windows that the Hyltons had added in the early eighteenth century when the castle was much enlarged. Also at that time a north and then a south wing had been added, creating a symmetrical facade with sash windows to the central block and crenellated parapets to the wings. These were demolished in the nineteenth century having fallen into decay. Inside the floors have gone, but visitors can ascend a circular stair to see the remains of some of the rooms, including a chapel on the east front. This was for private devotions, for the family chapel of St Catherine, now a roofless ruin, stands to the north. It is mainly fifteenth-century with late sixteenth-century octagonal, transept-like bays. This two-storey feature was probably added when the building was used as a garden banqueting house after the Reformation; but in the early eighteenth century the building reverted to its original use and a doorway dates from this period. The ghost of the 'cauld lad' is said to haunt the grounds; he was a poor kitchen boy murdered by one of the early Hyltons in a fit of anger and thrown into the pond. In the late eighteenth century, Hylton belonged to the widowed Countess of Strathmore who became the victim of a determined and vicious fortune hunter, Lieutenant Robinson. With the deviousness worth of Valmont in *Les Liaisons Dangereuses*, he fed the most salacious stories of her personal life to a gullible newspaper, which published them. Thereupon he was able to earn the countess's misplaced gratitude by challenging the editor to a duel and wounding him. Having finally succeeded in marrying her, his forcible attempts to get her to sign away her property to him ultimately landed him in prison.

Hylton Castle

TYNE AND WEAR

ABOVE: the south-east view of Hylton Castle

RIGHT: the east end of Hylton Castle Chapel

The sad remnant of this once proud house stands, with its chapel, next to a housing estate on the edge of Sunderland. To nineteenth-century guidebook writers it was always particularly attractive, redolent with tales of love deceived, wills contested, violent death and the decline of a noble family. The building that we see today is the gutted shell of the splendid tower house keep built *c.* 1390–1400 by Sir William Hylton. It is especially interesting for the heraldic devices that adorn the façades, nor merely those of the Hyltons, barons of the palatinate, but those of other noble families in the area, together with the royal coat-of-arms. The entrance front

St Paul's Monastery, Jarrow

TYNE AND WEAR

The home of the Venerable Bede in the late seventh century and early eighth century, the monastery at Jarrow has recently been the subject of intensive excavations that have made it the best-understood Anglo-Saxon monastic site in the country. Today the area is surrounded by oil refineries and electricity pylons, but part of Bede's church can be seen in what is now the parish church of St Paul. The foundations only of the monastic buildings can be seen, but there is a model showing the reconstructed buildings in the Bede Monastery Museum, Jarrow House, which also contains finds from the site. Among them is a great deal of coloured glass, for Frankish glaziers were brought over to decorate not just the church but the refectory, guest house and other buildings. Internal walls had painted decorative plaster and the floors were made of *opus signum*, Roman-style cement containing crushed brick. Hitherto only a spiritual richness had been known of at Jarrow, but this must have flourished amidst much greater material comfort than had previously been suspected. The monastery was founded in 681 by Benedict Biscop, seven years after that at Wearmouth, with which it was considered part of one whole. The Venerable Bede, father of English history, spent most of his life at Jarrow where he wrote the *Ecclesiastical History of the English People*, and other works, some of which are now lost. He died at the age of sixty-three in 735, and the title of Venerable refers to his spirituality rather than to his age. After the Danish raids of 794, repeated in the following century, the monastery was destroyed. It was refounded by the Benedictines in 1074–83, but was abandoned whilst incomplete. Thereafter it became merely a cell of Durham with a Master and two or three monks. The east wall of the west range survives from this period.

Tynemouth Castle and Priory

TYNE AND WEAR

This dramatic rocky promontory has been a refuge, both spiritual and physical, since the seventh century and probably earlier. It was one of the major medieval fortifications in Northumbria, often besieged, and it continued in military use until 1960. Visitors enter by the brooding gatehouse keep, dating from the late fourteenth century. There were alterations in the eighteenth and nineteenth centuries but these accretions have been stripped away leaving it dour and forbidding. The plan is similar to that of Alnwick, begun about the same time in 1390. The curtain walls and towers were extended at this time, supplementing the fortifications of 1296, and were partly destroyed in Queen Elizabeth I's reign when earthwork bastions were added. The castle bailey is one of the largest in the country. There are extensive remains of the priory church, the nave of which was used as the parish church until the seventeenth century. The west end doorways are early thirteenth-century, and from the first Norman church of 1090–1130 the crossing and stone rood screen survive. The most spectacular remains are the late twelfth-century presbytery, rising almost to full height at the east end. Behind the presbytery is the mid fifteenth-century Percy chapel with its intricate stone-vaulted roof, decorated with bosses, and much restored by John Dobson *c*.1850. There is little to see of the claustral buildings to the south, but the views down the coast are very fine. The exact date when the site was first colonised is unknown, but it was certainly one of the earliest Christian settlements and was occupied by the mid seventh century at the latest. The body of the King and martyr St Oswin, murdered in 651, was buried here, and attracted many pilgrims. In the ninth century the monastery was repeatedly sacked and plundered by the Danes and the site was abandoned by the eleventh century when it was used as a fortress by Earl Tostig. He was defeated by King Harold at the Battle of Stamford Bridge, 1066, and the monastery was refounded as a Benedictine priory in 1090. It was a daughter house of St Albans, and the priory served as a place of correction for unruly monks. One inmate wrote to a fellow monk lamenting his banishment, here '... spring and summer never come, the north wind is always blowing ... see you come not to so comfortless a place'.

ABOVE: the gatehouse of Tynemouth Castle and Priory

BELOW: the east end of the Priory church seen from the south transept

YORKSHIRE
AND THE NORTH WEST

Cheshire · Humberside
Lancashire · North Yorkshire
South Yorkshire

The Sandbach Crosses
CHESHIRE

These two ninth-century crosses stand in the centre of the market square at Sandbach. Though rather battered, they are among the few examples of these early commemorative crosses that can still be seen in the open, rather than in museums. Animals, dragons, biblical scenes and decorative patterns are carved on the shafts. That they originated here in Sandbach is fairly certain, but where they stood before the Reformation when they were moved to the market square is not known. Perhaps in the churchyard, for this type of cross was carved to commemorate some important event in church history or to honour a patron saint. In the early seventeenth century the Puritans set about destroying crosses such as these, which they considered idolatrous, and the Sandbach crosses did not escape their attentions. They were smashed to pieces, parts of which were reused as building material, and two large fragments found their way into a garden grotto. In 1816 an attempt was made to restore the crosses and the fragments were rescued from various buildings in the town. Pieces of three other cross shafts and two tomb slabs, all Saxon work, can be seen in the churchyard. The church itself was rebuilt in the nineteenth century.

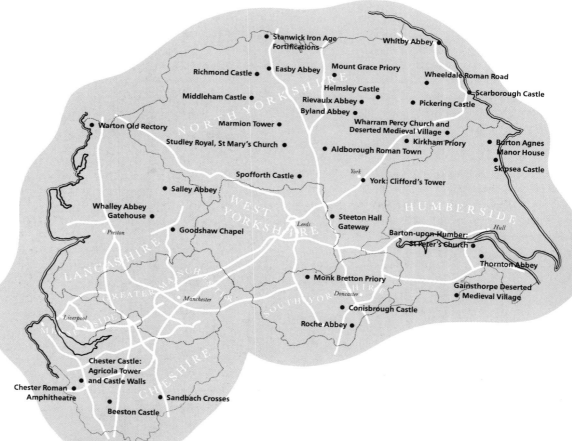

Beeston Castle

CHESHIRE

From the ruins of Beeston Castle on Peckforton Hills eight counties can be seen. The castle stands on an outcrop of red sandstone rock that rises 500 feet above sea level. It was built by Ranulf de Blundeville on his return from the Holy Land in 1220. (He also built *Bolingbroke Castle*, Lincolnshire.) Later in the century it was strengthened by Edward I who had the towers raised and crenellated. The castle occupies the summit of the crag and the land drops sheer away on two sides. The east and south fronts are protected by a curtain wall with the remains of seven towers and a gatehouse. In the north-west corner of the outer bailey stands a curtain wall enclosure with towers and a gatehouse on the bailey side. The gatehouse is the best preserved part of the castle. Beeston was described as derelict in the sixteenth century but it was garrisoned by the Royalists during the Civil War and changed hands twice. From here, Charles I watched the battle of Rowton Heath. In 1645 the garrison held out for eighteen weeks and was reduced to eating cats before it surrendered with full military honours. The following year the castle was slighted.

Chester Castle: Agricola Tower and Castle Walls

CHESHIRE

Most of the visitors to Chester Castle go to see the work of Thomas Harrison, who largely rebuilt it between 1785 and 1822. The splendid neo-Classical barracks, armoury, county hall and gateway, or Propylaea, form one of the best surviving groups of Greek Revival buildings in the country. They are still in use and not in the care of English Heritage. The original castle was a motte and bailey affair of *c.*1070, set in the angle of the city walls (which are still visible in many places). It was later strengthened by Edward I. The Agricola Tower was built as a gatehouse, probably in the twelfth century, and later converted into an ordinary curtain wall tower and was refaced by Harrison in 1818. It contains three rooms — in the upper one is the late twelfth-early thirteenth-century chapel of St Mary de Castro which is vaulted, with fragments of wall-paintings. In the guardhouse nearby is an exhibition on the history of the castle, and further material can be seen in the Weaver Hall Museum, and the Grosvenor Museum, Chester.

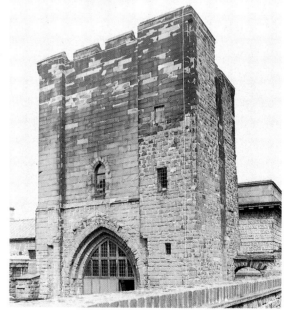

OPPOSITE: the Sandbach Crosses

ABOVE: the inner ward of Beeston Castle with the castle well

LEFT: the Agricola Tower, Chester Castle

Barton-Upon-Humber: St Peter's Church

HUMBERSIDE

Famous for its Anglo-Saxon tower and baptistry, the former parish church of St Peter closed in 1970 and has since then been subjected to an intensive archaeological investigation, together with the adjoining Anglo-Saxon and later graveyard. A fascinating picture is being built up of the evolution of the fabric, which is documented in a photographic exhibition in the church. From the exterior, St Peter's is a fine fifteenth-century church with an unusual Anglo-Saxon tower. Just how the Anglo-Saxon church evolved into what we see today is being revealed in far more detail than would ever have been possible from documentary evidence alone, or from the investigation of a building that is still in use. The church as built in the tenth century consisted of the tower flanked by the baptistry and chancel. It was extended east in eight stages, from which the tower and baptistry have miraculously survived. The latter is extremely rare. The construction of the tower, for instance, can now be described with certainty, for the use of internal scaffolding is clear from the putlog holes that were hitherto concealed. As the tower was built up, scaffolding poles were built into the walls on which the scaffolding planks rested. When the structure was complete, the poles were sawn off flush with the wall and rendered invisible by the coats of lime-wash which are now known to have covered the interior walls. The development of the church also mirrors that of the village; and the relationship of the nearby church of St Mary, formerly a chapel of ease and now the parish church, is full of interest. Although there is nothing for the visitor to see in the graveyard, 1,326 graves have been subjected to palaeopathological investigation (like criminal pathology but with only bones and earth to work on), and much important information has been gathered. There were no grave goods, though some of the coffins were filled with flowers. It is, for instance, possible to work out the family relationships between the deceased, even though they have been dead for over a thousand years, and the evidence of arthritic diseases in the bodies may provide information that can assist doctors working in this field today.

Chester Roman Amphitheatre

CHESHIRE

This was the largest amphitheatre in Britain, seating about 8,000, but half of it is unexcavated so its size is not immediately apparent. The north part of the arena wall, the north and south entrances, some steps and the 'nemeseum', a small room used as a shrine to the goddess Nemesis, are visible. Now partly encircled by a road, the amphitheatre stands just outside the Roman city walls on the south-east side, near Newgate. Chester (Deva) was founded in the late AD 50s as a marching camp that became a fortress. Here the XXth legion transferred from *Wroxeter* c. AD 88 and a large civilian population grew up outside the fortress. The amphitheatre was for both soldiers and civilians; not just as a place of entertainment but for military training. Skilled squads of soldiers would demonstrate manoeuvres to be copied by the recruits, as well as practising hand-to-hand fighting. It was built of stone c. AD 86, replacing an earlier earthen structure erected soon after the city had been founded by the Romans, and was only rediscovered in 1929. Excavating and conserving the amphitheatre presented many problems. A visit to Grosvenor House Museum (not English Heritage) will enlighten visitors, and there are various finds from the site on display as well as material on the development of Roman Chester. Here was the headquarters for the continuing battle to control North Wales, and until the River Dee began to silt up, Chester was also a seaport. (The fortress was abandoned partly for this reason.) The command GHQ for southern Wales was Caerleon, Gwent, which has the best preserved Roman amphitheatre in Britain; it is instructive to compare the two.

Burton Agnes Manor House

HUMBERSIDE

In 1601 Sir Henry Griffiths began to build himself a splendid new brick mansion at Burton Agnes. The stone manor house built by his Norman ancestors looked quite insignificant beside it and was soon encased in brick, demoted to a service building. Further indignities took place in the eighteenth

The undercroft, Burton Agnes Manor House

century when the walls were raised to insert another storey and all the windows replaced. For many years it served as a laundry. If it were not for the fifteenth-century-style doorway ground floor left, and the odd placing of the ground-floor windows, this would seem a Georgian property. A walk around the building would make one think again though, for as so often with old buildings, the most informative details are to be found at the back. Here a large chimney is corbelled out at first-floor level and there are many blocked openings. Inside, visitors find themselves in the restored undercroft of a first-floor hall house of *c.*1170-80. The room is divided by a row of three circular columns with waterleaf capitals, from which spring the stone vaults carrying the floor of the hall above. The undercroft floor is laid with bricks, dating from its laundry days. Diametrically across the room a tiny newel stair rises in the thickness of the wall. The main entrance to the hall would have been by an external stair, and the hall walls would only have risen to just above the top of the lower row of windows, with a steeply-pitched roof of thatch. In the fifteenth century the walls were raised and it is to these late medieval proportions that the room has been restored. It was always heated by a fireplace, never by a central hearth. No original features survive in the hall, which is quite empty. One should now visit the church close by which contains a wonderful collection of memorials to the Griffiths family, and to the Boytons who inherited the estate in 1654.

Gainsthorpe Deserted Medieval Village

HUMBERSIDE

Gainsthorpe was the first deserted medieval village to be discovered by aerial photography. That was in 1924. By and large this is still the best way to view it, for at ground level there is not a great deal to see. The first documentary reference to Gainsthorpe is in the *Domesday Book*, 1086. In 1616 a survey of the area noted that 'there is nowe neyther tofte tenemente or cottage standinge ... it keepes neer 1500 sheepe'. The village had probably been abandoned in the fifteenth century, not necessarily because of the Black Death the previous century, but more probably because of changes in farming and the switch to sheep pasture. For the general visitor, the site can be recommended as a good spot for leaning on a gate and contemplating the transience of earthly things. '*Iam seges ubi Troja fuit*'.

Skipsea Castle

HUMBERSIDE

Skipsea, a motte and bailey castle, had been completed by the time the *Domesday Book* was compiled in 1086. It was built by Drogo de Bevrère, who married a niece of William the Conqueror, murdered her, and fled. It is said that having poisoned her, Drogo then had the effrontery to go to William in order to borrow money from him for a trip abroad; ostensibly to take his wife on a visit to her relations. News of her death did not break until after he had fled the country. Not surprisingly she is believed to haunt the locality, dressed in white and moaning piteously. By the thirteenth century the castle had already been demolished. Today it consists of a gorse-covered hillock in the middle of a muddy field. Cows graze over the earthworks of the outer bailey. It would make a fine subject for a

watercolour, for the light along this flat stretch of coastline has a shimmering, pellucid quality, especially at dusk and dawn.

Thornton Abbey

HUMBERSIDE

Thornton has one of the finest monastic gatehouses in the country, and the remains of what must have been a very beautiful chapter house. The abbey was founded as an Augustinian priory in 1139 and achieved abbey status soon after in 1148. It was always very wealthy as the gatehouse, an extravagant confection in stone and brick testifies. Three storeys high, the gatehouse is rectangular in shape; the crenellated top was originally ornamented with

LEFT: Skipsea Castle

RIGHT: Aerial view of Gainsthorpe Deserted Medieval Village

When the room was broken into he was discovered seated at a desk, but the body fell to dust upon contact with the fresh air. The same writer tells us that after the Dissolution, Sir Vincent Skinner built a large house to the west of the abbey, the Great Hall of which collapsed for no apparent reason as soon as it had been completed. More of the abbey stone was taken to build Ferriby Sluice which was another disaster. The abbey survived intact until the reign of Edward VI as it had been chosen by Henry VIII as one of two colleges of secular canons that were to be maintained as schools and homes for aged civil servants. However, the scheme did not survive the 1540s.

statues as at Alnwick, and the façade too was covered with statues in ornamental niches, most of which have gone. It was probably begun in the 1360s and it is one of the earliest uses of brick for large-scale building in the Middle Ages. Inside there is a fascinating collection of little rooms tucked away, and some finely-carved details, for instance the roof of the main spiral staircase. An exhibition of medieval floor tiles and pieces of sculpture recovered from the site is housed here. A surprising distance from the gatehouse, about a five-minutes walk away across a field, are the foundations of the church and cloister buildings. The remains of the octagonal chapter house are the most impressive. There are three bays of panel tracery surviving and this same design would have been filled with coloured glass on the other side. It was begun in 1282 and the floor tiled in 1308. In the confused remains of masonry between the chapter house and the south transept, a small room can be detected. Here, so a seventeenth-century writer informs us, was found a monk who had been walled-up alive.

Thornton Abbey gatehouse from the barbican

Goodshaw Chapel

LANCASHIRE

This early Baptist chapel was recently rescued from decay and completely restored. Situated on Swinshaw Moor, it was built in 1760 and reseated in 1800 to accommodate a larger congregation. The textile workers in the cotton factories of the valleys were strongly nonconformist and chapel building to a certain extent mirrored the fortunes of the industry. A larger and much more imposing chapel was built in 1861, but this has since been demolished. Externally the building appears to be a two-storey pair of semi-detached cottages with the two entrances side by side and twelve pane sash windows. The reason for this modest exterior was due partly to lack of money, but also to the clandestine nature of all religious activity outside the Established Church in the eighteenth century and a desire not to attract attention by a provocatively grand exterior. Inside, the visitor finds one large room with galleries on three sides and box pews — an interior of elegant simplicity.

Sawley Abbey

LANCASHIRE

Pronounced 'Sally', the remains of this Cistercian abbey lie between the main road and the River Ribble, with the Forest of Bowland to the north. All the facing stones have gone and only the much eroded rubble core of parts of the church remains. The monastery was suppressed in 1536 but was refounded during the Pilgrimage of Grace under a new abbot, William Trafford. Henry VIII was so incensed by this that he sent specific instructions to the Earl of Derby 'without further delay' to 'cause the said Abbot and certain of the chief monks to be hanged upon long pieces of timber, or otherwise, out of the steeple'. William Trafford was executed on 10 March 1537, the monks dispersed and the buildings dismantled. The outline of the claustral buildings can be seen and part of the church walls. The tradition of the old faith continued to endure in Lancashire and resurfaced after the Catholic Emancipation Act with the support for the Roman Catholic school at Stoneyhurst (formerly the Jesuit English College from St Omer, which had finally found refuge at Stoneyhurst in 1794). Until the recent boundary changes, Sawley was in the North Riding of Yorkshire, but was closely linked with

Whalley Abbey to the south. Sawley was founded some thirty years before Whalley, in 1147, and had a scholarly tradition. It was never very large, nor very wealthy, and the nave was drastically shortened, probably after the Black Death had reduced the availability of lay brothers. By 1381 there were fifteen monks and two lay brothers. The aisled chancel was extended in the early sixteenth century. A gatehouse, about 250 yards north of the church, was constructed from materials found on the site when it was excavated in 1848 by the local landowner, Lord de Grey, who was also the first President of the RIBA. His vast estates included *Wrest Park* in Bedfordshire which he had rebuilt to his own designs in the 1830s. By showing an archaeological interest in the Gothic in the 1840s he was obviously keeping abreast of the times.

RIGHT: Goodshaw Chapel and its interior seen from the galleries

Warton Old Rectory

LANCASHIRE

Across the road from the parish church in Warton stands the old rectory built in 1825. Behind it are the ruins of the even older rectory built in the fourteenth century. The gable ends survive to full height and walls to roughly first-floor level, so it is possible to understand the layout of this typical medieval stone house quite easily. Above the entrance the eaves line of the former porch can be seen. Entering the building one is facing the entrance in the rear wall that would have opened on to the staircase. To the right would have been a wooden screen separating the hall from the through corridor; this has vanished and one has to imagine the hall open to the roof, probably with a central hearth and the smoke escaping through a louvred vent in the ceiling. To the left is a stone wall with three pointed arched doorways. The central one opened into a passage, the blocked door of which can be seen in the gable end wall. The other openings led to the buttery and the pantry, separated from the passage by timber partitions with little lancet windows in the gable end. This end was two storey, hence the staircase. There is evidence that the upper room, which was the drawing room or solar, had an inner chamber with a garderobe opening off it. In this period the kitchen would have been a detached building because of the risk of fire.

Warton Old Rectory looking at the service end

Whalley Abbey Gatehouse

LANCASHIRE

The remains of the Cistercian abbey at Whalley are quite extensive, but only the outer gatehouse is in the care of English Heritage. The inner gatehouse, the abbey ruins and the house built amongst them are administered by the Manchester Diocesian authorities and a Roman Catholic group. The outer gatehouse stands about quarter of a mile to the west of the abbey and the main road in fact passes through it. It is a particularly fine example of early fourteenth-century work, eight bays long with chamfered rib vaults. The upper storey is roofless and has window openings in the east and west gable ends. This large room over the gateway might have been a court or schoolroom, though in Cistercian monasteries gatehouse chapels were sometimes provided for the use of the lay brothers. The last abbot of Whalley and two of the monks were executed at the monastery in March 1537 for their adherence to the Pilgrimage of Grace. These events are described in Harrison Ainsworth's *The Lancashire Witches*, where they are linked with the famous seventeenth-century witches of Pendle. Though the prose style is rather leisurely, this late nineteenth-century novel is interesting for its depiction of the area, and also as an example of how the Victorian Anglican view has coloured our perception of medieval monastic life.

ABOVE: detail of mosaic pavement, Aldborough Roman Town

Aldborough Roman Town

NORTH YORKSHIRE

Two mosaic floors and a section of the town wall survive at Aldborough (Isurium), the tribal capital of Brigantes. The Iron Age hill fort at *Stanwick* had been the previous headquarters of this warlike tribe, until they were conquered by the Romans in the early AD 70s. Aldborough does not seem to have begun as a fort but had started to develop by the late first century AD. Its street pattern was possibly laid out in the reign of Hadrian (AD 117-138). Like other tribal capitals it was laid out on the grid system and an area of forty-four acres was enclosed by the town walls. Much of it now lies beneath the present village but the south-west section of the walls survive and the site museum stands by the south gate into the town. The defences first took the form of a ditch and earthen bank to which a stone wall was added in the third century. Mid fourth-century semicircular bastions were added, as can be seen at *Burgh* and other Saxon Shore Forts, but none are visible here. There is a pleasant tree-lined promenade beside the walls, whose remains are modest, and a bench to sit upon and reflect. A five-minute walk away in the middle of a field are the two mosaics, housed in two small modern buildings. They both belong to a large fourth-century town house and were discovered in the nineteenth century when a farmer was digging a pit to bury a calf. Unfortunately the pit broke through the centre of one mosaic which depicted a lion. The other, a geometric design, is intact. Several mosaics were discovered in the eighteenth century and nineteenth century which have since disappeared, though one of particular interest can now be seen in Leeds City Museum. It shows the only known Romano-British mosaic depicting the legend of Romulus and Remus. The wolf is grinning hugely, possibly at the fact that he is disguised as a horse. The site museum contains a variety of objects: coins, cooking pots, a backscratcher, a spatula for holding down a patient's tongue, and examples of Samian ware, the French red glazed pottery which was found on all 'the best Roman dining tables. There is also a milestone, reminding us that this was on Dere Street, the important road north to Catterick and *Corbridge* by *Hadrian's Wall*.

Byland Abbey

NORTH YORKSHIRE

The Cistercian abbey at Byland was originally founded by monks of the order of Savigny in 1134. They did not, however, arrive at Byland until 1177, having made three earlier unsuccessful attempts to settle. The monastery was originally planned for thirty-six monks and a hundred lay brothers, but after the Black Death numbers had fallen to twelve monks and three lay brothers. The ruins of the church, completed in 1225, are impressive, culminating in the great circular window remains at the west end. Large areas of glazed floor tiles are still *in situ* and others from Byland can be seen in the British Museum. From the carved stiff-leaf capitals displayed in the site museum, some idea can be gathered of how fine the interior must have been. The Rule of the Cistercian order called for plain churches and simple vestments, for they had begun as a reform movement emphasising the spiritual above all else. Nevertheless, with the light falling through the great west window on to the glazed green and yellow floor tiles, the whitewashed walls and piers painted with red lines to imitate ashlar masonry, and the crisply carved capitals picked out in red, the nave must have been very handsome. The foundations of the claustral buildings can be readily identified, the lay brothers' range being conspicuous by its length. The lay brothers performed the manual labour in the monastery. In 1322 the abbey was pillaged by the Scots. They narrowly missed capturing Edward II who had just been dining at the abbot's table.

Byland Abbey from the south-west

Easby Abbey
NORTH YORKSHIRE

This abbey of the Premonstratensian canons was founded *c.*1155. The remains are extensive and are compressed into a small site on the left bank of the River Swale. The restrictions of the site have produced an unusual plan. Many of the buildings rise almost to full height, including the early fourteenth-century gatehouse which gave access to the now-vanished outer courtyard of the monastery. This contained the parish church, which had been built before the monastery was founded, and which is still in use today, containing, among other features of interest, a good Norman font. Much remains of the infirmary wing and abbot's lodging standing to the north-east of the abbey church, while the guest house and the refectory to the south are particularly impressive. Little survives of the abbey church above foundation level. The refectory was largely rebuilt around 1300 and the walls rise almost to eaves' level over the remains of the original early thirteenth-century vaulted undercroft. The east window which retains so much of its original geometrical tracery has always been much admired. There is evidence that in the later Middle Ages the canons only used this magnificent room on feast days and had a smaller first-floor dining room for everyday use. Remains of the reader's pulpit can be seen in the refectory, for the canons ate their meals in silence, listening to readings from religious works as was the custom in all monasteries. To communicate their needs a system of sign language was employed. Documentary evidence survives for the sign language used by the members of another order, the Cluniacs, which seems to suggest that meals must have had their humorous moments in houses where discipline was strict. 'For bread, make a circle with the two thumbs and forefingers, because bread is usually round ... for cherries, put the finger under the eye ... for raw onions, press the finger on the mouth half open, on account of that sort of smell ... for honey, put your tongue out a little way, and pretend to lick your ear ...'

LEFT: the interior of the refectory, Easby Abbey

RIGHT: the south front of Helmsley Castle seen from Duncombe Park

FAR RIGHT: the east end of Kirkham Priory church

Helmsley Castle

NORTH YORKSHIRE

Helmsley has a very unusual rectangular earthwork dating from the time when motte and bailey castles were the norm. It was erected in the late eleventh century and this rare plan with double ditch may have partly resulted from the rock formation on which the castle stands. Visitors enter from the town side and have to walk humbly along the outer ditch in order to enter the castle via the fine barbican on the south-east front. This dates from the mid thirteenth century, while the keep with curtain walls and towers were built between 1186 and 1227, in the time of Robert de Roos. The keep, commanding the entrance from the town, also has an unusual plan being not rectangular but apsidal on the town side. This front has largely been destroyed but the square front that overlooks the inner bailey is well preserved. Remains of the Great Hall and other buildings face the keep across the bailey. They were altered in the late sixteenth century and some plasterwork and other internal fittings can still be seen. In the Civil War the castle belonged to the Duke of Buckingham and considerable damage was done to the buildings during the siege directed by General Fairfax. The Duke later married Mary, the daughter of General Fairfax, but there were no children. On his death the estate was sold to Sir John Duncombe, whose family built the nearby Duncombe Park (not in the care of English Heritage). Helmsley Castle looks across the fine eighteenth-century parkland of Duncombe, a house whose grounds in the eighteenth century contained not only a ruined castle but a ruined abbey as well. Two little Grecian temples were erected c.1758 and they still survive in the care of the National Trust, guarding either end of the terrace that looks down on the ruins of *Rievaulx Abbey* — one of the loveliest views in Yorkshire.

Kirkham Priory

NORTH YORKSHIRE

Kirkham was founded between 1122 and 1130 as a house of the Augustinian canons. Its famous gatehouse, dating from the late thirteenth century, is decorated with carvings and the coats of arms of its founder and patrons, the lords of *Helmsley Castle*. The priory was founded by William l'Espec, who later founded *Rievaulx*, and legend has it that the foundation was in memory of his only son, who was killed near this spot by a fall from his horse. As at *Rievaulx*, an extensive rebuilding programme took place soon after the priory was founded, and by the late thirteenth century the priory was heavily in debt. Kirkham had adopted one of the usual means of financing building, the sale of corrodies. These were annuities that lay people purchased in exchange for a lump sum, entitling them to live out their old age in the monastery, enjoying a comfortable standard of living which was carefully agreed in advance. There was also the added benefit of burial in the priory churchyard, in monastic garb, which assured a remission of days in purgatory. Financially this was a gamble for the monastery for some corrodians might live to a considerable age and Kirkham in the early fourteenth century may have contained as many corrodians as canons. (In 1380 there was a prior and sixteen canons, and this number was probably roughly the same earlier in the century.) One result of the rebuilding programme was the enlargement of the presbytery in the thirteenth century, and the east end is the major surviving feature of the church. The remains of an attractive vaulted porch gives access to the west side of the cloister and the sloping site that Kirkham enjoys provides interesting views.

Aerial view of Mount Grace Priory from the west

Mount Grace Priory

NORTH YORKSHIRE

Mount Grace is the best-preserved Carthusian monastery in England, founded in 1398. The unique life-style of the monks can be seen from the layout of the cloister where each monk lived a solitary existence in his own little dwelling with a garden at the back. One of the dwellings has been reconstructed: the two storey building had piped running water and a privy at the bottom of the walled garden where vegetables were grown. Beside each entrance can be seen the dog-leg opening through which food was passed to the monk without him being able to see or speak to the lay brother who brought it. Like so many hermits' cells, the buildings were laid out around an inner courtyard or cloister, overlooked by the oriel window of the prior's lodgings adjoining the church. The monks ate together once a week on Sundays when they went for a walk and conversation was permitted for a short time. Otherwise they lived in silence. This called for a deep spiritual commitment and understandably the number of Carthusian houses were few. They were particularly important in spreading the teachings of the mystics through translations, and the Carthusian monasteries in urban settings also played a more active role as preachers. This emphasis on solitude and a strict adherence to principle earned them the respect of the general public in the fifteenth century and down to the Dissolution, at a time when the other monastic orders had largely fallen into disrepute through too great an involvement in everyday life.

Middleham Castle

NORTH YORKSHIRE

Richard III was thirty-three when he died at the Battle of Bosworth, and he had been King for only two years, yet no other English monarch has aroused so much controversy. While his responsibility for the death of the little princes in the Tower is still debated, almost his every act is open to conflicting interpretations. The majority of his adult life was spent at Middleham, and part of his childhood. Here he lived after his marriage in 1472 and here his son was born and in 1484 died, the same year as his wife. For those who find the mid fifteenth century rather confusing there is an exhibition devoted to Richard, set amongst the extensive remains of the castle. Richard's was not an open nor a friendly personality, yet it was said of him that where he was most known he was most liked. Middleham shares something of his withdrawn, introspective character. The Norman keep is closely bounded by an impressive curtain wall with ranges of gaunt and blackened buildings filling most of the bailey and giving a rather claustrophobic feeling. The curtain wall is thirteenth century, heightened in the late fourteenth century-early fifteenth century when the gatehouse was added in the north-east corner. The castle stands on the edge of the moor and the village occupies the outer bailey. The road between Middleham and Richmond has some magnificent scenery, especially fine in the autumn, and the delightful castellated Middleham Bridge, a suspension bridge of *c.*1830, acts as a prologue to the Castle. One of the last stories told of Richard was on the eve of the battle of Bosworth. Going the rounds of the sentry posts he found a sentry asleep and stabbed him with the remark, 'I found him asleep, and have left him as I found him.'

Marmion Tower

NORTH YORKSHIRE

This beautiful little gatehouse was erected early in the fifteenth century by Elizabeth Marmion, wife of Sir William FitzHugh. It overlooks the river and commanded the ferry crossing that was in use before the bridge was built in the eighteenth century. The building is roofless and consists of a three-storied gatehouse-tower with a single room on each floor. There is a pretty little oriel window above the gateway, looking past the church to the village, and on the river frontage a garderobe projects. More accommodation would have been laid out around a courtyard to the west. The nearby parish church contains a large collection of memorials to the Marmions, including a fine pair of fourteenth-century alabaster effigies of a knight and his lady. They lie beneath one of the few surviving examples of an iron hearse, upon which candles and wreaths were set. The figures are thought to be Sir John Marmion, who died in 1387, and his wife. The knight's feet rest upon a very supercilious-looking lion, whose face seems vaguely familiar.

ABOVE: Marmion Tower

LEFT: interior of the keep at Middleham Castle

Pickering Beck. Here upon occasions the romantic whistle of a steam train can be heard as it threads its way through the woods below. On a clear day there are fine views across the moors from the keep. The moors, largely forested in the Middle Ages, were the domain of the castle. Hunting was the chief sport and occupation of the king and aristocracy who jealously guarded their rights. Clearing timber or trapping animals carried heavy punishments and the castle functioned as an administrative centre to control the forests, also as accommodation for the king and his retinue when they were hunting in the area. There was a fine collection of castles in the area for wider defence. After the dramatic events of 1322 when Robert Bruce laid waste the north of England, it was decided to strengthen the castle. The inhabitants of Pickering had felt it safer to buy off the Scots rather than trust to the castle for defence. Detailed accounts survive for this period 1324-46, and again for the 300 years after 1413 when the castle became part of the Duchy of Lancaster. These documents give a vivid insight into the life of the castle, some details of which are reproduced in the guidebook. By the early sixteenth century the keep was described as 'evil rent, riven and perished', and the whole was too overgrown and decayed to be worth garrisoning during the Civil War.

Pickering Castle

NORTH YORKSHIRE

ABOVE: Pickering Castle keep seen from the south

RIGHT: Piercebridge Roman Bridge

The ruins of Pickering Castle are worthy of a textbook on castle building. Here we can see clearly the classic development of a motte and bailey castle, erected in the early years of the Norman Conquest, where the timber palisade on the motte was replaced late twelfth-early thirteenth century by a stone curtain wall forming a shell keep. The timber palisade enclosing the bailey was replaced by a curtain wall with towers, 1323-26. The east side of the castle facing the town is the best preserved, while on the west there is a sharp drop down to

Piercebridge Roman Bridge

NORTH YORKSHIRE

Here at Piercebridge on the south bank of the River Tees are the remains of an early Roman by-pass. The Roman road of Dere Street that ran north from York originally crossed the River Tees by a bridge about 400 yards to the east. The chronology of events is not certain, but the road was realigned to by-pass the large fort that was constructed on the north bank, across the path of the road. It is the remains of this later road bridge that we see today. The banks of the Tees have altered considerably over the centuries and the piece of masonry abutment that survives is now about thirty yards from the river. Remains of one of the stone piers that carried the wooden bridge, similar to the first bridge at *Chesters*, are also visible, and there are various pieces of stonework excavated when the site was discovered in 1972. There are quite extensive remains of the Roman fort to be seen on the north bank of the Tees, in County Durham (not in the care of English Heritage).

Richmond Castle

NORTH YORKSHIRE

How pleasant to be in Richmond Castle and gaze across the River Swale at dusk. There is a contentment in the air befitting a castle that has never seen bloody deeds. Begun c.1071, much of Alan the Red's castle still survives. Indeed, except for the White Tower and Colchester, no other castle contains so much masonry from the first twenty years after the Conquest. This is not the traditional motte and bailey castle, for the natural defensive properties of the site made this unnecessary. Rather it is a triangular enclosure, curtain walls on two sides converging on the gatehouse with the steep drop to the river on the third. The ruins of the Great Hall, named after Alan's steward Scolland, stand in one corner fronting the river. Here is a very

early example of Norman first-floor hall, and of particular interest to historians. The great tower that is such an imposing feature of the castle was built over the gatehouse by Conan the Little between 1146 and 1171. The gateway opening remains at ground-floor level looking into the castle courtyard; the vaulting was added in the 1330s when further buildings were erected on the river front, but they have largely disappeared. The Great Hall of the tower has been floored and re-roofed (partly glazed), so that for once one can get some idea of the perpetual gloom which must have been the lot of castle inhabitants. They must have gravitated like moths to the blazing torches and shunned the black dancing shadows. Quite a relief to climb on to the roof and inhale the fine Yorkshire air. Richmond is spread out below to the north-east while the moors stretch away to the west. Do not omit to see the castle from across the river, the most popular view for engravers and painters in the eighteenth and nineteenth centuries.

Richmond Castle from the south bank of the river Swale

Rievaulx Abbey

NORTH YORKSHIRE

The ruins at Rievaulx, founded by the Cistercians *c.*1132, are among the finest monastic remains in Britain. The east end of the church with its ribbed vaults of *c.*1230 is particularly beautiful, the walls standing almost to full height with an imposing grandeur that can be matched by few monastic sites in Britain. There are extensive remains of the claustral buildings, notably the refectory and the buildings that stood around the infirmary cloister. As the first Cistercian house in the north of England, Rievaulx accommodated a very large number of people — 140 monks and 500 lay brothers, and many foundations were colonised from here. During the first century or so of its existence the monastery acquired an unrivalled reputation for sanctity that owed much to St Ailred, one of the great figures of English monasticism and Abbot of Rievaulx from 1147 until his death twenty years later. A massive building programme also took place. At the beginning of the fourteenth century the monastery was heavily in debt and numbers were reduced. The setting of Rievaulx is famous for its beauty, and there is a landscaped walk along the hillside above the abbey created in the mid eighteenth century by the owners of Duncombe Park. The Rievaulx Terrace with its two little temples is in the care of the National Trust, and from the terrace glorious views of the abbey and valley can be obtained.

RIGHT: looking north-east from the cloisters to the abbey church

FAR RIGHT: the Abbey seen from the Rievaulx Terrace

Scarborough Castle
NORTH YORKSHIRE

If one had to choose the English Heritage site with the finest view, Scarborough Castle would certainly be in the front running. On a clear day one can see as far south as Flamborough Head, and the coastline to the north is full of interest. In 1136 William le Gros began to improve the natural defensive properties of the site with earthworks, but such a fine location was quickly taken into royal possession. Henry II built the great keep that partially survives today, while the barbican of 1243-45 is the most recent major addition. The castle was frequently attacked and often capitulated — Piers Gaveston, the favourite of Edward II, being one unlucky custodian. During the Rising of the North in 1567 it was taken by subterfuge, for the rebels gained entry disguised as peasants, but only managed to hold out for three days. Subsequent events gave rise to the phrase 'a Scarborough warning' — a word and a blow, but the blow comes first. In the Civil War the castle changed hands upon a number of occasions, including twice in one day which was something of a record. The Royalist attack of 1645 led to the collapse of the north transept and choir of St Mary's Church in the town below. The ruins of the east end still adjoin this fine church, which contains much of interest. Another feature of the castle for visitors is the remains of the Roman signal station — an outline only — which was in use for about thirty years at the end of the fourth century. A small chapel was built here on the headland c. 1000, and this was twice rebuilt with some of the masonry still surviving.

Spofforth Castle
NORTH YORKSHIRE

Spofforth was the original home of the great Northern family of Percy, Dukes of Northumberland of the first creation, who arrived in England in 1067. In the Middle Ages their vast estates included Alnwick and *Wharram Percy*. Harry Hotspur, son of the first Earl, is said to have been born at Spofforth, which is a small fortified manor rather than a castle, now in ruins. The site is unusual in that the visitor approaches across a mound, the site of now vanished buildings, to the fifteenth-century great hall set at ground level. Continuing round the northern end of the building by the solar block, the land drops away and the hall now appears at first-floor level on the west side. A stream runs past this front of the building, but the landscape has been drastically altered since the Middle Ages by the addition of the large railway embankment across the southern end. The twelfth-century undercroft to the hall is built into the living rock with dramatic effect. On

ABOVE RIGHT: Scarborough Castle, looking north across the castle well to the keep

RIGHT: Spofforth Castle, the solar block with garderobe turret

Steeton Hall Gateway
NORTH YORKSHIRE

A small manorial gatehouse dating from *c.*1360 survives intact at Steeton, but the rest of the manor house was much altered in the eighteenth and nineteenth centuries and is not in the care of English Heritage. The gatehouse is a fine example of its type; it is two storey with a carriage entrance and a smaller pedestrian entrance beside it. There is a chimney to the first floor room and a crenellated parapet, both carried on corbels decorated with carved faces which were renewed in the nineteenth century. A stone ribbed vault covers the carriageway, and on the rear elevation an external stair gives access to the first-floor room via an ogee-headed doorway. This is probably a later insertion. Another doorway at ground-floor level gives access to an internal stair. The first-floor room has an oriel window overlooking the courtyard.

Stanwick Iron Age Fortifications
NORTH YORKSHIRE

the floor of the undercroft can be seen the bases of pillars that were inserted when the roof was vaulted to carry the rebuilt hall in the fourteenth century. The solar block and garderobe tower were added at the same time. This was probably done around 1308, the year Henry Percy received permission to fortify the house, and the year before he purchased Alnwick. The hall was rebuilt again in the fifteenth century.

This may have been the site of one of the major battles of the Roman Conquest, the defeat of the Brigantes under Venutius by the 9th Legion in the early AD 70s. The vast earthworks at Stanwick were the tribal stronghold of the Brigantes. They developed from an Iron Age hillfort, and by *c.*AD 50 enclosed an area of 850 acres. The impossibility of defending such a long perimeter was demonstrated by the Romans. The Brigantes were later settled at *Aldborough*, though they continued to cause the Romans many problems. Some idea of the fortifications can be gained just south of Stanwick Church at 'the Tofts', the earliest section of the earthworks, although the site is low-lying and much obscured by trees. Part of the ditch can be seen north of the Stanwick-Fawcett road at NGR NZ 179 112. Finds from the site are on display at the Yorkshire Museum, York, and in the British Museum.

ABOVE RIGHT: Steeton Hall Gateway

LEFT: part of the earthwork fortifications at Stanwick

St Mary's Church, Studley Royal

NORTH YORKSHIRE

The magnificent High Victorian Church of St Mary's, Studley Royal, was built 1871–78 by William Burges for the Marquis and Marchioness of Ripon. Their house at Studley Royal was demolished after a fire in 1945 but its beautiful eighteenth-century landscaped grounds, which include Fountains Abbey (National Trust, but maintained by English Heritage), still remain. The axis of the main drive centres on a view of Ripon Cathedral to the south, and it was on the site of an eighteenth-century obelisk that closed the northern view that Burges' church was built. Unlike the almost contemporary church that the Marchioness's mother built at Skelton, Studley does not appear to have had any purpose other than that of estate church and maus-oleum for the founders. The exterior of the church with its lofty west tower shows Burges' imaginative use of Early English and French Gothic, and he used features copied from the east and south fronts of Ripon Cathedral as a sort of distant echo at the end of the long drive. The interior of the church is very splendid: all the surfaces of the chancel are alive with colour and gilding; over the sanctuary is a wooden domed roof, covered with gilding and painted figures, similar to his work at Cardiff Castle; coloured marbles, stained glass, painting and gilding fill the choir with its painted ceiling, while the nave is more sober, though only by contrast. The great organ with its spiral staircase to the organ loft is an extraordinary structure in its own right.

ABOVE: detail of a corbel in the choir of St Mary's Church, Studley Royal

RIGHT: clustered marble shafts in the sanctuary

FAR RIGHT: the south front of Whitby Abbey

Wharram Percy Church and Deserted Medieval Village

NORTH YORKSHIRE

Wharram Percy lies in a fold of the moors, a lovely setting for a village which has everything to recom-mend it apart from buildings. The growth and decline of the medieval village can best be seen in the alterations to the church, which is now a roof-less shell. It was enlarged as the village prospered but sections were demolished as the community shrank. In the nineteenth century only a farmhouse remained on the site of what had once been a thriving community. The outlines of some building foundations and garden walls can be identified and

and north transept remains, there is little to be seen of the claustral buildings of the medieval monastery. Like the west end of the church they were destroyed to build a mansion at the time of the Dissolution. This house, the home of the Cholmley family, was often rebuilt and it survives as a roofless ruin to the south-west of the church.

the medieval millpond beside the church has been reconstructed. Excavations are in progress which have provided a great deal of information about the evolution of the village, one of the 3,000 deserted village sites that have so far been identified.

Whitby Abbey

NORTH YORKSHIRE

The ruins of the Benedictine church built in the thirteenth and fourteenth centuries dominate the headland above Whitby. They stand on the site of the religious community founded by St Hilda in 657. This was a double monastery, and burial place of the kings of Northumbria, which became famous for its scholarship and learning. The poet Caedmon, who wrote in the language of the Northumbrian people, was one of the community, and in 664 the important Synod of Whitby was held here. This was summoned by the King of Northumbria, Oswy, to decide between the Celtic and Roman methods of dating Easter, symbolic of deeper differences that threatened to split the English church. The Roman method was chosen. Some two hundred years later the community was destroyed by the Danes and only ruins remained, but roofless buildings are described in the foundation charter in 1078 when the community was refounded as a Benedictine priory. While much of the east end of the church

Clifford's Tower, York

NORTH YORKSHIRE

Bursting with self-importance on its neat conical mound, the keep of York castle has a rare quatrefoil plan. It was built between 1245 and 1270 on the site of a timber motte and bailey castle that had burnt down. In fact William the Conqueror had erected two castles in York 1068-69, for the Normans experienced considerable trouble in subduing the north of England and much of Yorkshire was laid waste in the process. Evidence of the other castle can still be seen. The quatrefoil plan with a splayed base and turrets corbelled out at the junction of the foils was never repeated in England, and its precedent seems to have been the Château d'Etampes, near Paris. More or less from the time it was built, Clifford's Tower was used as a prison and it is named after one of its inmates, Sir Roger de Clifford, one of those executed by Edward II after the Battle of Boroughbridge in 1321. The interior of the keep has been gutted, initially by the sixteenth-century prison jailer who ran a good business in secretly selling the interior fittings and stonework of the castle for building materials. In 1684 the keep was burnt out and fell into disuse until it briefly became a prison again in the early nineteenth century. The palatial group of eighteenth-century buildings to the south were built as the debtor's prison, the female prison and the Assize courts. The Castle Folk Museum is now housed here.

ABOVE: Wharram Percy church

ABOVE RIGHT: Clifford's Tower, York

Wheeldale Roman Road

NORTH YORKSHIRE

In many ways Wheeldale is one of the most impressive Roman monuments in Britain. Lying on the moorland far from human habitation, this mile-long stretch of roadway brings home the heroic nature of Roman road building. How they managed without maps and compasses, without explosives, in a country that they hardly knew, to create the magnificent network of straight roads is quite extraordinary. Many of the roads like Watling Street are routes we still use today. The paving stones have gone but the 'agger', the cambered core of the road, flanked by drainage ditches remains. It was built in the first century AD.

ABOVE: Wheeldale Roman Road

TOP: the western range of claustral buildings at Monk Bretton Priory

Monk Bretton Priory

SOUTH YORKSHIRE

The Cluniac order, to which Monk Bretton belonged, differed from other monastic foundations in its overriding preoccupation with the worship of God. The almost continuous celebration of divine service, in the most beautiful surroundings, took precedence over everything else. The houses were dependent on the mother house at Cluny, France, and for various reasons the order was never very popular in England. Its influence was already waning when Monk Bretton was founded in the year of King Stephen's death, 1154. Now it is part of the suburbs of Barnsley and the red sandstone ruins are etched with grime, making it difficult to imagine these liturgical splendours, particularly since most of the church has disappeared. The early days of the monastery were darkened by very unspiritual wrangling with the priory at Pontefract, from whence the first monks had come. The references to the election of the prior in the foundation charter were open to conflicting interpretations, upon which devolved the question of an annual payment. Physical violence marred the dispute, and at one stage the whole of Monk Bretton was excommunicated. In 1281 the quarrel was finally settled by the priory joining the Benedictines. This was an auspicious choice and at the Dissolution Monk Bretton was one of the very few houses where monks' piety led them to wish to continue their monastic existence. They banded together, purchased 148 books from the library, and continued their communal life at the home of one of the brethren. The monastery itself was partly converted into a residence. Visitors today enter by the gatehouse. To the south is the detached prior's lodging with its crenellated mid fourteenth-century fireplace. The remains of the cloister buildings, including the refectory with service hatch to the kitchen can be seen, and the east range with chapter house.

Conisbrough Castle

SOUTH YORKSHIRE

The spectacular keep at Conisbrough is one of the finest English buildings of the twelfth century. It is thought to have been erected by Hamelin Plantagenant, half-brother of Henry II, *circa* 1180. The castle had been granted at the Conquest to the de Warenne family, who also held *Castle Acre*, but nothing of their fortifications now survive. The unique plan is cylindrical with a splayed base and six solid buttresses rising full height, also with splayed footings. The fine ashlar finish of the walls gives it a sculptural purity. Access is at first-floor level by a stairway which was originally broken with a drawbridge. Below the first floor, which was used for storage, lies the vaulted basement with the hall and private apartments on the two upper floors. Each of these rooms has a hooded fireplace, a laver recess and a garderobe. A tiny chapel with a fine vaulted stone roof stands in one of the buttresses. The sleek exterior of the keep is marred by few window openings and consequently these rooms must have been extremely dark. The conical roof and parapet have gone, but visitors can ascend to the walkway. The buildings in the inner bailey would have provided normal living accommodation and the foundations of the single aisled hall and other buildings can be identified. Conisbrough has an unusually well-preserved collection of privies, including a fourteenth-century double latrine and one that uses a deep fissure in the rock as a chute. Various alterations were carried out in the fourteenth century but some time around 1500 part of the curtain wall collapsed, rendering it undefendable and thereby preserving Conisbrough from destruction during the Civil War.

Roche Abbey

SOUTH YORKSHIRE

The remains of the Cistercian abbey at Roche lie in a lovely secluded valley, with a little cascading brook chattering by. The 'capabilities' of the site were recognised in the eighteenth century and

included in the landscaping around Sandbeck House, (not in the care of English Heritage). The monastery was founded in 1147 and was built of the fine local stone. The name St Mary of Roche, or St Mary of the Rocks, was thus derived. Immediately beneath the cliff are the remains of a twelfth-century gatehouse in the north-west corner of the site. Only the lower storey survives. The most prominent feature at Roche are the east walls of the transepts of the church, which stand almost to their full height. They date from *circa* 1170 and are pierced by openings to the transept chapels, which are interconnected by an aisle. Adjoining are part of the chancel walls, which were embellished in the fourteenth century with a fine sedilia and piscina beneath an ornate canopy. The remainder of the church and the claustral buildings are only a few feet high, but their layout can easily be identified. A sorry picture of the last days of the monastery has come down to us, and one which must have often been repeated elsewhere. 'All things of price' were 'either spoiled, carped away, or defaced to the uttermost ... it seemed that every person bent to filch and spoil what he could,' as one eye-witness recorded long after the event. The library was pillaged for missals to patch the covers of wagons, the monks tried to raise a little ready money by selling off the contents of their cells, and the choir stalls were burnt in order to melt the lead from the roofs. A former friend and supporter of the abbey who took much of the timber from the church roof, when asked in later years why he had done so, replied, 'I did see all would away; and therefore I did as others did.'

TOP: Conisbrough Castle from the south-west

LEFT: Roche Abbey from the south-east

THE HEART OF
ENGLAND

Gloucestershire
Hereford and Worcester
Oxfordshire · Shropshire · Staffordshire
Warwickshire

Over Bridge, Gloucester
GLOUCESTERSHIRE

One of the later bridges built by the great engineer, Thomas Telford. The single-arch masonry bridge was erected in 1825-27 over the Maisemore Channel of the River Severn. As a tidal river that floods frequently, the Severn poses many problems for bridge builders. Telford produced a novel design based upon Peronnet's five-arch bridge over the River Seine at Neuilly, built 1768. This is how Telford explained it in his autobiography: 'The general body of the arch (is) an ellipse, 150 feet on the chord line, and 35 feet rise, while the voussoirs, or external arch stones, being in form of a segment, have the same chord, with only 13 feet rise. This complex form converts each side of the vaults of the arch into the shape of the entrance of a pipe, to suit the contracted passage of a fluid, thus lessening the flat surface opposed to the current of the river whenever the tide or upland flood rises above the springing of the middle of the ellipse.' One can now admire his ingenuity from the new road bridge that carries the A40 west of Gloucester.

LEFT: Over Bridge, Gloucester

BELOW: Cirencester Amphitheatre

Cirencester Amphitheatre
GLOUCESTERSHIRE

Cirencester (Corinium) was the largest town in Roman Britain after London, and some idea of the wealth of the city can be gained from a visit to the Corinium Museum with its fine collection of mosaics. The town's amphitheatre was probably erected early in the second century and was an earthwork with stone terraces and wooden seating. The perimeter survives with grass-covered banks rising to a height of twenty-five feet above the arena floor, with entrances at the north-east and south-west ends. Here 8,000 spectators enjoyed gladiatorial combats and watched condemned criminals mauled to death by wild animals. In the fifth century the legions withdrew to defend Rome and for a short period the amphitheatre was fortified against the invading barbarians, but to no avail.

Greyfriars, Gloucester
GLOUCESTERSHIRE

Built in the early sixteenth century, only a few years before the Dissolution of the Monasteries, this Franciscan friary church has undergone surprising transformations. Only the nave walls now remain. Seen from the west it is an early nineteenth-century ashlar-fronted town house, yet the north and south return walls are the buttressed nave and north aisle walls, two bays forming the house and two bays open to the sky. The east end stops at the chancel arch, and looking down the nave one is faced with a twentieth-century curtain wall. Strangely enough this is the part of the building that is in the worst state of repair. The north aisle wall has cartouches below the four-light windows, with trefoil-headed panels between. The church would have been the gift of a rich patron, for the friaries did not administer great estates as the monasteries did, but followed St Francis's teachings on poverty. The rest of the friary was to the south where the technical college now stands; but to the north and west, buildings of many periods have created an informal quadrangle with some fine old trees.

Blackfriars, Gloucester
GLOUCESTERSHIRE

Here is a good example of the fate that befell monastic foundations at the Dissolution. While the Benedictine monastery of St Peter became the cathedral, the much smaller Dominican friary was purchased by the Sheriff of Gloucester and converted into a house for himself, with a cloth factory attached. He drastically shortened the nave and inserted floors and fireplaces into the church to make a fine house, externally altered in the eighteenth and nineteenth centuries. The floors have now gone and the thirteenth century nave rises once more to the original scissor-braced collar-beam roof — a rare survival. The friars (unlike the monks and canons) became especially noted as preachers and evangelisers in the growing towns; their closest modern counterparts would be the Salvation Army. Based in the towns, they walked through the countryside preaching at wayside crosses and nominally living by charity alone. The buildings of the friary are set around a grassy quadrangle, the west side of which was rebuilt in the eighteenth century with something of the feeling of a French town square. In the south range there is another rare survival, the monks' study cubicles, eighteen in number, and at present undergoing restoration.

Hailes Abbey
GLOUCESTERSHIRE

Part of the cloisters and the foundations of one of the great Cistercian abbeys survive at Hailes. It was founded in 1246 by Richard, Earl of Cornwall, a

ABOVE LEFT: interior of Blackfriars showing the fine thirteenth-century roof

ABOVE RIGHT: the north aisle of Greyfriars

RIGHT: Hailes Abbey, the cloister from the west

brother of Henry III, in fulfilment of a vow made after being shipwrecked off Sicily. One of the richest men in Europe, he became King of the Romans in 1257 and attempted to rule in Germany – the Holy Roman kingdom – until his death in 1272. In 1270 his son gave the abbey a relic authenticated by Pope Urban IV as being the Holy Blood of Christ. The mass appeal of the holy relics held by every monastery and church sometimes became, in crude terms, the basis of their economy. Hailes was soon one of the main pilgrimage centres in this country and consequently very rich, for the possession of such a highly venerated and popular relic attracted substantial donations from the faithful. After the Reformation there was much dispute concerning the Holy Blood. One ex-monk maintained that it was duck's blood, renewed weekly, which was contained in a glass phial, one side of which was thicker than the other. Since the godly would be able see the Blood more clearly than the ungodly, the thicker side of the glass was revealed to those who it was felt had 'room for improvement', and might yet make larger donations. The east end of the church was rebuilt to house the relic and this took the form, rare in England, of a chevet, or cluster of chapels around an ambulatory facing the shrine, the foundations of which can be seen today. Floor tiles from the chevet, decorated with heraldic designs, are on display in the British Museum. The wealth of the abbey is reflected in the very high quality of the carved bosses and sculptural fragments rescued from the church and housed in the museum, which is laid out like a small cloister. The church was demolished at the Reformation and most of the other surviving buildings disappeared in the eighteenth century. The nearby parish church, which incidentally predates the abbey, contains medieval floor tiles and some wonderful heraldic wallpaintings. They include the personal emblems of Eleanor of Castile, a castle, and for Richard, the abbey's founder, the eagle, symbol of the Holy Roman kingdom. (This kingdom later became an empire, the first reich.)

only rediscovered in 1871. The survival from this early date of a cycle of frescoes in their entirety is quite unique. In the nave there are some thirteenth-century tempera paintings, including the Wheel of Life and Ballam and his Ass. Among the other notable features are a fourteenth-century wooden porch protecting a medieval wooden door with early ironwork, while the tympanum above is carved with the Tree of Life. Here one gets a very good idea of how exciting a medieval church must have seemed to its worshippers, most of whom lived in dreary hovels. It was full of colour, with carvings and pictures evoking the vast fund of stories and parables that were the basis of the medieval churchgoers' world. (Rather like going to the picture palace during the Depression.) Since the church has to be kept locked, visitors would be advised to ring the Area Office before planning a trip.

St Mary's Church, Kempley

St Mary's Church, Kempley

GLOUCESTERSHIRE

This is a fine Norman church with a remarkable collection of wallpaintings. In the chancel is a beautiful cycle of fresco paintings *c.* 1130–40, whitewashed over at the time of the Reformation and

Odda's Chapel, Deerhurst

GLOUCESTERSHIRE

A rare survival of an Anglo-Saxon chapel, built by Earl Odda during the reign of Edward the Confessor and dedicated to the memory of his brother in 1056. The chapel was subsequently incorporated into farmbuildings and was only rediscovered in 1885. At that time the nave was in use as the kitchen of the half-timbered farmhouse it still adjoins. The rectangular nave and partly rebuilt square chancel adjoining it have been restored. The chapel is empty, but the nearby priory church of St Mary is also an Anglo-Saxon foundation containing much of related interest. There is a ninth-century font for instance, which for many years, if not centuries, had served as a washtub until rediscovered in 1844. Odda was also a benefactor of nearby Tewksbury Abbey which no visitor to the area should miss seeing.

ABOVE: Odda's Chapel and the farmhouse adjoining

RIGHT: Kingswood Abbey Gatehouse

Kingswood Abbey Gatehouse

GLOUCESTERSHIRE

All that remains of the Cistercian abbey at Kingswood is the early sixteenth-century gatehouse. The original roof survives on the upper storey, which is accessible to visitors. Of particular interest is the window above the vaulted gateway, for the mullion is fancifully carved with flowers emerging from foliage like that found on top of a pineapple, the whole set in a vase. In fact they should probably be described as lilies, flowers of the Virgin, to whom Kingswood was dedicated, as were all Cistercian monasteries. The abbey was founded in 1139 by William de Berkeley and was the first daughter house of Tintern. The early days were difficult but in the thirteenth century it became very prosperous due to the wool trade. In 1291 there were eight granges, or outlying farms worked by the monks and lay brothers. The Cistercians were major wool producers in the Middle Ages. Their Rule which ordered them 'to seek out the wilderness' as the site for their monasteries sent them to the uplands of Yorkshire, Wales and Lincolnshire — ideal sheep pasture. The order included a large body of lay brothers who tended the flocks, grew food and acted as building labourers. They worshipped separately from the monks, were not allowed to learn to read, and could not become monks. But the Black Death badly undermined the economic basis of the order, for this pool of cheap labour dried up. Kingswood, for one, never fully recovered its former prosperity; the granges were leased out to tenants and the abbey became a landlord thereby subtly altering its relationship with the local people. The prior's behaviour at the Dissolution reflected little credit on the abbey. First he sent Thomas Cromwell a pamphlet he had written in support of the Royal Supremacy, and then this was followed by a friar that he had taken prisoner for preaching in favour of Papal Supremacy.

Above this the body of a young woman had been interred soon after. The site was excavated in 1881 and 1934-35 and the fragments of Neolithic pottery discovered are on display in the Cheltenham Museum.

Nympsfield Long Barrow

GLOUCESTERSHIRE

Here also the earthen mound has disappeared from this Neolithic burial site. Aligned south-east/north-west and ninety feet long, there was originally a horn-shaped forecourt with the walls curving back from the east entrance. This gave access to a square forecourt within the barrow, from which three burial chambers opened out in a clover leaf plan. Evidence of fires and pig bones were discovered in the forecourt, which shows that some sort of ritual feast accompanied the internment. It is generally thought that the bodies interred in these Neolithic sites were left in a special place to decay, or until some appropriate time, and then the tomb was filled and permanently sealed on one single occasion. Of the twenty-three people interred at Nympsfield, a large number seem to have had problems with their teeth. Inflamed gums, septic teeth and abscesses were common complaints. There is now a picnic area beside the Barrow which stands on the edge of a wood, on the west side of the B4066.

Looking south-east through Nympsfield Long Barrow

Notgrove Long Barrow

GLOUCESTERSHIRE

The earthen mound has been removed from this Neolithic barrow leaving a few monolithic stones, largely obscured by vegetation, marking out the original plan. The exact length of the mound is uncertain, but it was rather more than 160 feet and was surrounded by a dry stone wall like *Belas Knap Long Barrow*. Internally, however, it was quite different, belonging to the type of Cotswold-Severn tombs known as transepted gallery tombs. Entered from the east end via a shallow forecourt and ante-chamber, two burial chambers lay on either side of the gallery with another at the west end. These contained the remains of six adults and two children. Later a domed circular cairn was constructed adjoining the western burial chamber in which was found the crouched skeleton of an elderly man.

Hetty Pegler's Tump (Uley Tumulus)
GLOUCESTERSHIRE

A 'tump' is a mound or barrow, and Hetty Pegler was the wife of a seventeenth-century owner of this well-known Neolithic site. It is one of the most interesting because the mound is still intact and visitors can enter two of the four chambered tombs, having first obtained the key from nearby. The plan is similar to that of *Nympsfield Long Barrow*, a mile to the south. Both belong to the Cotswold–Severn group of chambered tombs and are of the type known as transepted gallery where pairs of burial chambers face each other off a central passageway, or gallery. Uley is one of the earliest in the group, dating from sometime after 3000 BC. The barrow is aligned south-east/north-west and is approximately 120 feet long. In 1821 and 1854 excavations were carried out which produced evidence of about twenty-three bodies; the finds can be seen in Guy's Hospital Museum, London. After this subterranean excursion, there is a splendidly bracing walk to be had over Uleybury Iron Age Fort, half a mile to the south-west.

The interior of Hetty Pegler's Tump

Offa's Dyke
GLOUCESTERSHIRE

Offa's Dyke was built in the eighth century as a defensive boundary between the kingdom of Mercia and the ancient British and Welsh tribes in Wales. Offa was King of Mercia 757–796 and he achieved great things through a judicious mixture of murder, marriage and military campaigns. The dyke ran from the Severn estuary to the Welsh coast and consisted of a ditch with a bank on the east side. It was not continuous, but made use of natural defensive features like rivers. The dyke was built by local levees and was at least partly fortified with a system of beacons and watch towers. Many sections can still be identified. The best-preserved piece is at Knighton but the section in the care of English Heritage is set in the lovely country south-east of Tintern Abbey. It is possible to walk along some sixty miles of the dyke itself following the Offa's Dyke footpath, marked by wooden finger-posts with yellow acorns. This is one of the twelve official long-distance footpaths in England and Wales, and runs 168 miles from Sedbury Cliffs near Chepstow to Prestatyn on the north Welsh coast. Stout walking shoes and an OS map are needed for the dyke, including the English Heritage section above Tintern.

Belas Knap Long Barrow
GLOUCESTERSHIRE

Not for the faint of heart, nor weak of feet. A brisk twenty-minute climb up through a coppice and across windy fields brings one to this Neolithic chamber tomb, one of the best restored of the Cotswold group, with the mound intact. The orientation is roughly north-south with a false entrance at the higher northern end to mislead tomb robbers. The five chamber tombs have been opened up so that visitors can see inside. They lie on the perimeter of the barrow, two on the east side and one west, with a conjectural reconstruction at the southern end. The remains of thirty-one people were found in these tombs and six more, a man and five children, had been hastily interred blocking the false entrance.

St Briavels Castle
GLOUCESTERSHIRE

St Briavels, with its splendid views across the Wye Valley, standing in the midst of marvellous walking country, was once the administrative centre of the

Royal Forest of Dean. The thirteenth-century gatehouse is the main surviving feature, and its present use as a youth hostel helps to preserve something of the atmosphere that it had when occupied. The Forest of Dean was a favourite royal hunting ground, and it also functioned as a royal arsenal, supplying timber and iron bolts for crossbows, and stones for missiles. The castle was begun in the twelfth century and was a royal possession by 1160 at the latest. Little remains of the square Norman keep which collapsed in 1752, and the moat surrounding the castle has been filled in. The three-storey gatehouse, however, built in the 1290s, is quite substantial. It is roughly square with the entrance wall curved to form two towers flanking the gateway. It belongs to the gatehouse keep type that could be separately defended. The south-east corner has been demolished but numerous small rooms still survive inside the towers, some with interesting fireplaces. An old dog-wheel spit can be seen in the west tower. Eighteenth-century engravings show four sinister posts like gibbets projecting from the eaves of this tower. For many years the castle was a prison, as inscriptions bear witness, and the dungeon below the east tower can still be seen. The gatehouse was reroofed c. 1900 when the west wing and chapel were extensively restored. The church opposite is dedicated to St Briavel, the fifth-century Welsh saint who gave his name to the village and castle. The Norman arcade and the Warren memorial, where the husband and wife lie beside each other as on an Etruscan tomb, are among the features of interest. Here is the setting each Whitsun for the St Briavels bread and cheese ceremony, when bread and cheese are thrown to those waiting outside the church. Differing accounts are given as to the origin of the custom, but they all revolve around the hard-heartedness of the constable of the castle, and the kindness of his wife.

TOP: the gatehouse of St Briavels Castle

BELOW: the entrance to Belas Knap Long Barrow

H-plan facing south-east, subsequently enlarged to include, among other things, a luxurious bath house complex in the south-east corner. This is the main interest of the site. The key to the two little twentieth-century buildings covering part of it can be obtained from the house nearby, though an imperfect view can be had through the windows. The cold room, frigidarium, has a cheerful mosaic of dolphins and fishes. Here the owners would have undressed and then entered the tepidarium. They could then have either chosen a steam bath in the caldarium or the dry heat, like that of a sauna, in the sudatorium. The latter had a hot plunge bath attached, partly surviving in the other little twentieth-century building. Perhaps they might have preferred the cold plunge bath which opened off the frigidarium? Beside it there was a water closet. This was all encompassed in a very small area, but how many houses can boast such luxury today? To the north of the bath house are the foundations of a shrine, thought to be dedicated to the local water nymphs. The spring that supplied the water for house and bath can be heard singing and gurgling above the villa. Often in the past, water pouring down the hillside has threatened to wash the villa completely away, but so far the water nymphs have protected it.

Rodmarton Chambered Tomb (Windmill Tump)
GLOUCESTERSHIRE

Also known as Windmill Tump, this Neolithic stone cairn lies to the west of Rodmarton, on the south side of the road to Cherington, set in a field and surmounted by a clump of trees. An estimated 5,000 tons of stone are contained in this small hump, of which only the false portal at the east end is now visible. The site was excavated in 1863 and 1939, and then backfilled. It was discovered that two rectangular tombs stand behind the false portal, entered from passages on the north and south sides. The remains of ten middle-aged adults and three children were found within.

Arthur's Stone, Dorstone
HEREFORD AND WORCESTER

Set on a ridge about a mile north-north-east of Dorstone church lie the remains of a Neolithic chambered tomb. The mound, which was probably orientated north-south and about sixty feet in length, has disappeared, leaving the polygonal-shaped tomb and remains of the passageway entrance. It belongs to the group of chambered long barrows known as the Cotswold type found in the area that includes South Wales and stretches as far south as *Stoney Littleton* with *Waylands Smithy* to the east and Arthur's Stone as the most northerly

Witcombe Roman Villa
GLOUCESTERSHIRE

ABOVE: Windmill Tump

RIGHT: the foundations of the water nymphs' shrine, Witcombe Roman Villa

Normally known as Great Witcombe, the foundations of this Roman villa are set on a hillside overlooking a delightful valley. The view can have changed little since the villa was built *c* AD 250-70. The site slopes steeply and the house is entered from the upper level; there were probably terraced gardens laid out below. The original villa was

example. Tradition has made this the tomb of King Arthur, or of a giant killed by him.

Edvin Loach Old Church

HEREFORD AND WORCESTER

Edvin Loach is a hamlet so unfrequented that the main access is along a gated and unmetalled lane. The churchyard contains the ruins of the old church and St Mary's, the new church being built by Sir George Gilbert Scott *c.* 1860. A photograph of St Mary's taken soon after consecration shows the earlier church beside it, roofed and intact. Built in the eleventh century with the east end reconstructed in the twelfth century, the old church consists of a single space containing nave and chancel, with the west end tower always open to the nave. The tower survives almost to full height, but the nave and chancel walls are much lower, particularly on the north side which has a beautiful view across to the blue hills. The south door has a large tufa stone lintel, and there is a lot of herringbone masonry, typical of the eleventh century. It is a very peaceful spot.

Arthur's Stone

Goodrich Castle from the south

Goodrich Castle

HEREFORD AND WORCESTER

A splendid castle. Built of red sandstone, it springs from the living rock high above the empty moat. Great spurs thrust the towers skywards. The grey sandstone keep is twelfth century but the curtain walls and towers are of the late thirteenth century. Entered through the barbican and gatehouse, the bailey is roughly square in plan with towers at each corner and the gatehouse set beside the north-east tower. The scale of the Edwardian castle is here, but not the order and symmetry, and Goodrich seems all the more aggressive in its irregularity. For many years the castle was the principal residence of the Talbot family who were created Earls of Shrewsbury in the fifteenth century. By the early seventeenth century, when it passed by marriage to the Earls of Kent, it was no longer inhabited. This was made permanent after the Civil War when it was slighted by the Parliamentarians following an unsuccessful siege. There are very fine views across the Wye Valley to the north.

Mortimer's Cross Water Mill

HEREFORD AND WORCESTER

This eighteenth-century mill has been altered externally, but the interior contains the corn-grinding machinery that was in use until the 1940s. The mill is driven by an undershot waterwheel and the mill leat is fed by the River Lugg. The whole process of corn milling can be readily understood within this small two-storey building. Although there is now only an inn sign to remind us, Mortimer's Cross was the site of a very important battle during the Wars of the Roses. Here in 1461 Edward of York intercepted the Lancastrian Earls of Pembroke and Wiltshire with their forces en route to join Queen Margaret, and annihilated them. Three thousand men were slain. Edward and the centre section of his troops were drawn up on the site where the water mill now stands, and fought their way to victory near the crossroads. Among those beheaded afterwards was Owen Tudor, grandfather of Henry VII. Edward was proclaimed King as Edward IV.

Rotherwas Chapel
HEREFORD AND WORCESTER

This modest little building was formerly the private chapel to Rotherwas House. It was largely rebuilt in 1589 for the Bodenham family who owned the estate until 1913. The house was demolished in 1926. The Bodenhams were orginally Anglicans, but in 1606 Roger Bodenham was cured of leprosy after a visit to St Winifred's Well, Flintshire, and he converted to Roman Catholicism. His descendants were active supporters of the Old Faith, and one of them endowed a large convent outside Hereford in the nineteenth century. The nave of the chapel dates mainly from 1589, the date on one of the tie beams, and the hammerbeam roof with its moulded beams is a fine piece of workmanship. The little west tower was added in the late seventeenth to early eighteenth century, and the chancel was rebuilt in 1868 by E.W. Pugin, son of the more famous A.W. Pugin, both of whom were responsible for many Roman Catholic churches. The chancel is quite simple with a patterned tile floor, stencilled dado and wooden altar. A side chapel with a fireplace was added in the nineteenth century which would have been the Bodenham family pew. The whole is empty of fittings and now stands rather sadly on the edge of an industrial estate, created out of the grounds of Rotherwas House. There are some tantalising remains of estate buildings, much altered (not English Heritage) but of the house, rebuilt in the eighteenth century and attributed to James Gibbs, only a neat mound of turf remains. Visitors should contact the Area Office before planning a visit since the chapel is kept locked.

Longtown Castle
HEREFORD AND WORCESTER

The ruins of this twelfth-century castle command a magnificent view across the River Monnow valley to the Black Mountains, which on a summer's evening seem to be clad in green velvet. The castle

ABOVE: Longtown Castle keep

was built c. 1180–85. It is a cylindrical keep with the remains of two of three semicircular buttresses visible. One of them contained the spiral staircase, and at the upper level there is evidence of the garderobe which was corbelled out. The walls are fifteen feet thick and life in the interior of the castle must have been very cramped. The castle stands on a motte, with the inner bailey enclosed by the remains of the thirteenth-century curtain wall and gatehouse with two circular towers. The cylindrical keep was not a common form, though it is found most frequently in Wales and the Marches.

Witley Court

HEREFORD AND WORCESTER

Witley Court is one of the most impressive ruins in the country, for in the late nineteenth century, here was one of the grandest houses in England. This vast Italianate mansion was created by Samuel Daukes for the 1st Earl of Dudley in the 1860s. He employed the style made popular by Prince Albert at *Osborne House* on the Isle of Wight, but the interiors were more opulent. Daukes was in fact remodelling an earlier house, one which had briefly been the residence of the dowager Queen Adelaide, and which had already been extended twice before. The Ionic portico on the south front belongs to the work done *c.*1800 by Nash, and in the interior the brick core of the house that belonged to the Foleys between the mid seventeenth century and early nineteenth century can still be seen. Their fortunes were largely dissipated by gambling in the eighteenth century. The chapel and also the parish church survive as their monument, however, for they escaped the fire of 1937 that brought about the ruination of the house. Built in 1735 but refaced by Daukes in the 1860s, the chapel has a remarkable interior. In 1747 Lord Foley asked James Gibbs to fit it out using materials from the chapel that he had earlier built for the Duke of Chandos at Canons, another architectural extravaganza, demolished in that year. Ten early eighteenth century stained-glass windows illuminate this white and gold confection, and there is an imposing monument by Rysbrack to its creator, the 2nd Lord Foley. Part of the gardens still survive at Witley Court, laid out by W.H. Nesfield to complement Daukes's work, and include the enormous Perseus Fountain sculpted by James Forsyth, and the Flora or Triton Fountain that could be viewed from the main apartments where Edward VII, when Prince of Wales, often stayed.

ABOVE: *the interior of Witley Parish Church, rebuilt by the Foleys and also used as the chapel to Witley Court*

RIGHT: *the interior of the conservatory*

OPPOSITE: *the south front of Witley Court and the Perseus Fountain*

Abingdon County Hall

Abingdon County Hall

OXFORDSHIRE

'A Market house of most curious Ashler workmanship which may challenge the Preeminence of any in England', as one eighteenth-century writer aptly described this fine building. In the seventeenth century there was great rivalry between Reading and Abingdon as to which would be recognised as the county town of Berkshire. Abingdon hoped to secure this title by housing the Assize courts in a fine new courtroom constructed over an open market hall in 1678-82. The mason-contractor was Christopher Kempster, who worked with Sir Christopher Wren on the City churches and St Paul's. Either of them may have been the architect. The plan consists of an open four-bay loggia for the market over storage cellars. The ceiling of the market is well worth looking at; it is a fine piece of workmanship in an earlier style that looks rather quaint after the handsome classical exterior. Access to the courtroom is via a stair turret containing a solid rather than elegant staircase, recently enlivened with painted decoration, reproducing the original design that was overpainted in the nineteenth century. The courtroom is unadorned apart from an attractive internal porch with Corinthean columns. Above there is an attic storey with cupola (not accessible to the public). The building was first known as the Market Hall and then in the eight-

eenth century the County Hall because the County Courts as well as the Assizes and Berkshire sessions were held there. They were all transferred to Reading in 1868. In the 1920s the building became a museum. The Museum of Abingdon Life contains much of interest, including a section on the Benedictine abbey that gave the town its name and one on the MG sports cars that were built here until 1969. There is also a small collection of stale currant buns dating back to 1887. They are relics of the famous Abingdon Bun Throwing Ceremony, but to find out more you have to visit the museum, or a bakers in Abingdon.

Deddington Castle

OXFORDSHIRE

In 1277 Deddington was described as 'an old demolished castle' and in 1310 as 'a weak castle containing a chamber and a dovecote'. Matters have not improved since. Already in 1312 it was considered too delapidated to contain Piers Gaveston, Edward the II's favourite, en route to his murder at Blacklow Hill. Edward's barons hated him for many reasons; his arrogance and introduction of the table fork were two, and he was confined in the rectory. Today, all that is left of the castle is a small hillock beside the village sports field, which occupies the site of the bailey. The decline of Deddington is at

first surprising when one considers its importance at the time of the *Domesday Book*. The castle had been built by Bishop Odo of Bayeux as the centre of a large estate and was strengthened in the twelfth century. In 1275-76 the town became a borough and in 1302 returned two members to Parliament. The proximity to Banbury, however, was its undoing; one declined as the other prospered, but those who now only think of Deddington as a set of traffic lights on the Banbury-Oxford road should think again. To the east lies the pleasant village centre with the parish church and wide market street preserving the medieval town plan, while the castle earthwork is tucked away, a ten-minute walk to the south-east.

Minster Lovell Hall and Dovecot

OXFORDSHIRE

The Windrush valley is as lovely as it sounds. Here at Minster Lovell, on the banks of the Windrush, stand the remains of Lord Lovell's fifteenth-century house. The manor house was built *c.*1431-42 on land that had belonged to the Lovells for many generations. It lies about a courtyard, looking south, and had a watergate on to the river, which was then navigable. The Great Hall on the north side had a central hearth. Some fine window tracery still

survives. Backing on to the hall and solar, on the church side, is an unusual arrangement of a two-storey block, containing the chapel set above two rooms. The porch, with its handsomely-carved stone vault, is still much in evidence, approached by a patterned pebble pavement, also fifteenth-century. Little remains of the east range containing the kitchens, or the lodgings of the west range, but in the late fifteenth-century south-west tower, the oriel window of Lord Lovell's great chamber can still be seen. This was probably built by the last Lord Lovell, a friend and loyal supporter of Richard III. He survived the battle of Bosworth, led an unsuccessful revolt against Henry VII the following year, and then supported Lambert Simnel. His fate after the defeat at Stoke Field is unknown: some say he fled to Flanders, others that he returned in secret to Minster Lovell and lived concealed in a room that was only accessible from the exterior. One faithful servant alone knew of his presence and supplied him with food. But one day death overtook the servant before he was able to pass on the secret, and Lord Lovell died from starvation. It was reported that in 1708, when a chimney was being rebuilt, an underground chamber was discovered containing the body of a man, with books and papers beside him. The house was dismantled in 1747 by its owner Thomas Coke, Earl of Leicester, whose new house at Holkham in Norfolk was nearing completion. Many years before he had spent his honeymoon at Minster Lovell, a house that had hardly been altered since the fifteenth century. To the north-east lies a circular dovecot, part of the medieval farmbuildings. It has a good stone roof and is complete with nesting boxes.

ABOVE LEFT: the interior of Minster Lovell Dovecot

ABOVE: gable end of the North-West Building at Minster Lovell

North Leigh Roman Villa
OXFORDSHIRE

A mosaic floor with its underground heating system intact is the most interesting feature that remains of this large Roman villa. The villa was arranged around three sides of a courtyard with servants' quarters and three separate baths; the fourth side was closed by a wall with a gateway. In the Roman period the word villa should be understood as a country estate, for all the 600-700 villas known to survive from this period were dwellings whose economic base lay in agriculture. North Leigh began in the second century AD as a simple corridor house with a detached bath house, and expanded up until the fourth century when the surviving mosaic was laid. The geometric design was probably laid by the mosaicist who worked at Chedworth (not English Heritage), and shows affinities with the work at Cirencester in its Museum. The hypocaust, or underfloor heating system, which caused hot air to circulate beneath the floors, supported on pilae, or pillars of tiles, is perfectly preserved, and part of the floor has been cut away to reveal it. This room was probably the dining room, and part of a bath complex adjoins it. Foundations on two sides of the courtyard can be seen, which would have supported timber-framed buildings, probably single storey. Normally in Romano-Britain it was only military and public buildings that were built of stone, which is why, by and large, only the rubble foundations of the timber-framed houses survive today. The villa lies in the bottom of a vale, about a mile from the carpark on the ridgeway above.

Uffington Castle, The White Horse and Dragon Hill
OXFORDSHIRE

ABOVE: Mosaic floor at North Leigh Roman Villa

RIGHT: North Hinksey Conduit House

These sites lie in a group along the old Prehistoric route, the Ridgeway. The White Horse is the only figure of this kind, carved from chalk, which is known for certain to be Prehistoric. The shape of the horse is similar to those depicted on Belgic coins and it may have been cut as the tribal emblem of the Dobunni, or Atrebates. The horse is 360 by 130 feet and is best appreciated from a distance. The regular scouring ceremony to keep the chalk clear of vegetation used to be accompanied by celebrations and sports at Uffington Castle to the south. This is an Iron Age hill fort with a double bank divided by a ditch. Excavations in the nineteenth century revealed that the inner bank was faced with sarsens and there were postholes forming some sort of timber fortification. A little to the north is the flat-topped mound known as Dragon Hill. It is natural rather than man-made, but was used by Prehistoric man for purposes unknown. The name comes from the legend that this is where St George slew the dragon. Thomas Hughes in the opening chapters of *Tom Brown's Schooldays* paints an attractive picture of the Vale of the White Horse and the village of Uffington.

North Hinksey Conduit House
OXFORDSHIRE

This little conduit house, eighteen feet long, was part of the new water supply system given to the city of Oxford in 1616-17 by the lawyer, Otho Nicholson. The main conduit at Carfax in the centre of the city was an elaborately carved affair topped with crocketed, ogee-shaped flying buttresses, like a coronet, and reminiscent of the market cross at Malmesbury. It was transferred to Nuneham Courtenay around 1790 and became a garden ornament. The North Hinksey conduit house was in the depths of the country when built and is consequently a modest little building. Since North Hinksey is divided, rather than by-passed, by the Oxford ring road, locating the conduit house is not easy. It stands on the southern side of the ring road on the lower slopes of Boar's Hill, almost submerged by evidence of twentieth-century civilisation.

Rycote Chapel
OXFORDSHIRE

The interior of this mid fifteenth-century chapel is famous for its unique collection of seventeenth-century fittings. The chapel served the great house at Rycote which was built in the sixteenth century and largely destroyed by fire in 1745. The rest of the house was demolished c.1800, apart from part of the stable wing which survives today as a private house. The great house lay to the north and covered the distance from the stables to the church on its shorter front. In the early seventeenth century the estate passed to the Earl of Berkshire from Lord Norreys, who lies buried in a sumptuous tomb in Westminster Abbey. He probably refitted the chapel around 1610. The fabric of the chapel with its wagon roof remained unaltered, as did the benches in the nave, but the west gallery, pulpit and north pew were added. The latter served as the family pew and it contains painted panels and stencilled decoration, crowned with a singing gallery. The southern pew with its crocketed ogee ribs and painted decoration is believed to have been built for King Charles I when he stayed at Rycote in 1625. The two are linked by a strapwork screen resting on the base of the old rood screen. Later in the century the estate passed to James Bertie, created first Earl of Abingdon in 1682. He replaced the early seventeenth-century reredos that is preserved at the west end of the church with a much larger and more elaborate version, fronted by new altar rails.

Waylands Smithy
OXFORDSHIRE

This Neolithic burial site is an interesting example of two different grave types superimposed one upon the other. The earliest burial consisted of a wooden structure containing fourteen bodies on a stone floor, covered with a mound of earth and stones. Within half a century, c.2800 BC, a long barrow of the Cotswold type was placed over it, orientated south-east/north-west, and containing a pair of transepted burial chambers and a terminal one. Visitors can enter the tomb, which is fronted by massive sarsens. Many legends are connected with the barrow and it is associated with Wieland or Wayland, the only Teutonic hero who firmly established himself in England. He is a fire spirit who will come to man's assistance — here mending broken tools or shoeing horses. He is said to have made the shoes for the *White Horse* at Uffington. The barrow is surrounded by a grove of beech trees but a mid nineteenth-century guidebook writer tells us that 'the modern proprietor of this curious Druidical remain has had the good taste to plant a small wood of fir trees round it, throwing the whole into a deep gloom well suited to its ancient character ...' The barrow can be reached either by a one-mile walk along the Ridgeway from *Uffington Castle*, or via the track that runs south of the B4507 at Compton Beauchamp, joining the Ridgeway quarter of a mile north-east of the site.

ABOVE: Waylands Smithy

LEFT: Rycote Chapel

Acton Burnell Castle

SHROPSHIRE

Entered through a tunnel of rhododendrons beside the church, this warm red sandstone shell survives amidst the eighteenth-century landscaping of Acton Burnell Hall. It is all that remains of the moated castle built by Robert Burnell, Lord Chancellor to Edward I and Bishop of Bath and Wells. He received a licence to fortify his house at Acton in 1284. What remains was probably always the centrepiece of the resulting castle, and formed a free-standing residence for Burnell himself. The main accommodation, a square hall occupying the eastern half, with private chambers to the west, was on the first floor. Access was by an external stair in the north-east corner. The rectangular plan with corner turrets has echoes of earlier keeps, though this building was not intended to be defensible. It would have been served by a kitchen to the east, probably connected only by a bridge at first-floor level. Nearby are the end gables of a great medieval barn. Here, it is said, Edward I held his 1283 Parliament, the first at which 'commoners' were present and when a statute safeguarding the rights of merchants was passed. When Burnell's hunting park developed into the parkland of the later Hall to the north, the ruins of both castle and barn were carefully incorporated as landscape features.

ABOVE: the east wall of Acton Burnell Castle

ABOVE RIGHT: the crossing at Buildwas Abbey church, looking north-east

Buildwas Abbey

SHROPSHIRE

Although by no means a large abbey, the remains of Buildwas, a Cistercian monastery built between 1135 and 1200, possess a remarkable grandeur. Nearly all of the church walls survive to their full height, except those of the aisles. The nave arcade, frequently depicted by eighteenth and nineteenth-century painters, conveys much of the dignity and austerity of the earlier years of the Cistercians. The west end, without a doorway because of the sloping site, has a heroic quality. The cloister lay to the north, between the church and the River Severn. Tolls from the bridge across the river formed part of the abbey's income. The east range of cloister buildings comprise a crypt below the north transept, the sacristy-cum-bookroom, and the chapter house, which is vaulted with some nicely carved capitals. In the chapter house the monks met every morning to discuss spiritual and business matters, seated on benches around the walls. Thus the size of the chapter house is a fair indication of the number of monks in the monastery, at least at the time when it was built. Buildwas was in fact founded for the Savignac order in 1135, who merged twelve years later with the Cistercians. It was never a very wealthy foundation and suffered periodically from the Anglo-Welsh hostilities. In 1350 the abbot was carried off by Welsh soliders and had to be ransomed. His predecessor had been murdered — not by the Welsh, but by a renegade monk.

Boscobel House

SHROPSHIRE

Ever since the Restoration, when the story of King Charles hiding in an oak tree after the Battle of Worcester became known, Boscobel has been attracting visitors. The original oak tree that stood near the house died in the eighteenth century, largely as a result of the attentions of souvenir hunters, but it has since been replanted. In 1651 Boscobel was a modest little hunting lodge belonging to the Giffords of *White Ladies*, and tenanted by the Penderell family. They concealed King Charles at Boscobel for a short time and then assisted him in his escape to France. In the seventeenth century the house was enlarged on the south side, and again in the early nineteenth century when the farm

buildings were added to the north-east. The latter now contains an exhibition about King Charles and the Penderells. In the house is a splendid collection of priests' holes — under the stairs, beside the chimneybreast, behind the panelling — three at least, which would have provided the Penderells with enough priests to start a seminary. However, it seems that most of the hiding places were constructed in the nineteenth century when the house belonged to the Evans family. Walter Evans pur-chased the property in 1817 and being very inter-ested in its past history, he decided to restore and furnish the house as it once had been and he enthusiastically acquired many seventeenth-century fittings and artefacts. These were dispersed at a sale in 1918, but Boscobel is now being restored as it was when the Evans family had it — a romantic nineteenth-century interpretation of the seven-teenth century, and very enjoyable it is too.

The west front of Boscobel House

Cantlop Bridge
SHROPSHIRE

This little cast iron road bridge over the Cound Brook was completed in 1812 to designs by Thomas Telford. It is very similar to other bridges that William Hazeldine cast for Telford at Long Mill (1812), Cound (1818) and Meole Brace (1811–12). The bridge is quite narrow although it is known that Telford wished it to be wider. Traffic now runs beside Cantlop Bridge, carried on a twentieth-century road bridge.

Haughmond Abbey
SHROPSHIRE

Although the church was demolished at the Reformation, there are quite extensive remains at Haughmond. These were preserved through their incorporation into a house that has now disappeared. The abbey was founded c1135 for a community of Augustinian canons by William Fitzalan, a connection which greatly helped the abbey to prosper during the reign of Henry II. In the late twelfth century there were twenty-four canons. The chapter house with its three fine arched openings date from this period. The abbot's great hall is early fourteenth century and at the same time two large statues were added to the south-west door of the church, the only part of that building which now survives. In the late fifteenth to early sixteenth centuries a good deal of work was done at the abbey including the addition of the bay window that greets visitors upon their entry to the site. The plan of the abbey is unusual in that the buildings have been laid out around a double cloister. The site museum contains some fragments recovered from the ruins. If one includes the church, it is apparent that building work was almost continuously in progress at Haughmond. Indeed it would be rare to find a large monastic foundation in the Middle Ages where there was not some building work going on somewhere, which must have greatly detracted from their tranquillity. In the sixteenth century a house was built out of the abbot's great hall and lodgings, which was gutted by fire during the Civil War. The chapter house roof survives from this post-monastic period.

Iron Bridge
SHROPSHIRE

The world's first iron bridge spans the River Severn at Coalbrookdale. This graceful structure was built between 1777 and 1781 to the designs of Thomas Farnolls Pritchard; and financed by the ironmaster Abraham Darby, whose grandfather had first used coke to smelt iron at Coalbrookdale. Woodworking joints were used in the bridge's construction and 378 tons of cast iron were needed. In the 1780s and '90s the bridge was a symbol of the optimistic view of the industrial revolution as the provider of work and wealth for all. The romantic scenery of the Severn Gorge combined with the drama of the blast furnaces, Blake's Satanic mills, made this the thrilling crucible of a new age. Even before the bridge was complete Abraham Darby had commissioned the artist Michael Angelo Rooker to do a painting so that a print could be engraved to spread its fame. Thomas Jefferson purchased a copy of this print in 1786 and it later hung in the presidential residence in Washington. The depression that followed the Napoleonic Wars and the many critics of the 1840s who exposed the horrors of the Industrial Revolution, have led us to forget the energetic optimism of the late eighteenth century. Today the Iron Bridge is the centrepiece of the fascinating collection of industrial monuments that have been preserved in Coalbrookdale and the surrounding area. Amongst them are the Iron Museum, Blists Hill Open Air Museum, the Jackfield Tile Museum and the china works at Coalport.

Langley Chapel

SHROPSHIRE

Standing alone in a field is this little chapel, whose chief delight is a complete set of early seventeenth-century fittings redolent with the smell of beeswax polish. The chapel served the occupants of Langley Hall, home of the Lee family; and both chapel and house have stood on their respective sites, in various guises since the thirteenth century. A date of 1564 once existed on the exterior of the chapel, while one of the trusses of the arch-braced collar-beam roof is

dated 1601. The chapel is an undivided space with a moulded tie beam distinguishing the chancel from the nave. The raised floor of the former is inlaid with medieval floor tiles. There is seating for about eighty people; a desk at the west end for the musicians, benches with poppyhead finials for the servants and labourers, and box pews for the tenant farmers, as well as a larger one for the Lee family themselves. The late sixteenth to early seventeenth-century changes in Anglican worship are reflected in the fact that the altar is no more than a wooden table (a replica) brought forward into the body of the church with seating all around it — including the east end. A square structure open on two sides with a flat roof has variously been identified as a boxed pulpit with tester, a lectern without a reading desk, and the Lees' family pew. Langley had become the main seat of the Lee family in 1600, and in 1620 Sir Richard Lee was one of the patriotic group of Englishmen who sought to rescue King James from his financial difficulties by purchasing a baronetcy. It seems quite possible that the chapel was fitted out in commemoration of the event. He died in 1632 and, like his father, has a fine memorial in Acton Burnell church. By the end of the century the estate had descended through the female line and Langley Hall was occupied by tenants: thus the chapel escaped alteration. Much of the charm and interest of the chapel is that the contents are all of one period, in contrast to the more lavish fittings at *Rycote*, Oxfordshire, which span the seventeenth century and include some earlier fittings. Langley Place was demolished in 1868 and only the gatehouse now remains.

Mitchell's Fold Stone Circle

SHROPSHIRE

This Bronze Age stone circle has a beautiful setting on high ground. Heathland encompasses the site on three sides and to the west the land falls away sharply with Welsh hills rising in the far blue distance. Of the circle, sixteen undressed stones survive, ten of which stand erect. There are other, possibly related, sites in the area, though not all are on common land. The name, Mitchell's Fold, derives from Medgel or Medgley, a giant who is reputed to have milked his cows here.

Lilleshall Abbey

SHROPSHIRE

Founded in the mid twelfth century for Arrouasian canons, a reforming French group, Lilleshall was colonised from Dorchester, Oxfordshire. Soon after they were absorbed into the Augustinian order. Much of the church survives, dating from the twelfth and thirteenth centuries, together with parts of the east and south ranges of the cloister buildings. The thirteenth-century west end has a deeply moulded round arched opening, a conserva-

tive, not to say out-of-date choice for the period, but suitably imposing for a facade with only one entrance. There were no side entrances because there were no aisles. An aisleless nave was a common arrangement in the early churches built by the canons, of which this is one of the largest. Remains of the east end of the nave are substantial, including a very fine Romanesque processional doorway in the south-east corner opening into the cloister. The twelfth-century east end wall of the presbytery had almost vanished when the enormous east window was inserted in the fourteenth century, and it still has quite an impact today, even without its tracery. One of the interesting features in the south range of the cloisters is a little book locker; two openings rebated for doors, with a shaped projection to hold a bolt. The abbey was well-endowed and had a reputation for scholarship. One of the canons, John Mirk, wrote a number of religious works, one of which is numbered among the first works printed in England for it was included by Caxton in *The Golden Legend*, published in 1483. At the Dissolution the buildings were partly stripped and a dwelling erected in the cloisters. During the Civil War it was hastily fortified by Sir Richard Leveson for the King, and stoutly defended for several weeks. Finally the Parliamentarians fought their way in through the north transept and many of the buildings were destroyed.

The west end of Lilleshall Abbey church

Moreton Corbet Castle

SHROPSHIRE

This is a ruined medieval castle with the remains of a splendid late sixteenth-century mansion adjoining. The castle occupies a roughly triangular site beside the church where many of the Corbet family are buried. The square castle keep dates from *c.*1200 with remains of a fine hooded fireplace projecting at first floor level. To the north-east is the gatehouse, possibly thirteenth century, altered 1579 as an inscription states. A range along the east side was added in the mid sixteenth century but has now largely disappeared. The pièce de resistance is the ruined south front range dated 1579. It was begun by Robert Corbet, inspired by his visit to Italy, and is a wonderful mixture of classical and mannerist with carved dragons and grotesques, shaped gables and pedimented mullioned windows. It is a shame that not more of the building survives. Camden, the sixteenth-century historian, knew the building: 'Where within our remembrance, Robert Corbet, carried away with the affectionate delight of Architecture, began to build in a barraine place a most gorgeous and stately house, after the Italians modell … but death, countermanding his design, took him off, and so his project was left unfinished.' Robert Corbet died of the plague after visiting his ailing uncle in London. Moreton has affinities with Kirby Hall and Sir Thomas Tresham's Rothwell Market Hall, both of which were built in the 1570s, an exciting decade for English architecture. The house was partly completed in the early seventeenth century and was besieged during the Civil War when it sustained considerable damage.

White Ladies Priory

SHROPSHIRE

It is hard to imagine, looking at the shell of this twelfth-century priory church, that in the seventeenth century it was part of the large house belonging to the Roman Catholic Giffards, where King Charles sought refuge after the Battle of Worcester. The hunting lodge at *Boscobel*, a couple of miles to the north-east was part of their White Ladies estate. The house was demolished in the eighteenth century but Roman Catholic families continued to be buried in its graveyard. Here is the headstone to William Penderel, died 1707, whose father had sheltered Charles at Boscobel, and a nineteenth-century replica of Jane Penderel's headstone inscribed 'Here lieth the bodie of a friende the king did call Dame Joane but now she is deceased and gone interred Anno Do 1669'. St Leonard's Priory was founded towards the end of the twelfth century for the nuns or canonesses of the Order of St Augustine, who were known as White Ladies because of their white habits. It was a small foundation: the number of nuns dwindled from nine in 1377 to four at its dissolution in 1538. Enough remains of the church, with some of its walls rising to full height, to get a good impression of a small cruciform conventional church of the twelfth century. Two features of architectural note are the round-headed arch to the north transept, and the north-west doorway from the nave which has an unusual lobed surround, rarely seen in England.

ABOVE: White Ladies Priory from the east

LEFT: Moreton Corbet Castle, the south range

Old Oswestry Earthworks

SHROPSHIRE

Aerial view of Old Oswestry Earthworks

This is a magnificent Iron Age hillfort covering about sixty-eight acres, an area similar in size to that occupied by *Maiden Castle*, Dorset. However, unlike Maiden Castle, Old Oswestry has never been scientifically excavated so not a great deal is yet known of its history. The hillfort was begun *c.*300 BC enclosing an oval area with a double rampart, ultimately increased to four ramparts, with a fore-work of six ramparts on the west guarding the entrance. It is not thought to have been a tribal capital, but it was abandoned after the Roman Conquest and the evidence of the major legionary fortress recently discovered nearby at Rhyn Park suggests that this was possibly a region of resistance – in an area that has been fought over for centuries. In the Dark Ages after the Romans left, the hillfort was again reoccupied for a short time. Present-day Oswestry to the south is a Saxon settlement. It is named after the Christian King of Northumbria, Oswald, who was defeated by Penda of Mercia, and died nailed to a tree. His martyrdom took place near here, and he was later canonised. A few years later in the early eighth century Wat's Dyke was constructed, marking the boundary of Mercia. Predating *Offa's Dyke*, it ran from near Holywell on the north Welsh coast, to just south of Oswestry. A section of the dyke adjoins the south-west corner of Old Oswestry hillfort, and it is also visible about 500 yards away to the north. This is excellent walking country.

Wenlock Priory

SHROPSHIRE

The ruins of the Cluniac priory at Much Wenlock stand on the site of the eighth-century religious foundation of St Milburga, to whom the priory is dedicated. It was founded by Merewald of the Mercian royal house and his daughter Milburga — subsequently canonised — was the second abbess. The monastery was refounded between 1079 and 1082 by Roger, Earl of Shrewsbury, and in 1102 the patronage passed to the Crown. The buildings date from the twelfth and thirteenth centuries, though the prior's lodgings (now a private residence and not accessible to the public) were rebuilt on a lavish scale c.1500 and are a notable example of late medieval domestic architecture. The priory church was completely rebuilt in the 1220s and was vaulted throughout. Parts of the south aisle and transept stand almost to full height. At the west end of the south aisle there is a unique example of a first-floor room, thought to be a chapel dedicated to St Michael accessible directly from the church. Between the west wall of the south transept and the cloister is a room, believed to have been a library. The chapter house adjoining remains from the 1180s and contains some good Norman work, blind arcading in three tiers, and an unusual doorway in the south wall which is carved with dragons above the lintel. The only other piece of twelfth-century work is the lavatorium in the south-west corner of the cloister. It is circular but stood within a free-standing octagonal building. Two delightful sculptured panels, reproductions of the original pieces, remain. The lavatorium was where the monks washed their hands before meals and a fountain of water probably rose in the middle of the basin. Since the monks, like everyone else in the Middle Ages, ate with their fingers, clean hands were particularly important. Food was served in bowls, two people to a bowl or cover, and medieval works on etiquette are strong in their condemnation of those who put partially-eaten bits of meat back into the communal bowl or scratch themselves while eating. Spoons and napkins were provided and the cupboards in which they were kept survive in some refectories, for instance at Tintern. The monks ate in silence and it is known that at Wenlock they were fined tuppence for breaking the silence on ordinary days and tuppence a course on feast days. Where they obtained the money from to pay the fines when they ostensibly had no property is not clear. Of the refectory itself, little remains. For obscure reasons it was set at an angle from the cloister. Topiary work, dating from the time when the abbey ruins were part of the gardens of the residence formed from the priors' lodgings, ornaments the cloister and the whole composition is very pleasing.

Wenlock Priory, the lavatorium in the cloister garth and west end of the priory church

Stokesay Castle

SHROPSHIRE

This fortified manor house, largely built by a wool merchant, Laurence de Ludlow, in the last years of the thirteenth century, must be among the most photographed buildings in the land. Anyone with an interest in architecture will know its distinctive features: a Great Hall with gabled windows, a polygonal stone turret at one end, and a second at the other with a unique oversailing upper storey, now known to be original. But what comes as a surprise to anyone visiting for the first time is the scale of the buildings: they seem distinctly cottage-like at first sight but are in fact remarkably large. Inside, the Great Hall, with its fine cruck-built roof, is breathtaking; and the solar boasts a magnificent Elizabethan fireplace with elaborately carved over-mantle. The whole has a wonderful mellow atmosphere. It is a remarkable survival. The castle stands in a delightful group formed with the parish church and its own splendid Jacobean gatehouse.

Wroxeter Roman City

SHROPSHIRE

Here at Wroxeter can be seen the best example of a Roman public bath in England. Wroxeter (Virconium) was founded as a legionary fort AD 58, an important base for the campaigns against the Welsh

tribes. Thirty years later the XXth legion moved to Chester and the fort was rebuilt as the tribal capital of the Cornovii. These important settlements, second only to the 'coloniae' founded for retired Roman soliders, were fine examples of urban planning. They were laid out on the grid system with public lawcourts, a market, bath house, water supply and drainage. For this the Cornovii left their hillfort on the Wrekin. Aerial photographs show the Virconium occupied a large area of which only a fraction, around the public baths, has been excavated. Here visitors can admire one of the largest surviving pieces of Roman civilian masonry in England. It is the wall that separated the exercise hall from the frigidarium, or cold room, in the baths. The entrance to the baths was here, through double doors. The foundations of the warmer tepidarium and caldarium to the south can be seen, and in the south-west corner an unusual feature, an open-air bathing pool. It was not more that three feet deep and was lined with a fine sandstone which looks like marble when wet. Indeed the bathers may well have said to each other, as they jumped in and out, that it was almost as good as the Emperor Hadrian's pool at Tivoli, though he had

in 1176 at Cotton, five miles away, and moved to Croxden three years later. Its history was uneventful and in common with other Cistercian houses the abbey kept large flocks of sheep. The church was begun when the abbey moved here; it was consecrated in 1250. The east end had a chevet, or cluster of radiating chapels around the chancel now marked out in the grass. This was a rare feature though it also existed at two other Cistercian houses, Beaulieu in Hampshire and *Hailes* in Gloucestershire. The south transept wall and the west end both rise to a good height and have the tall lancet windows of the later twelfth to early thirteenth centuries, like extended arrow slits. Their verticality is imposing, but once the monks had seen traceried windows, how they must have longed to open up these austere paths of light and let colour and light flood in. The south range includes the sacristy-cum-library, the chapter house, and undercroft of the dormitory.

BELOW: Croxden Abbey, remains of the south transept of the abbey church and chapter house seen from the cloister

better weather there. Adjoining the public baths were the public lavatories, and to the south-west a small shopping precinct built around a courtyard. Perhaps here were sold oils and perfumes for use in the baths, sponges from the Aegean, and little cosmetic tools. Certainly they sold pottery (some of which can be seen in the site museum) looking as if it were made only yesterday. Cooking equipment and armour is also to be seen, while finds from the nineteenth-century excavations are on display at Rowley House Museum, Shrewsbury.

Croxden Abbey

STAFFORDSHIRE

Two isolated sections of this Cistercian abbey rise to almost their full height, and part of the east range of the cloisters, including the chapter house, still survive. A road bisects the church diagonally, but it is nonetheless a pretty spot. The abbey was founded

Wall Roman Site
STAFFORDSHIRE

The foundations of the bath house and the inn can be seen at Wall, which was a small posting station on the important Roman road of Watling Street. This was the route taken by the imperial Roman couriers from Richborough on the Kent coast, via London to Wroxeter, and on to Chester. Close-by was the junction with Ryknield Street which ran from Bourton, north to Alcester. The posting stations provided accommodation and a change of horses for both the messengers and travellers, and a small town grew up here beside the road, covering twenty to thirty acres. The absence of inscriptions means, among other things, that it is not even clear whether the town lay within the territory of the Coritani, whose tribal capital was at Leicester, or the Cornovii at Wroxeter. The local tribe was obliged to maintain the posting houses and the roads in its territory. The foundations of the inn (mansio) at Wall are of the third building on the site, the earlier two having been of timber. The inn was probably two-storied with rooms around a courtyard, the upper rooms opening on to a first-floor gallery. In the courtyard was a statue on a semicircular plinth. The windows were glazed and some of the rooms had painted plaster walls. Elsewhere on the site there must have been extensive stabling, probably a grander inn or hotel for important travellers, and granaries. The other building whose foundations can be seen is the bath house. It has the same basic sequence of rooms as the larger baths at Wroxeter. Finds from the site can be seen in the museum: others are in the museums in Lichfield (the City Library), Birmingham and Wolverhampton.

ABOVE: remains of the mansio at Wall

OPPOSITE: the Great Hall and State rooms seen from the south-east

BELOW: the keep at Kenilworth

Kenilworth Castle
WARWICKSHIRE

Vying with Warwick as the most important castle in the Midlands, Kenilworth was one of the grandest castles in England. The red sandstone ruins are very impressive, rising above the rich green pastureland that once formed a vast lake. The earliest building to be seen is the mighty twelfth-century keep. A huge suite of State rooms was added in the late fourteenth century by John of Gaunt, and the Great Hall was second only to that at Westminster in size and magnificence. Even as a roofless shell, it is an imposing structure. Private chambers led off it in a chain that was ultimately to be extended by the addition of an extra block of stately rooms built by the Earl of Leicester. These were intended as accommodation for Queen Elizabeth when she visited. He also built the fine gatehouse at the north entrance to the castle as well as the barn-like stables. One of the most notable features of the castle was its extensive water defences covering over 100 acres. The two entrances to the castle, on the north and, more noticeably, on the south are reached across causeways. These held back the water, forming a huge lake stretching away nearly a mile to the west of the castle. The system was completed with lower pools around the east side of the castle. It was these defences that enabled the castle to withstand a siege of nearly nine months in 1266 during the rebellion against Henry III. Subsequently the lakes assumed a more recreational role: Henry V liked to take a boat across to a moated lodge or 'pleasaunce' that he built at the far end. A water pageant formed one of the highlights of the spectacular events arranged for Queen Elizabeth on her notable visit in 1575. She spent nineteen days at the castle on that occasion and was entertained by masques, banquets, hunting and poetry. The great siege of 1266 was not repeated in the Civil War, although the castle was left with its keep slighted to render it indefensible, and the great dam was breached, draining the lakes and moats to create farmland.

EAST MIDLANDS

Derbyshire · Leicestershire
Lincolnshire · Northamptonshire
Nottinghamshire

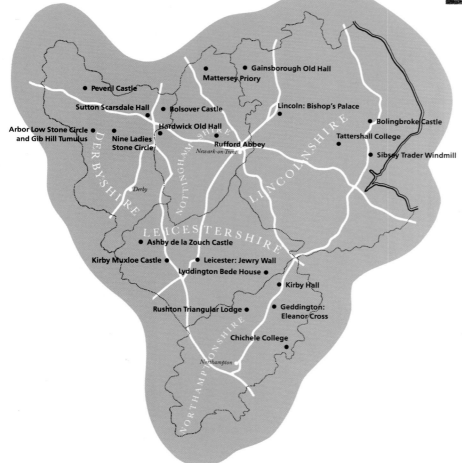

Peveril Castle

Sutton Scarsdale Hall

Arbor Low Stone Circle
and Gib Hill Tumulus

Nine Ladies
Stone Circle

Bolsover Castle

Hardwick Old Hall

Mattersey Priory

Gainsborough Old Hall

Lincoln: Bishop's Palace

Bolingbroke Castle

Tattershall College

Rufford Abbey
Newark-on-Trent

Sibsey Trader Windmill

Derby

DERBYSHIRE

NOTTINGHAMSHIRE

LINCOLNSHIRE

LEICESTERSHIRE

Ashby de la Zouch Castle

Kirby Muxloe Castle

Leicester: Jewry Wall

Lyddington Bede House

Kirby Hall

Rushton Triangular Lodge

Geddington:
Eleanor Cross

Chichele College

Northampton

NORTHAMPTONSHIRE

Bolsover Castle

DERBYSHIRE

Derbyshire is full of interesting country houses, but Bolsover with the painted and gilded interior of the Little Castle is very special. Dominating the surrounding landscape of collieries and towns, Bolsover stands on the site of a medieval castle which was largely destroyed in the early seventeenth century by the Cavendishes, son and grandson of Bess of Hardwick. It belongs to the fascinating world of romance and chivalry that flourished in the later sixteenth to early seventeenth centuries. The literary origins are to be found in Spenser's *The Faerie Queene*. Bolsover has similarities with the castle at Heidelberg — home of James I's daughter, the tragic Winter Queen — which provided a perfect setting before it was torn apart like much of northern Europe during the Thirty Years War. Set around the inner bailey of the medieval Bolsover Castle are the Riding School, the Terrace Range and the Little Castle. The latter is a conscious attempt to create a fairytale castle with its painted decoration,

carved stonework and marble chimneypieces, some like small castles in themselves. It was begun *c.*1610 for Sir Charles Cavendish and was completed for his son in 1634. The Smythsons — father, son and grandson, were the architects. The walls of the medieval keep form the Fountain Garden on the east side of the Little Castle, with rooms set in the thickness of the walls on the site of earlier towers. The fountain is dedicated to Venus. A suite of state rooms, including a magnificent Long Gallery, was included in the long Terrace Range on the west front. Gutted in the eighteenth century, the unusual carved decoration still survives on the façade. To the south is the famous Riding School (1630-34), with its fine roof. The building is still used for its original purpose by Riding for the Disabled, and there is an exhibition space in the adjoining block. It was made famous by William Cavendish, Bess's grandson, who became the first Duke of Newcastle. Having fought bravely on the Royalist side during the Civil War, he followed the court into exile, where he wrote an important book on the art of horsemanship. This was published in 1658 with engraving that used Bolsover and Welbeck, another Cavendish mansion nearby, as backdrops to pictures explaining the movements of dressage.

ABOVE LEFT: the Terrace Range, Bolsover Castle

ABOVE RIGHT: the Pillar Chamber in the Little Castle at Bolsover

RIGHT: window reveals in the Star Chamber of the Little Castle, decorated with paintings of the saints

Arbor Low

DERBYSHIRE

Known as the 'Stonehenge of Derbyshire', this late-Neolithic henge is spectacularly sited, enjoying tremendous views across open country. The henge consists of a circular plateau, slightly tilted, surrounded by a ditch and bank with opposing entrances on the north-north-west and south-south-east sides. These are aligned to the west of the centre of the circle. Set in the centre are three recumbent stones, remains of a 'cove' as at *Avebury*. In a circle about them lie forty-two recumbent stones, massive slabs of limestone, which were not excavated in the immediate vicinity but which were brought here. It has been calculated that the ditch alone, cut from solid limestone bedrock, would have occupied fifty people for at least six months, and some of the boulders in the bank weigh nearly a ton. There is very little doubt that the stones were originally erect. Henges are unique to Britain, and it is not yet possible to point confidently to their purpose. They acted as communal assembly points; trade was carried out at them as well as magic and religious ceremonies. At many there are alignments that indicate an understanding of the movements of the heavenly bodies, although there are no obvious connections at Arbor Low. A later Bronze Age tumulus has been set in the south-east corner of the bank, and a linear earthwork adjoins the south side of the henge — its purpose unknown. The earthwork runs in a curve towards Gib Hill to the south-east. This is another Bronze Age barrow, partially excavated, which at one time was the site of a gibbet and gallows. Finds from the site can be seen in the Sheffield Museum.

Hardwick Old Hall

DERBYSHIRE

Dazzled by the magnificence of Hardwick Hall (National Trust), visitors sometimes fail to notice the blackened shell to the east, the remains of Hardwick Old Hall. However, both historically and architecturally, in the old hall are to be found the origins of the new. Somewhere in the ruins lies the small manor house of John of Hardwick from which his daughter Bess rose, through four marriages, to become the Countess of Shrewsbury. But in 1584 when she returned to her childhood home, her affairs were not prospering; she was separated from her fourth husband, the Earl of Shrewsbury, who was keeping her very short of money, and her right to occupy Chatsworth (her own property from a previous marriage) was in dispute. In addition, it was entailed upon her eldest son with whom she had quarrelled. Following the well-tried policy of when things look bad, spend money to

Arbor Low

cheer yourself up, she decided to transform Hardwick into an ancestral home for her second and favourite son, William (who later built *Bolsover Castle*). Bess seems to have acted as her own architect and evolved the plan as she went along. A legal settlement in her favour in 1587 greatly accelerated matters, and the house was finished by 1591. Many of the ideas found in the old hall were to reappear in the later building. The arrangement of the hall for instance, set axially in the centre of the house is a rare feature, possibly appearing for the first time here. The planning of the two great chambers on the upper floors of the east and west wings, the Hill and Forest Chambers, distinguished by the tall window openings, are the development of plans at Chatsworth and Worksop. Some of the plasterwork still survives, probably executed by Abraham Smith who worked in the new hall. The house was almost completed in 1590 when the Earl of Shrewsbury died, and his death increased her income by a third. Within weeks of his death, and possibly even in anticipation of it, she had begun the new hall a hundred yards away to the north-east. Now she knew exactly what she wanted, and with the aid of Robert Smythson, architect, she got it — one of the masterpieces of sixteenth-century architecture. Bess watched the house rise from the comfort of her old hall and in 1597, when she was in her mid-seventies, she moved across to the sound of pipes and tabors. The old hall continued in use for guests and servants and descended, via her elder son, to the Dukes of Devonshire. By the late eighteenth century the east wing was destroyed and partially demolished, and by the mid nineteenth century the west end was roofless.

Nine Ladies Stone Circle, Stanton Moor

DERBYSHIRE

Stanton Moor is an Early Bronze Age burial site where at least seventy stone cairns have been found, twenty of which have been excavated, indicating that between 300 and 400 people were buried in this area. The cairns were laid out according to a plan which is scarcely discernible, but the Nine Ladies Stone Circle was part of it, as were a number of other circles since lost. Nine Ladies is about fifty feet in diameter with entrance gaps to the north-east and south-west. A single stone stands about thirty yards away to the south-west known as the King Stone. In common with many other stone circles, this is reputedly the site where women who danced on the Sabbath were changed to stone, the isolated stone being the fiddler. This small stone circle with its outer bank seems to be a tiny henge monument, but there was once a small burial mound within the circle and it can be seen as transitional between the old Neolithic traditions and those of the Bronze Age single round-barrow burial. In the eighteenth century there were at least three other smaller stone circles in the vicinity. Access to this Bronze Age stone circle is from the west via the Stanton-Birchover road. Visitors equipped with the OS map number 119 will feel more confident during their fifteen-minute walk.

LEFT: plasterwork surviving in Hardwick Old Hall

RIGHT: the east front at Hardwick Old Hall

Peveril Castle

DERBYSHIRE

The castle is best approached through Winnats Pass, as from here one can quite appreciate why it is known as the Castle of the Peak. Visitors should be nimbly footed and sensibly shod. If the ten-minute path from the ticket office seems steep going up, it feels perpendicular going down. Of course there are marvellous views to compensate. The castle was founded soon after the Conquest by William Peverel on a small triangular site bounded on two sides by a steep gorge and enclosed by a curtain wall. Its purpose was to protect the Peak Forest and the valuable lead mines. His grandson William was disinherited for poisoning Ranulf, Earl of Chester, though he was probably framed, and his estates were forfeit to the Crown. In 1176 Henry II added the square tower which still stands to its full height, denuded only of floor and roof. Numerous other buildings stood within the bailey, though all are now reduced to foundation level. One of the ruined thirteenth-century towers above the Cave Dale precipice shows that Roman building materials have been brought from Brough, about two miles away, and reused. The entrance was always via a main bridge beside the keep spanning the gorge. Beyond the bridge was an outer bailey containing the stables and other service buildings (not in the care of English Heritage). The present entrance was made when the village of Castleton was laid out in the twelfth century. It was intended principally as a sally port, but was doubtless used by castle servants going to and from the town. The castle ceased to be of importance around 1400 though it was frequently used thereafter as a prison, being virtually impregnable. Walter Scott's novel *Peveril of the Peak* should be read if one has a lot of time in hand, which may very well happen if the back road to the south of the castle is used, without exercising extreme care. It should be avoided.

Sutton Scarsdale Hall

DERBYSHIRE

High on a cold and windy promontory, the gaunt shell of this proud house stares grimly straight ahead, as if trying to ignore the existence of the M1 rushing far below to the east. The house was designed in 1724 by Francis Smith of Warwick for the 4th Earl of Scarsdale, but it incorporates the earlier house of the 1st Lord Scarsdale, which was besieged and damaged during the Civil War. The 1st Lord Scarsdale, an ardent Royalist, was reputedly so depressed by the execution of King Charles that he dressed in sackcloth thereafter; and having ordered his grave to be dug, lay in it every Friday in order to reflect upon the sorry state of earthly affairs and the glory of the life to come. His descendant, the 4th Earl, created a magnificent house here. Built from the local tawny, biscuit-coloured Rang quarry stone that carves so beautifully, the house contained excellent stucco work by Vassalli and Adalbertus Artari, two samples of which still survive. The 4th Earl doubtless intended to re-site the medieval parish church which still adjoins the house, but the heavy expenses of building, coupled with an unlucky addiction to gambling, bankrupted him. At his death, without issue, in

ABOVE: Peveril Castle, the keep seen from the inner bailey

RIGHT: Sutton Scarsdale, detail of window opening on the south front

1736, the house and estate were split up and sold. This had dire consequences for the house: without an estate to maintain it, Sutton Scarsdale was only viable for those with enormous 'independent means'. Fortunately, in the nineteenth century it was bought by just such a family, the Arkwrights, descendants of the inventor of the 'spinning jenny', but in the twentieth century no such purchasers could be found. Put on the market in 1920 by the Arkwrights' executors, the house was up for sale for thirty years without success. Eventually everything movable was stripped and sold. American visitors can see three of the first-floor rooms preserved in the Philadelphia Museum of Art. The house was only saved from complete destruction through vandalism and neglect when Sir Osbert Sitwell purchased the ruined shell in the 1950s. His valiant attempts to get the house preserved for the nation achieved posthumous success in 1970.

Kirby Muxloe Castle
LEICESTERSHIRE

The builder of Kirby Muxloe, William Hastings, was Edward IV's closest friend. This friendship, plus his skills as a diplomat, earned him a peerage, the position of Lord Chamberlain, and in 1464, the estate at *Ashby de la Zouch* which he embellished with the Hastings Tower. However, the modest family home at Kirby Muxloe was not forgotten and in 1480 Lord Hastings began to convert it to a quadrangular castle. The courtyard plan has square angle towers and a large gatehouse set centrally on one of the longer sides. It is built of patterned red brick and the building accounts tell us that the master mason and his assistant were sent to look at Tattershall Castle, Lincolnshire. The grand gatehouse, with provision for a drawbridge, had reached its second storey and the west tower with its early gunports had been completed, when Edward IV died. His friend followed him soon after, though not from natural causes. Today the remains of the castle stand encircled by its broad moat. Only the west tower and the gatehouse survive, and the foundations of the original house. One of the interesting features of Lord Hastings' house was that the privies were designed to discharge into purpose-built cesspits that could be emptied, rather than into the moat. This was a great improvement; castle moats that were not fed by rivers must have been as objectionable to the occupants as they were to attackers.

Ashby de la Zouch Castle
LEICESTERSHIRE

The ruins at Ashby are of interest to visitors for many reasons. The buildings began as a manor house in the twelfth century and did not achieve castle status until the fifteenth century. The hall and buttery were enlarged with a solar to the east in the thirteenth century and a large kitchen to the west in the fourteenth century. This was rather innovative since it was normal to have detached kitchens because of the risk of fire. The keep, Hastings Tower, was added in 1474 by Lord Hastings, Edwards IV's Lord Chamberlain and the owner of *Kirby Muxloe*. It framed a self-contained and self-defensible lodging: a castle-within-a-castle. And equally, it acted as a physical declaration of its owner's status. At the same time he built the chapel,

Kirby Muxloe Castle, the west tower and gatehouse

which in 1907 became the Hastings family mausoleum. Only half the Hastings Tower survives — it was literally split in two during the Civil War, which enables us to view the finely carved details, but only from ground-floor level. Lord Hastings' son was made Earl of Huntingdon by Heny VIII and the sixteenth and seventeenth century Huntingdons enjoyed life to the full. The delightful red-brick towers on the south side mark the extent of the famous gardens. Here Anne, Countess of Huntingdon and builder of the *Countess Pillar* in Cumbria, held a masque in honour of her mother, one of the many lavish entertainments which delighted James I and others. During the Civil War the castle played an important part in the Royalist defence of the Midlands. Underground passages were constructed, one of which can be seen to connect the main kitchen with that in the Hastings

Tower. After a long and dramatic siege, 1644 to early 1646, the castle was mined and partly demolished in 1649. The family moved to Donnington Park, but an eighteenth-century Countess of Huntingdon, Selina, resided here. She was of a different turn of mind from that of her predecessors and inclined towards the Methodists. She founded her own evangelical sect — the Countess of Huntingdon's Connection — which was responsible for a number of interesting chapels. Sir Walter Scott used Ashby de la Zouch as the setting for many of the scenes in one of his best novels, *Ivanhoe*. The grateful residents name their magnificent spa baths 'Ivanhoe' in his honour, but unfortunately only his honour now remains, the baths having been demolished.

Ashby de la Zouch, the north range with the tall kitchen building adjoining the earlier pantry and buttery next to the Great Hall

Lyddington Bede House

LEICESTERSHIRE

A bede house, or house of prayer, is the early name for an almshouse where prayers are said for the soul of the founder by the grateful inmates. The house at Lyddington, next to the parish church, was an alms-house until 1936, but when built it was part of the palace of the Bishop of Lincoln and dates from the fifteenth century. It contains a fine first-floor hall, or audience chamber, which was originally open to the roof. After the Reformation when the house passed into private hands, an attractive framed wooden ceiling was inserted, its coved cornice decorated with carving. There is an oriel window looking towards the church and some fifteenth-century stained glass, as well as a collection of funeral hatchments on the walls. On the other side of the framed partition wall is an inner chamber with a privy chamber beyond. The latter was the bishop's wardrobe where he kept his many costly

Lyddington Bede House from St Andrew's churchyard

Jewry Wall, Leicester

LEICESTERSHIRE

ABOVE: *the bishop's audience chamber, Lyddington Bede House*

BELOW: *the Jewry Wall and Church of St Nicholas, Leicester*

How this thirty foot high stretch of Roman masonry came to be called Jewry Wall is unknown as it has no Jewish connections. The jurats, or medieval aldermen, have been suggested as a possible derivation. Leicester was the tribal capital of the Coritani and was originally founded as a fort on the Fosse Way, the Exeter-Lincoln road via Bath and Cirencester, near its junction with Watling Street. By a strange coincidence, this section of wall forms part of the exercise halls at the public baths, almost the same part of the building that survives at *Wroxeter*, another tribal capital. Excavations have shown that the baths at Leicester were unusually large and had separate facilities for women. The normal arrangement was that the public baths were open to women in the morning and to men for the rest of the day. Little else remains above ground of the Roman town, but the adjoining Jewry Wall Museum (not English Heritage) contains many interesting finds. In particular there are some notable mosaics, including an unusual and elegant second-century design where the tesserae are made from broken Samian pottery. Two very striking sections of painted wall plaster removed from a house in 1958 are also on display. Dominating the Jewry Wall to the north is the Anglo-Saxon church of St Nicholas, built over part of the Roman forum. It was altered by the Normans and the Victorians and is well worth a visit.

garments, and there was a garderobe with a laver, or little wash basin, built into the wall. Visitors can now ascend to the roof space and admire the construction of the arch-braced collar-beam roof that the bishop originally gazed upon in his audience chamber. The building was converted into an almshouse by Lord Burley in 1602. The parish church is worth a visit to see the acoustic jars set into the chancel wall, the medieval version of a loudspeaker system.

Bishop's Palace, Lincoln
LINCOLNSHIRE

Time has dealt cruelly with the palace of St Hugh at Lincoln. The hall, with its marble columns and painted-glass windows, where he warmed himself at the great central hearth, are low foundations now; the great kitchens are just a hollow shell. During the Civil War the palace was badly damaged, the chapel then became a private house and in the early eighteenth century the whole site was turned into a quarry to repair the cathedral. In the nineteenth century, however, it was decided to rebuild the palace on land adjoining to the west. The much decayed fifteenth-century Alnwick Tower and former chapel range were rebuilt at the same time, leaving the foundations of the medieval palace to twentieth-century archaeologists. Set within an angle of the Roman city walls, the ruins look down the hillside on to walled gardens below — at a glance recapturing something of the atmosphere of medieval Lincoln. Visitors enter through the Alnwick Tower and are faced with the foundations of the East and West Halls set at angles to a narrow yard. Changes in level make the site difficult to understand at first. On the west side lie the remains of the thirteenth-century Great Hall with the aisle posts marked out and the foundations of the great oriel added in the fifteenth century. At the lower end are the openings to the buttery and

RIGHT: Alnwick Tower and Lincoln Cathedral

OPPOSITE: Sibsey Trader Windmill

pantry from the screens passage, now the foundations of Ewan Christian's chapel of the 1880s (not accessible to the public). The kitchen stood on the other side linked by a bridge whose vault survives. The floor of this very early detached kitchen has gone and visitors admire it from the undercroft. Both levels have the remains of ovens and fireplaces. To the east lies the Lower Hall with its barrel-vault roof. Despite appearances, it was not an undercroft or cellar but a proper hall with a great chamber opening out at the south end, beyond the spiral stair. This range pre-dates that of St Hugh and was erected sometime around 1180.

Sibsey Trader Windmill
LINCOLNSHIRE

Built in 1877 by Saundersons of Louth, this six-storey tower mill stands seventy-four feet high and contains its original machinery for grinding corn. It is constructed of red brick, tarred outside and whitewashed inside, and is one of the few six-sailed windmills surviving. It, or to be more precise she, contains an exhibition of windmills in the area. An adjacent building houses an exhibition which explains the working of the mill by dividing the machinery into its component parts. The tower mill is the successor to the earliest form of windmill, the post mill. In the latter, the whole mill structure revolves, as at *Saxtead Green*, Suffolk, but in the more substantial tower mill, the tower itself is stationary and only the cap revolves. Along a groove around the top of the tower runs the fantail, which automatically veers the main sail into the face of the wind. The shutters on the main sails can be adjusted to control the speed of their rotation. The miller can operate the chain mechanism that controls these shutters from his balcony on the second floor; like the captain of a sailing ship, reefing in the sails. Before the mid eighteenth century the fantail was unknown, and automatic reefing was invented in 1807. Tower mills, with their extra height to catch the wind, were first introduced in the seventeenth century. As a power source, the wind's main disadvantage is its capriciousness. In favourable conditions eight hours' power out of twenty-four can be expected. In the nineteenth century the flat grainlands of Lincolnshire were covered with windmills, however the influx of cheap imported grain from America in the latter part of the century soon altered this. Steam-driven mills at the ports milled the flour which was distributed by train and the grain-growing areas had to consider different crops.

The Eleanor Cross, Geddington

NORTHAMPTONSHIRE

In 1290 Eleanor of Castile, the wife of Edward 1, died at Hardby, Nottinghamshire. She was then forty-seven years old, and had never fully recovered from the birth of her thirteenth child earlier in the year. Although Edward's betrothal to a Spanish princess had been politically unpopular, there is no doubt that in personal terms the marriage was a great success. Very little is known of Queen Eleanor except that she accompanied her husband everywhere, including his expedition to the Holy Land where she was popularly reputed to have sucked the poison from his wounds. This story was not told until many years after her death. Another version relates that Edward was suffering from an infected wound for which a nasty operation was the only possible cure. Eleanor was removed screaming from the room whereupon Edward remarked sardonically that it was better that she should wail than England should mourn. The beautiful tomb that he erected to her memory in Westminster Abbey, with its gilded bronze effigy, can still be seen today, and the places where her funeral cortège rested on the journey from Hardby to Westminster were marked by crosses where, until the Reformation, prayers were said on the anniversary of her death. The cost of these twelve finely carved crosses was met by Eleanor's executors but assuredly the noble thought was Edward's. Some twenty years earlier his aunt had caused a smaller series of similar crosses to be erected along the funeral route of her husband, Louis IX of France, afterwards canonised, who died returning from the same crusade that Edward and Eleanor had supported. Only three of Eleanor's crosses now remain intact: in the centre of Waltham Cross, Herts; at Hardingstone, near Northampton; and in the centre of Geddington. The latter is particularly graceful and elegant, a tapering triangular shaft, similar in feeling to Eleanor's tomb, William Torel's masterpiece in Westminster Abbey.

The Eleanor Cross, Geddington

Chichele College, Higham Ferrers

NORTHAMPTONSHIRE

Only part of this college founded by Archbishop Chichele for secular canons in 1422 survives, and of that, only the exterior is accessible to visitors. The college was built around a quadrangle; the east range with the entrance fronted the street, while the hall was on the west side, lodgings to the north and the chapel to the south. There was accommodation for the Master, seven chaplains, four clerks and six choristers; two of the chaplains or clerks taught grammar and singing. Only the east wall with entrance remains and part of the south range. The building has undergone many alterations and restorations over the centuries and little remains internally of the original features. In the early eighteenth century it was an inn known as the Saracen's Head, and in 1914 it was extensively restored. Archbishop Chichele (1363-1443), Archbishop of Canterbury during the reigns of Henry V and his son Henry VI, and founder of All Souls College, Oxford, was a generous benefactor to his native town of Higham Ferrers. The College of the Blessed Virgin, St Thomas of Canterbury and St Edward the Confessor now bears his name. It was founded for the same reason that Sir Ralph Cromwell established a college at *Tattershall*: in order to say masses in perpetuity for the soul of the founder. To facilitate this, the Archbishop repaired and enlarged the parish church. He also refounded the school in 1422, and the Bede House (1428) which survives today (not English Heritage). The latter is a very pleasing small building of banded ironstone and whiteish limestone.

Chichele College

Kirby Hall

NORTHAMPTONSHIRE

Kirby Hall is a magnificent ruin. No attempt was ever made to demolish the house, it simply fell into decay through neglect during the nineteenth century, so the walls all rise to their full height, while the Great Hall and south-west wing are still roofed and retain a few original features. The house, begun in 1570, is built around a courtyard, one room deep, in the medieval fashion with the Great Hall on the south side, lodgings on the east and west, and a gateway to the north. However, this is a period of transition so a Renaissance loggia was erected on the courtyard side of the entrance front and the hall range is symmetrical with a grand porch flanked by walls of windows. Giant pilasters unite the two-storey north and south blocks for the first time in England, and everywhere one looks there are fascinating carved details derived from a plethora of sources. Inside, the hall contains a fine roof, and

Kirby Hall: the north front of the inner court facing the Great Hall

though stripped of all fittings except for the mid seventeenth-century gallery, it is an imposing room. The north front by which the visitor enters was rebuilt rather unsuccessfully in 1638-40 by Nicholas Stone, who worked with Inigo Jones. In the south-west corner is the late sixteenth-century wing with two full-height circular bays overlooking the gardens. This was the work of Christopher Hatton I, later Lord Chancellor, who bought the house after the death of its builder, Sir Humphrey Stafford. The house continued in the Hatton and Finch-Hatton families until the 1920s. The gardens on the west front have been restored in outline and planted with roses. They were the pride of Christopher Hatton IV, a seventeenth-century governor of Jersey who acquired many rare and wonderful plants from all over the world. Once he had retired to Kirby he was very loathe to leave his garden and on two occasions the House of Lords had to send for him to explain his non-attendance. The fine avenues of trees cut down in the nineteenth century to repay Finch-Hatton gambling debts have been replanted and a good time to visit Kirby Hall is when the chestnut trees are in flower.

Gainsborough Old Hall

LINCOLNSHIRE

Built by Sir Thomas de Burgh in the mid fifteenth century, this is one of the largest and most complete houses of its time to be seen anywhere in the country. It has a magnificent Great Hall and two cross-wings containing a suite of formal rooms and lodgings for guests and retainers. Much of the building was timber-framed originally, although the wings were later largely clad in brick. However, dating from the fifteenth century is a huge brick-built kitchen standing at one end of the hall range, and a polygonal tower at the other. This too is of brick; handsomely and elaborately built. It was not self-contained nor strictly defensible, but provided a symbolic declaration of the owner's status, over and above the sheer size of the main buildings. The Hall contains displays belonging to the Lincolnshire Museums Service, who are responsible for the day-to-day running of the building.

Tattershall College Building

LINCOLNSHIRE

A smidgen of a building this, and one of rather doubtful origin. As well as building Wingfield Manor and Tattershall Castle (National Trust) for his earthly comfort, Sir Ralph Cromwell, Lord Chamberlain of England, also looked to his future spiritual needs, and those of his villagers. He rebuilt Tattershall church and endowed it with a college of secular canons to serve in the church and act as chantry priests to pray for his soul in the hereafter. He also built a grammar school, which provided choristers for the church, and almshouses for the poor. At the Reformation the college was disbanded but the grammar school survived until the late seventeenth century, and the almshouses remain. It is not certain whether the brick walls known as Tattershall College belong to the school or the college, or to a related structure. One of the walls is twentieth-century, but another contains a fifteenth-century doorway. In the eighteenth century the building was part of a brewery and subsequent alterations have removed all other features of interest.

Bolingbroke Castle

LINCOLNSHIRE

Bolingbroke Castle

Only the foundations survive of the castle built 1220-30 by Randulph de Blundervill, Earl of Chester, the builder of *Beeston Castle*. Bolingbroke has none of the natural defensive advantages of Beeston. The countryside is gentle and the castle rose sheer from the moat, which has long since disappeared, as at *Nunney*. The plan is hexagonal with five bastion towers at the angles, and two towers on the north front flanking the entrance. The ground inside the castle has been artificially raised. In 1311 the castle passed by marriage to the Duchy of Lancaster to whom it still belongs. Here, John of Gaunt's son Henry of Bolingbroke, later Henry IV, was born. The fourteenth and fifteenth centuries were the great days for Bolingbroke for it was the administrative centre of the Duchy. This is reflected in the history of the nearby parish church which was then three times its present size. What we see today, hinted at by the odd positioning of the tower, is only the south aisle. The nave and north aisle were demolished in the seventeenth century, partly as a result of damage sustained during the Civil War. At the outbreak of the War the castle was so decayed as to be barely habitable and it was used as a prison. In October 1643 it was besieged, but capitulated after a couple of days following the Royalist defeat at nearby Winceby. By 1650 it has been completely dismantled and the land sold for pasture. The ruins became no more than grassy mounds and remained such until dug out again in the 1960s and early 1970s. An undefended outer bailey extends to the south. Within it is an unusual moated pond, probably dating back to the eighteenth century, and intended for breeding duck. Although it is not a spectacular site, it is nonetheless interesting as all the walls and towers, bar one, can be traced out, and the lower levels of some of the towers are accessible.

awaken in the informed visitor memories of the texts from which they spring. It is not only the quotations themselves that are important, but their context too. References in these texts, combined with images on the building, would create further ideas, giving the visitor much to think about. Although hardly anyone today can hope to understand the full meaning of Sir Thomas's personal philosophy, the building is nevertheless quite beautiful. In a way it still partly fulfills his original idea, for it provokes the visitor to think; not just about his philosophy but in general terms about buildings that have been designed to embody ideas, whether consciously or not. The plain whitewashed interior of Rushton Triangular Lodge seems a good place to discuss building and philosophy, although during Sir Thomas's lifetime one of his estate workers lived here. Rushton was the only building that Sir Thomas completed, but he also built much of Lyveden New Bield, a house designed to show the harmonious structure of the universe, and the Market House at Rothwell — for the good of the inhabitants.

Rufford Abbey
NOTTINGHAMSHIRE

The remains of Rufford Abbey stand in the middle of a Nottinghamshire County Council Country Park, created out of the Rufford estate. The large country house of the Saviles that grew out of the abbey remains was largely demolished in the 1950s, and out of the rubble emerged the undercroft of the lay brothers' dormitory, now in the care of English Heritage. This undercroft contains the cellarium, or storeroom, and the lay brothers' refectory, which is one of the best preserved in the country. The abbey was founded in 1146 in the wild lands of Sherwood Forest, and little is known of its history. The lay brothers did the manual work in a Cistercian monastery. When the number of lay brothers declined dramatically after the Black Death these ranges were often demolished or converted to other purposes, which is probably what happened at Rufford. The monks' refectory and dormitory were grander first-floor buildings, which were more frequently preserved after the Dissolution through their incorporation into dwellings. Features survive here that were common to both refectories, for instance the spoon and linen cupboard recess in the north wall, though the fireplace was added later when the room became part of the servants' quarters of the Saviles' house. At the Dissolution the property was bought by the Talbots, the Earls of

Rushton Triangular Lodge
NORTHAMPTONSHIRE

Built between 1593 and 1597 by the Roman Catholic Sir Thomas Tresham, this small building is a manifesto of his ideas. These ideas were mystical and somewhat abstruse, evolved during the twelve years that he had spent in confinement for his religious views. He was released in 1593, the date on the building, and construction began the following year. The Trinity is the central theme, made manifest through the use of the number three. Not only physically in the three-sided building, but also throughout his life Sir Thomas found references to it: his nickname, Tres: the number of his children, three times three, three sons and six daughters, and in countless other ways. Although he created a building whose form is dictated by his ideas, he had no wish to make these ideas accessible to everyone, only to those who shared his interests. Thus the Latin quotations along the cornice would serve to

Rushton Triangular Lodge

Shrewsbury. The 6th Earl, one of the husbands of Bess of Hardwick, converted the lay brothers' dormitory into accommodation and *c.*1610 his son added the range to the south which survives today in a modified form. By 1679 the house had descended to the Saviles and all the other remaining abbey buildings had been swept away. The house was extended over the years so that by the late eighteenth century it was described as 'gloomy and ill-managed'. Of the surviving nineteenth-century additions and alterations, the Jacobean-style entrance between the lay brothers' range and the south block is by Salvin 1838-40, who also added the little cupola to the south range. This work was done for the 8th Earl of Scarborough who lived at Rufford with his mistress Agnes and their six children. The couple had met in the most romantic of circumstances, for the Earl has rescued Agnes from drowning in the Serpentine. One of their sons became the 1st Lord Savile. The grounds of the house, now a Country Park, contain much of interest both in terms of landscape and architecture.

Mattersey Priory
NOTTINGHAMSHIRE

There is not a great deal to see at Mattersey. Remains of the vaulted undercrofts of the canons' refectory and dormitory stand amidst flat farmland, almost encircled by the River Idle. However, Mattersey must always be of some interest to visitors for it is the best surviving remains, open to the public, of a Gilbertine house, the only monastic order of English inspiration that was founded in the Middle Ages. Founded by Gilbert of Sempringham in Lincolnshire it was originally a double order, created for nuns to live in seclusion aided by lay sisters, with canons to perform Divine Service and lay brothers to perform the menial tasks, as in the Cistercians. Gilbert had hoped to get the original house absorbed into the Cistercians but as a double foundation it was not acceptable. The Pope, however, encouraged him to found a new order, which he did in 1149. The segregation of the sexes involved separate cloisters and a divided church, so that neither sex was visible to the other. At Communion the holy wafer was received by the nuns from a turntable in the wall that separated them from the canons. At the Dissolution there were ten of these double monasteries and fourteen for canons only. Concentrated in Lincolnshire and the surrounding counties, they were active in caring for orphans and the sick, particularly lepers. Mattersey

was one of the two houses for canons only, founded in 1185. Like most of the other Gilbertine houses it was never well endowed and a disastrous fire in 1279 encumbered it with an expensive rebuilding programme which it could not afford. The order never achieved widespread popularity; without influence in Rome it was unable to acquire papal privileges (such as indulgences to remit days in purgatory) which would have attracted lay benefactors, thereby ensuring its success. Had Gilbert been able to link his order to a larger and more successful one — such as the international and well-organised Cistercian order — things might have been different. The advantages would have been similar to those of a small company joining a multinational corporation.

Mattersey Priory, the south wall of the refectory

EAST ANGLIA

Cambridgeshire · Essex
Norfolk · Suffolk

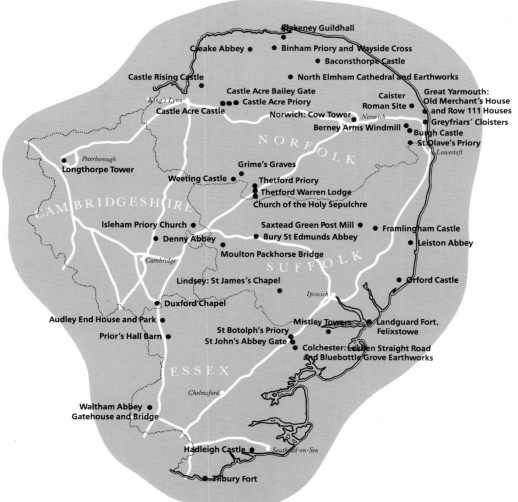

Blakeney Guildhall

Creake Abbey ●   ● Binham Priory and Wayside Cross
                        ● Baconsthorpe Castle

Castle Rising Castle   ● North Elmham Cathedral and Earthworks

             Castle Acre Bailey Gate   Caister   Great Yarmouth:
King's Lynn ●●● Castle Acre Priory   Roman Site ● Old Merchant's House
Castle Acre Castle   Norwich: Cow Tower ●   and Row 111 Houses
                                    Norwich   ● Greyfriars' Cloisters
                      Berney Arms Windmill ●   ● Burgh Castle
                                               ● St Olave's Priory
                                                     Lowestoft

Peterborough   ● Grime's Graves   NORFOLK
● Longthorpe Tower

    Weeting Castle ●   ● Thetford Priory
CAMBRIDGESHIRE   ● Thetford Warren Lodge
                       Church of the Holy Sepulchre

    Isleham Priory Church ●   Saxtead Green Post Mill ●   ● Framlingham Castle
         ● Denny Abbey   ● Bury St Edmunds Abbey   ● Leiston Abbey
    Cambridge   Moulton Packhorse Bridge   SUFFOLK

              Lindsey: St James's Chapel   ● Orford Castle
                                        Ipswich
         ● Duxford Chapel

Audley End House and Park ●   Mistley Towers ● ● Landguard Fort,
    Prior's Hall Barn ●   St Botolph's Priory ●   Felixstowe
                          St John's Abbey Gate ●
                             ● Colchester: Lexden Straight Road
                               and Bluebottle Grove Earthworks

              ESSEX

         Chelmsford

Waltham Abbey ●
Gatehouse and Bridge

         Hadleigh Castle ●   Southend-on-Sea

              ● Tilbury Fort

Denny Abbey
CAMBRIDGESHIRE

Denny underwent a remarkable number of changes during the Middle Ages and had one of the most varied histories of any monastic building. At different times it housed Benedictine monks, the Knights Templar and nuns of the Franciscan order, the Poor Clares, all of whom have left evidence of their occupation. At the Dissolution the buildings were converted into a farm, but these later alterations have recently been stripped away so that the interesting medieval features can best be appreciated. Only the eighteenth-century sash windows remain from the farmhouse period. Two detached buildings are to be seen; the Franciscan nuns' refectory of the mid fourteenth century, and the west end of the church, converted into lodgings in the fourteenth century. Disentangling the history of the latter, which at first appears to be an attractive stone-built farmhouse, is quite complicated. It consists of the north and south transepts of the Benedictine church 1160-70, part of the nave of the Templar church 1170-90, with a thirteenth-century building adjoining which was linked up into one block by the nuns, who converted it into rooms for their founder, the Countess of Pembroke. She rebuilt the church on a much grander scale to the east, all of which has now disappeared. Denny is the only surviving medieval Franciscan nunnery in England. It is a paradox that while the Franciscan friars lived and worked very much among the people (and have been likened to the Salvation Army today), the little sisters of St Francis were by contrast among the most exclusive of the conventual foundations, catering mainly for women of noble birth who wished to lead a devotional life, somewhat stricter than in the nunneries of the other orders. For various reasons they were never very popular in England and only three houses were established. The Knights Templar lands at Denny had been granted to the Countess of Pembroke by her cousin Edward III in 1327, some twenty years after the Templars had been ignominiously disbanded. The Countess had been widowed at an early age and devoted the rest of her life to charitable works, including the foundation of Pembroke College, Cambridge, which provided chaplains for the nunnery, and attempts to improve Anglo-French relations. Among the endowments of the nunnery she obtained another former property of the Knights Templar, now known as *Temple Manor* at Strood in Kent.

ABOVE: the east front of Denny Abbey seen from the site of the chancel: the blocked crossing of the twelfth-century church and a pier from the northern arcade of the Franciscan church are visible

LEFT: Interior of Denny Abbey, the nave of the twelfth-century Benedictine church

certain. What is interesting is that they are evidence that lavishly-painted domestic interiors were not uncommon, and not solely confined to royal apartments and churches, as had often been assumed. The paintings survive on all of the four walls in the Great Chamber and show a variety of secular and sacred subjects including the Wheel of Life, the Wheel of the Five Senses, the Labours of the Months, the Nativity and King David. Though faded to a pale image of their original beauty, they are definitely by the hand of a medieval master painter.

Duxford Chapel
CAMBRIDGESHIRE

This was the chapel of St John's Hospital, founded *c.* 1200. Nothing remains of the hospital except the thirteenth-century chapel which was externally much altered in the nineteenth century when the east window was bricked up and the roof rebuilt. The interior, however, is of interest. The nave and chancel is an undivided space containing thirteenth-century windows and a sedilia and piscina in the south-east corner.

Longthorpe Tower
CAMBRIDGESHIRE

ABOVE: Longthorpe Tower, the west wall depicting in the lower section a philosopher or teacher and a young man separated by two scrolls, above figures thought to represent St Anthony's encounter with two angels dressed as men, one working, one praying

RIGHT: the piscina and sedilia in the chancel of Duxford Chapel

There are only two rooms to see at Longthorpe but one of them is unique. It contains the finest example of fourteenth-century domestic wallpainting in the country, and there is little surviving in Europe from this period, 1300–1350, that can match it. The wallpaintings were discovered quite by accident after the Second World War. The building had been occupied by the Home Guard and when the tenant began redecorating he discovered evidence of the paintings under layers of whitewash and distemper. The tower, with the Great Chamber that contains the paintings, is part of a fortified manor house of the late thirteenth century. This solar tower was added *c.* 1300. (The rest of the buildings are much altered and not open to the public.) The paintings were commissioned by a member of the Thorpe family, but whether they were people of more than local importance is not

Isleham Priory Church

CAMBRIDGESHIRE

This is a rare example of an early Norman chapel, and all that remains of the Benedictine priory that was founded here in 1100. It has been reroofed and consists of a nave and a chancel ending in an apse. Some herringbone work masonry can be seen in the nave wall and the interior of the church (key obtainable nearby) is quite plain apart from the chancel arch and the arch to the apse. The priory belonged to St Jacut sur Mer, Brittany, and was dissolved in 1254. Monasteries which were dependent on a mother house abroad, like the Cluniac foundations, suffered considerable financial hardship during the thirteenth century because the wars with France placed them in the category of 'aliens', or enemy property. Thus they were subjected to heavy fines and the threat of confiscation. Poorly endowed, small foundations did not have the resources to meet these demands, and this may be the reason that Isleham priory was dissolved.

Audley End House

Audley End House and Park

ESSEX

This magnificent house was built between 1605 and 1614 by the Earl of Suffolk on the site of Walden Abbey, land given to his grandfather, Sir Thomas Audley at the Dissolution of the Monasteries. The house was built around two courtyards, but only part of the smaller inner court now remains. The Earl, who was Treasurer to James I, planned to entertain the King here, but in the event he was convicted of embezzlement and retired to Audley End in disgrace. King James had remarked earlier that the house was too big for a King but would do well for a Lord Treasurer. His descendants sold the house to Charles II, but he made little use of it and Audley End returned to the family in the early eighteenth century. They consulted Sir John Vanbrugh, and on his advice demolished the three sides of the outer court to make the house more manageable. Vanbrugh partly remodelled the Great

OPPOSITE: the Tea House Bridge by Robert Adam

Hall, adding the stone stairway and screen at the opposite end from the sumptuously-carved Jacobean screen. In the mid eighteenth century the house was acquired by Lady Portsmouth for her nephew, Sir John Griffin Griffin. She demolished the east side of the inner court leaving the house as we see it today. Sir John employed Adam to create the suite of rooms that includes the jewel-like Little Drawing Room, and reconstructed the chapel in the Gothick style. The final transformation came in the mid nineteenth century when the 3rd Lord Braybroke rearranged the other rooms and decorated them in the Jacobean style. Many of the pictures, furniture and other items, such as the 4th Lord Braybroke's collection of stuffed animals, are on loan from the family, giving the house a 'lived-in' atmosphere not normally found in English Heritage properties. The house is surrounded by fine eighteenth-century parkland, created partly under the direction of Capability Brown. There are a number of garden monuments, some by Adam, including the idyllic Tea House Bridge.

BELOW: the stone screen and Vanbrugh's staircase at Audley End

the most impressive remains, the two eastern towers, date from the 1360s. The plan is an irregular oval walled enclosure with towers, a barbican on the north front, and evidence of the Great Hall rebuilt at least twice on the west side. The southern third of the castle fell away in a landslide.

Hadleigh Castle

ESSEX

The setting of Hadleigh is its chief glory. After the interminable flatlands of Essex, the castle mound appears at the end of a bumpy track, rising behind some trees. Once inside the curtain wall the world is transformed. The land drops steeply away to the south, and spread out below in an arc of 180 degrees are the Essex marshes and the shipping on the Thames estuary. Here is another, quite different Essex. The remains of the castle itself are inconsiderable. It was founded by Hugh de Burgh, Chief Justiciar to King John and Henry III in 1230. The most powerful man in the kingdom, he quarrelled frequently with the young Henry III who on one occasion tried to stab him after it was discovered that there were insufficient ships for a proposed military expedition to France. Hadleigh was confiscated by the King when it was still unfinished. The surviving curtain walls date from this period, but

The towers of Hadleigh Castle

Prior's Hall Barn, Widdington

ESSEX

A handsome example of an aisled barn dating from the mid fourteenth century, extensively restored in the late twentieth century. It is timber-framed with a crown-post roof, eight bays long, and has excited much interest among those concerned with the history of carpentry. The use of the stop-splayed-scarf joint has dated it to the mid fourteenth century and the aisles of the barn demonstrate the use of the 'hanging knee' in their construction. Before restoration, Prior's Hall Barn was damningly cited as an example of 'the complete failure of the crown-post roof' to provide structural stability in long buildings. Happily it is now fully restored and structurally quite sound, housing a small display to initiate visitors into the arcane mysteries of timber-framing in Essex.

Lexden Straight Road and Bluebottle Grove Earthworks

ESSEX

This unlikely sounding duo are sections of the earthworks that were built *c.*50 BC–AD 50 to defend the important Iron Age settlement of Camulodunum (Colchester), capital of the Belgic tribe the Catavellauni. The settlement was protected on three sides by the arch of the River Colne and its tributary, Roman River, and the fourth side to the west was closed by a line of dykes. An area of twelve square miles was encompassed. The dykes were eight to fifteen foot ditches with ten foot high banks on the eastern sides, probably topped by timber palisades. They could not have been flooded.

With the aid of OS map number 168, parts of three dykes can be identified, though twentieth-century Colchester has engulfed them and they emerge intermittently, best followed on foot or by public transport. The best surviving dyke is the most westerly, Grymes Dyke, which is possibly a Roman addition to the defences. Part of it follows the line of King George V playing fields, which are off the west side of Lexden Straight Road. Visitors who enter Lexden Straight Road from the north, at the main road, will first pass the remains of Shrub End Triple Dykes, lying on the eastern side of the road. These are the Lexden Straight Road Earthworks in the care of English Heritage. As the name suggests, this was a triple ditch dyke of which now only the banks, not the dykes, are visible. At Bluebottle Grove Earthworks the reverse is true. A 100 yards of ditch can be seen, but not the bank. This is the southern end of Lexden Dyke and is reached via Heath and Beech Roads to Prettygate Road and Park Road bridle path. Little remains to be seen of the earliest Gosbecks dyke, nor of the most easterly Sheepen dyke, named after the Sheepen mound which has been identified as the centre of Camulodunum at NGR TL 988 256, off Sheepen Road in the grounds of the technical college. The importance of the settlement is demonstrated by the fact that the Emperor Claudius thought it the major British town and thus chose it for his triumphal entry after the Roman invasion of AD 43. The subsequent history of the Roman town can be seen in the Castle Museum, one of the most enjoyable in the country. Grave goods from the Lexden Tumulus give some idea of the civilisation of the Catuvellauni. This is believed by some to be the grave of their King Cunobelinus, who died in AD 40 and was succeeded by his bellicose son Caractacus; his attack on the pro-Roman Atrebates gave Claudius the excuse for the invasion of 43 AD.

Interior of Prior's Hall Barn

St John's Abbey Gate, Colchester

ESSEX

This fine fifteenth-century gatehouse is all that remains of the Benedictine abbey founded in 1096, three years after *St Botolph's*. It was a rich and important foundation and at the Dissolution the abbot was imprisoned in the Tower of London, accused of having stated that Henry's greed was such that 'if the Thames were flowing with gold and silver it would not suffice to slake his thirst for money'. Despite his protestations that such thoughts had never even crossed his mind, the abbot was executed that same year and the monastery hastily disbanded. The two-storey gatehouse has four crocketed turrets and a main carriageway entrance with a pedestrian, or postern gate, beside. The highly effective use of flushwork decoration on the façade is a feature of East Anglian churches of the later Middle Ages and is composed of knapped flint and ashlar stone. Sometimes a checkerboard pattern was created, other times a more ornate design, such as at St John's, with pale crocketed niches against a dark background; some of the niches are filled with elegant lilies in vases which have benefited from the ninteenth-century restoration. Standing on a slight eminence, the gatehouse offers its ornate facade towards the town, from which it is now separated by the rush and thunder of the ring road.

Mistley Towers

ESSEX

The towers at Mistley are the remains of the most important church built by the great neo-Classical architect Robert Adam. Here in 1776 he remodelled the existing church of 1735 for the local landowner, Robert Rigby. The church stands on the banks of the Stour estuary, at the entrance to the village of Mistley. The two towers contained the chancel and the west tower of the parish church, the nave between was demolished in 1870. To Victorian eyes it must have seemed a truely pagan temple with its lack of Christian symbolism and the classical portico, set equidistant between the two towers. Adam's design was as innovative as one would expect. Instead of entering the church via the west tower, or inconspicuously at the western end of the nave, worshippers entered boldly through the portico and found themselves in a semicircular bay looking at the middle of the nave. A similar bay opposite gave access to the stairs for the gallery. The entrance portico with its paired columns was repeated on the estuary frontage, so the building was thus symmetrical. The columns from the demolished porticos have been arranged around the two towers, complementing the existing disengaged columns, so the absence of the nave is not at first apparent. The church must have been an arresting sight for visitors approaching the village, while those sailing up the reaches of the Stour on a misty summer's morning might have thought themselves transported into a painting by Poussin. At Gunton in Norfolk, Adam had already designed a smaller church for Sir William Harbord in 1769. Here Adam's interior still survives, though the chancel was rebuilt in the nineteenth century. These were the only two churches for which he was responsible.

ABOVE: detail of the flushwork on St John's Abbey Gate

RIGHT: Mistley Towers

St Botolph's Priory, Colchester

ESSEX

Time has stripped away the covering from the twelfth-century priory church of St Botolph, revealing its constructional material — reused Roman bricks. Originally they would have been covered by plaster, both internally and externally; the internal walls with painted decoration similar to that in the nave at St Albans Cathedral, another church built in an important Roman town. At the Reformation, St Botolph's became a major parish church, but it was very badly damaged during the Siege of Colchester in 1643 and fell into ruins. Only the nave with the impressive west end survives today. The priory had been founded *c.* 1100 and was the first English house to adopt the rule of the Augustinian canons. Up until that date many 'minister' churches were served by groups of secular

canons who officiated as priests, but whose way of life had become rather irregular, many of them being married. The reform movement of the late tenth to eleventh centuries that produced the Cistercians, created the Augustinian or regular canons who lived a more monastic existence following precepts laid down by one of the Early Fathers of the Church, St Augustine of Hippo. Either a group of secular canons decided to adopt the rule of St Augustine, as at St Botolph's, or a patron purchased the advowson of a church and founded a priory to serve it, maintained by the church's tithes. Other benefices and endowments would then have to follow if the foundation was to prosper. Most of these foundations were quite small; there were 200 priories, but only thirteen other Augustinian foundations which achieved abbey status. The dedication of Colchester's priory to the East Anglian saint, St Botolph, was apposite since he was credited with being an early advocate of the monastic life. His ideas were in advance of their time and he lived a solitary life during the seventh century in a dismal hut in the Fens.

The west end of St Botolph's Priory

Isles, known as *King Charles's Castle*. However, it was under Charles II and his Chief Engineer, Sir Bernard de Gomme, that Tilbury became an important part of the Thames defences following the audacious Dutch raid up the Medway in 1667. The plan is a pentagonal fort with arrowhead bastions, though the water bastion projecting out into the Thames was never built. This is surrounded by a double moat with an embarkment between. Work began in 1670 and now, with the aid of the guidebook, such interesting objects as redoubts, redans and ravelins can be identified. This period of fortification is best appreciated by looking at the plan first, then the building. Because it is created for defence against artillery bombardment, the fort seems low and undramatic until the sophistication of its defences are understood. The fort is built of brick with a fine ashlar watergate, designed by Sir Bernard de Gomme and reminiscent of his work at the *Royal Citadel*, Plymouth. The main entrance is on the north, or landward side. Inside the fort there is the seventeenth-century guardhouse and chapel, the powder magazines largely remodelled in the 1860s, and the late eighteenth-century terrace of officers' quarters overlooking the parade ground. (The mens' barracks that stood opposite were destroyed in the Second World War, as were a number of smaller buildings.) Fine views can be had across the Thames to Gravesend and the New Tavern Fort by *Milton Chantry*. Partly due to the success of its design, and partly to the fact that the line of fortifications were pushed further east, Tilbury has never been directly under attack. The most violent episode in the fort's history was the Kent *vs* Essex cricket match of 1776, which left three dead and a number wounded.

Tilbury Fort

ESSEX

'Although I have the body of a weak and feeble woman, but I have the heart and stomach of a king, and a king of England too ...' Although Tilbury is irrevocably linked in people's minds with Queen Elizabeth I's stirring speech to her troops on the eve of the Armada, the fort that survives today is in fact a very good example of late seventeenth-century military engineering, complete with moats and earthworks. The site was first fortified by Henry VIII, who built a two-storey blockhouse similar in design to the one surviving on Tresco in the Scilly

Waltham Abbey Gatehouse and Harold's Bridge

ESSEX

The remains of the gatehouse and its bridge are the remnants of one of the great monastic foundations of the Middle Ages. The origins of this religious settlement are shrouded in legends connected with the miraculous holy cross, that was said to have appeared in the reign of King Canute. This cross had healing powers and one of the beneficiaries, Earl Harold, built a magnificent church here, the nave of which is now the parish church. It is the

first example of Norman architecture in England, completed five years before the Conquest. The other buildings have gone. Harold was reputedly buried at Waltham after the Battle of Hastings and thus his name became attached to the fourteenth-century bridge. The gateway, which bears the arms of Edward III, was probably a four-square structure with corner turrets. The abbey was immensely rich and enjoyed royal patronage, the abbot having a seat in Parliament. For some years before the Dissolution Thomas Tallis was organist and Master of the choristers at Waltham. Henry VIII, like Henry III and other Kings before him, enjoyed staying at Waltham and a story is told of one visit he made *incognito*. Disguised as a solider, the King arrived at the abbey and was invited to dine at the abbot's table. A fine saddle of beef was set before him which he consumed with gusto. 'Ah', said the abbot, 'What a pleasure it is to see a man with such a good appetite. Alas, my stomach gives me such trouble I can hardly manage a breast of chicken. I would give a hundred pounds to be able to eat like you.' Henry retired and considered this. A few days later he had the abbot arrested and confined in the Tower of London on a diet of bread and water. A week passed and a saddle of beef was set before the abbot, which he happily consumed. Henry then burst in and demanded his hundred pounds.

Berney Arms Windmill

NORFOLK

You have to ask the guard to stop the train at Berney Arms. This in itself is almost worth the trip. The windmill stands alone in the Fens at the head of Tile Kiln Reach, otherwise accessible only by boat, and now a nature conservation area. Standing seven storeys high, here is an excellent example of a tower mill, of the same type as *Sibsey Trader Windmill* (Lincolnshire), and probably built around the same time. The millwrights were Stolwothys of Great Yarmouth. The mill is built of red brick, tarred outside and whitewashed within, with four sails. All the machinery is intact. Berney Arms was originally built to grind cement clinker, dredged from the Fens, or brought by wherry from the cement works at Caister. The cement works closed in 1880. The windmill was then used to drain the Fens, which she continued to do until 1951 when she was presented to the Ministry of Works (now English Heritage) by the Lower Bure, Halvergate Fleet and Acle Marshes Internal Drainage Board. The big 'scoopwheel' that dredged up the water still stands in its casing beside the windmill, and there is an interesting exhibition inside the windmill explaining how this Herculean task was carried out. Now in England, as in Holland, the marshes are drained by electric motor-driven pumps with oil engines.

LEFT: Waltham Abbey Gatehouse

BELOW: Berney Arms Windmill and scoopwheel

Baconsthorpe Castle

NORFOLK

The Paston Letters give a wonderful view of fifteenth-century life, particularly in Norfolk. Among the many people with whom the Pastons were on bad terms was Sir John Heydon, the builder of Baconsthorpe. The Wars of the Roses were a time when the energetic and unscrupulous opportunist prospered, and Sir John, a lawyer by training, was one of these. He carved out a sizeable estate for himself in Norfolk where his descendants in the sixteenth-century grazed large flocks of sheep. Baconsthorpe is not actually a castle, rather a fortified manor house; there was never a licence to crenellate, nor was it properly defensible. The best surviving part of the outer gatehouse, erected in the 1560s by Sir John's grandson and inhabited as a dwelling until 1920 when one of the turrets fell down. Sir John's castle had been demoted to a walled garden in the seventeenth century, and it is now hard to know exactly how it looked beyond the ruined inner gatehouse and part of the adjoining walls. The last of the Heydons bankrupted himself in the Royalist cause and it was he who dismantled the castle to sell it for building materials. The remains of red brick and knapped flint look delightful reflected in the lake, which partly embraces the castle as a moat. Its clay bed soil has produced some interesting archaeological finds; however, the sandy loam that was ideal for sheep pasture has destroyed any evidence that survived within the castle itself.

Binham Priory and Wayside Cross

NORFOLK

The remains of the Benedictine priory church at Binham are quite extensive and the nave of the church fortunately continues in use as the parish church. The priory was founded *c.*1103 by a nephew of William the Conqueror, Pierre de Valoines. As normal, the church was built from east to west, and only the area west of the pulpitum screen survives intact. This separated clergy from laity for as with many Benedictine churches, the laity had the use of the nave. In the decoration of the three tiers of arcades can be seen the progression from the Norman to the Early English style, cul-

minating in the fine west front which greets the visitor. The facades only of the north and south aisles remain, the rest was demolished in the early nineteenth century, and late sixteenth century, respectively. The dating of the tracery of the west end windows has been the subject of much debate. This can only be of academic interest to the visitor since the windows in question were bricked-up in the early nineteenth century for structural reasons, and are not visible on the facade. However, the excellent church guide reproduces various engravings showing the west front in its original glory. The most recent opinion is that the west end is later than the *Chapter House at Westminster Abbey*, and is therefore no longer considered a pioneer use of bar tracery. The fittings of the church include a fine fifteenth-century font with sculptural panels depicting the Seven Sacraments, some unusually plump poppyhead bench ends, and the remains of a painted rood screen. At the ruined east end of the former church, the crossing piers survive to an impressive height. At the Dissolution the monastic buildings were purchased by Thomas Paston, whose family correspondence, *The Paston Letters*, provides much interesting information on medieval life. At attempt to build a house on the site was abandoned and the stone was removed for other buildings. Remains of the chapter house, warming house, refectory and cellarer's range can be seen. Beyond the west gateway, (which visitors may not have noticed upon their arrival since it frames a striking view of the church), can be seen the slender shaft of the market cross. This marks the site on the village green where an annual fair was held from the reign of Henry I until the 1950s.

ABOVE: Binham Priory from the south

OPPOSITE: The outer and inner gatehouses at Baconsthorpe Castle

Burgh Castle
NORFOLK

Burgh is a ten to fifteen-minute walk from the carpark beside the church. Just as one begins to doubt the path, the long low mass of the castle appears on the horizon to the right. Its size is as impressive as it is unexpected in the flat landscape. When built, it stood on the banks of a broad river estuary, facing the fort of *Caister*. Burgh, or Gariannonum, is one of a chain of Roman forts built from the 270s onwards because they were designed to repel attacks by Saxon raiders on the east coast. Excavations at *Portchester* and *Richborough* have produced a great deal of refuse but little evidence of buildings, suggesting that the forts were occupied intermittently, possibly by mercenaries. There were at least nine forts in the chain that stretched from the Wash to Hampshire, creating Britain's first coastal defence system. *Reculver* seems to have been the earliest, a rectangle with rounded corners and no bastions, while *Richborough* is a rectangle with angle bastions and square turrets, and *Portchester* the most impressive with twenty bastions. At Burgh the bastions were later additions. That only the upper courses of the bastions are bonded-in can be clearly seen. Three walls survive in varying degrees of verticality, but the west wall that overlooked the harbour has disappeared. It is said that in the seventh century St Fursey founded his monastery here, and after the Norman Conquest a motte and bailey castle was erected at the south end of the site, but this was levelled in 1839.

Blakeney Guildhall
NORFOLK

This so-called guildhall is in fact the undercroft, or basement, of a merchant's house built in the fourteenth century. It would have been similar in plan to *Burton Agnes Manor House*, Humberside. Nothing remains of the flint building above the basement, but the brick vaults and octagonal stone piers that divide the room into two aisles of four bays each are of some interest. The moulded doorway survives on the centre of what would have been the gable end of the building, facing the sea. Merchandise was probably unloaded directly into the undercroft to be stored, as in palaces of Venetian merchants. As in Venice, so in Blakeney, the harbour has silted up and trade routes have changed. Now it is a pleasant holiday resort with the mud flats a haven for seabirds, whereas once the harbour was full of ships that plied an energetic trade with the Low Countries. The bricks for the guildhall may well have arrived as ballast in these ships.

Burgh castle looking west to the site of the river estuary and harbour in Roman times

Caister Roman Site

NORFOLK

There is very little to see at Caister; most of the Roman town has been built over in the twentieth century and only the foundations of a gateway and what may be a hostel, or early boarding house, have been identified beside a section of Roman road. It is hard to imagine that in Roman times Great Yarmouth was beneath the sea, and Caister was a port on the north side of a large estuary, facing the Saxon Shore Fort at *Burgh*. Two or more navigable rivers emptied into the estuary and the Fen Causeway connected Caister with the important industrial area of the Nene Valley. The town was founded *c.*AD 125, about 150 years before *Burgh*, and had a good trade with the Rhineland ports. There was a Saxon settlement here between the fifth and seventh centuries but thereafter the site was abandoned as the rivers silted up and the landscape changed.

TOP: *The undercroft at Blakeney Guildhall*

ABOVE: *Caister Roman site*

Castle Acre Castle and Bailey Gate
NORFOLK

Recent archaeological excavations at Castle Acre have revealed a surprising sequence of building that brings into question the interpretation of many other Norman motte and bailey sites. It has always been assumed that the buildings erected by William the Conqueror's followers in the years after 1066 were castles. Yet here one of the greatest Norman magnates, William de Warenne, built himself a country house, and here his wife Grundrada died in childbirth in 1085. The house where she died was a two-storey building, parallel range in plan with gable ends and a ground floor entrance. The defences were a bank with timber palisade which was rebuilt in stone with a gatehouse soon after. Only in the 1130s, during the anarchy of Stephen's reign, was the house converted into the conventional keep. In fact the building was not completed to the original plan which incorporated all the house, since the keep rose over only the rear half. The foundations of the original house can be seen, also part of the curtain wall and remains of the west gateway to the lower bailey. The most memorable feature are the earthworks, raised twice from their original height and intriguingly bumpy and lumpy. The lower bailey extended south down to the River Nar which was navigable to this point. Now it is a shallow reed-filled stream that has absent-mindedly wandered away. Adjoining the castle to the west was the Norman town surrounded by its ditch and town walls. It was on the important Roman road, Peddars Way, that ran from the coast near Hunstanton to join the Great Road (London to Caister by Norwich) at Ixworth. A good stretch of it can still be walked today between Castle Acre and Fring. Peddars Way enters the town via the North Gate which still survives, erroneously called the Bailey Gate. It was built c. 1200 and has grooves for a double portcullis between two round towers. The town soon outgrew its walls, its prosperity increased by the existence of the Cluniac priory founded by William de Warenne's son. The parish church and the priory both stand to the west of the original town walls. After the Dissolution of the Monasteries the town declined and much of the stone was taken from the castle to build houses. It was already in decay by the fourteenth century and had never come under attack.

ABOVE: the Bailey Gate, Castle Acre

RIGHT: looking west down the Priory church at Castle Acre

Castle Acre Priory
NORFOLK

The ruins of this Cluniac priory are unusually extensive and sections including the prior's lodgings and the porch are roofed and accessible to the public. They adjoin the west end of the priory church which rises almost to its full height. Founded in the late eleventh century by William de Warenne, the priory was originally sited in the bailey of the Warenne castle at *Castle Acre*, but within a year it had moved to its present location. The church was built late eleventh to mid twelfth century and the west end is a particularly fine example of late Norman Transitional work, enriched with blind arcades. Little remains of the east end which was rebuilt in the early fourteenth century to accommodate pilgrims visiting the priory's most popular relic, the arm of St Philip. As anyone who has visited Westminster Abbey during the summer will appreciate, the problems of circulation and crowd control at the east end of a church were tricky ones for monasteries with popular relics. Pilgrims had made long and hazardous journeys and an added difficulty was that the healing powers attributed to some relics meant that pilgrims often wished to expose their afflicted limbs to the relics, and understandably they did not wish

to be hurried; much tact and careful organisation was called for. At Castle Acre Priory a square-ended chancel was adopted, and it is always interesting to see how monastic churches tackled this problem. Of the cloister buildings, the best-preserved range is the east side with the chapter house and dormitory over an undercroft, and an excellent example of a reredorter (latrine block) set at right angles over the stream. To the west lies the prior's lodgings and guest range. These buildings became a private residence after the Dissolution but they still contain various medieval features including fireplaces, a laver recess and newel stair. The remains of a handsome early sixteenth-century gatehouse of brick and flint greet the visitor upon arrival. Not a great deal is known of life at Castle Acre, and as a Cluniac foundation it was primarily concerned with the celebration of Divine Service. In the fifteenth century there was a dispute with one of the four cells, or houses dependent on the priory — St Andrew, Bromholm. Perhaps this was partly occasioned by jealousy, for the small settlement was famous for its relic of the True Cross, which rather put the arm of St Philip in the shade. Moreover, Bromholm showed a reluctance to pay certain dues to the mother house at Castle Acre. In the 1490s relations between the two houses had become very strained and the monks at Bromholm complained to the Pope that they were unable to celebrate mass because the monks from Castle Acre had come and stolen all their sacred vessels.

Castle Rising

NORFOLK

In 1138 William de Albini married the widow of Henry I, Alice Queen of England, and on his estate at Rising he built a castle worthy of this splendid match. Much of it still remains today surrounded by an impressive earthwork. The rectangular hall keep with its elegant forebuilding, similar in design to that at Norwich, was strengthened later in the twelfth century and slightly altered in the fourteenth century. Though roofless, the keep walls extend to their full height, and ascending the steep forebuilding stairway one senses something of William's pride in his newly-acquired status; on his marriage he was made Earl of Lincoln and soon after became Earl of Sussex. The grand entrance to the state apartments from the forebuilding vestibule was blocked in the sixteenth century by a fireplace. Earlier through the doorway had passed another dowager Queen of England, Isabella, widow of the murdered Edward II. Her widowhood was neither unwelcome, nor unexpected, and she had conspired with Roger, Lord Mortimer, to bring about her husband's imprisonment and eventual murder. A coup by her son Edward III ended their regency (and Mortimer's life), but Isabella spent the next twenty-odd years living in splendour at Castle Rising. Some fine architectural details still survive inside and out, and more of the same period can be seen in the parish at Castle Rising.

Castle Rising, the keep from the north-east showing the forebuilding

Creake Abbey

NORFOLK

The remains of Creake Abbey are not extensive. In the fifteenth century the abbey was cursed with ill luck after many years of prosperity. It had been founded *c.* 1206 as a chapel, and soon after a hospital and guest house for travellers were attached. In 1227 the whole was affiliated to the Augustinian order and in 1231 it was raised to the status of an abbey when the King became the patron. Henry III and his successors were very generous to the foundation and it was well endowed. The mid four-teenth century was its heyday; there were only about seven monks, though many more servants. Like most religious houses it suffered from finan-cial problems in the fifteenth century and in 1484 a disastrous fire broke out which is believed to have been started deliberately. What remained of the nave had to be demolished, together with most of the transepts. Plague then attacked the abbey,

ABOVE: Creake Abbey looking east through the north transept

RIGHT: remnants of the cloisters at Greyfriars

killing all the monks except the abbot. Other houses in the area were also affected and it was impossible to transfer new brethren. Finally the abbot himself was struck down, dying alone in 1506. The abbey property reverted to its patron, the Crown, and the revenues were transferred to one of the new colleges at Cambridge, now known as Christ's College. Only the remains of the truncated church can be seen. The remnants of the cloister buildings have been incorporated into a farmhouse and are now largely concealed behind a high wall. The parish church at North Creake is well worth a visit for its late fifteenth-century roof.

Greyfriars Cloisters, Great Yarmouth

NORFOLK

The scanty remains of this Franciscan friary include two bays of the elaborate stone-vaulted cloisters, and two tomb recesses with evidence of wall-paintings. These were accidentally discovered while repairs were being carried out after the Second World War. The site does not look very prepossess-ing; the remains that have escaped demolition and enemy bombing, and those that have not been incorporated into other buildings, are squeezed into a small railed enclosure. Little is known of the history of the friary; it is thought to have been founded about the same time as the one in Norwich, in the 1220s, and is known to have been enlarged in 1285-90. The community was badly hit by the Black Death in 1347 but recovered quickly. At the Dissolution, the buildings were not demolished but passed into private ownership. In 1593 they were purchased by the town council who began the process of sale and demolition. The fragment of the cloisters is of much interest since the Franciscans rarely had cloisters this ornate. They must have provided an elegant and tranquil retreat in the centre of medieval Yarmouth (as the convent cloisters still do in Italian towns today), for in the thirteenth and early fourteenth centuries this was a bustling port and one of the most properous towns in England. Behind a twentieth-century boarded door, rather like the entrance to an electricity station, can be found two tomb recesses set against what was the south wall of the church. One has a finely cusped tracery canopy with traces of painting, in the other painted figures can be distinguished.

Old Merchant's House and Row 111 House, Great Yarmouth

NORFOLK

These two early seventeenth-century houses are examples of a type of building unique to Great Yarmouth — the Row House; and one which was almost completely eradicated by bombing in 1942-43. Row 111 House contains many fixtures and fittings rescued from the rubble. These houses were the result of the peculiar development of Great Yarmouth. The sand bar blocking the estuary that led to the abandonment of Roman *Caister* had, by the time of the Norman Conquest, extended to link up with the north side of the mainland. A settlement here developed rapidly in the thirteenth century thanks to the herring trade, and a street plan of closely-spaced parallel alleys running to the main streets evolved. After decline in the later Middle Ages, a period of great prosperity returned with the herring shoals in the late sixteenth — early seventeenth centuries when all of the town was rebuilt in brick, flint and tile. The influence of the Dutch settlers, who also contributed to this prosperity, is evident and the houses, each with their little brick courtyard and pump, must have looked

very similar to those in paintings by Vermeer and de Hooch. Built about 1604, the Old Merchant's House has two fine plasterwork ceilings and oak panelling, whilst among the items on display in Row 111 are excellent examples of the iron ties in the form of numerals and letters which decorated many buildings before the War. Panelling, joinery, window catches and hinges are among the many interesting pieces of architectural salvage. Both houses also demonstrate the alterations that the Rows underwent in the eighteenth and nineteenth centuries when declining prosperity led to the division of the rooms into smaller units and the houses were occupied by many families rather than one.

ABOVE: exhibition of architectural fittings salvaged from the destroyed Row Houses, Row 111 House

LEFT: entrance to Row 111 House

RIGHT: *Grime's Graves*

BELOW: *North Elmham
Cathedral looking west*

Grime's Graves

NORFOLK

The earliest major industrial site in Europe, these eerie pits are the remains of flint mines worked between *c.*2300–1800 BC. There are about 400 shafts in a forty-acre site, the vast majority of which are shallow hollows, but a few have been excavated and the visitor can descend by an iron ladder to view the galleries some thirty feet below ground level. The Neolithic miners would have descended by a swaying ladder holding chalk cup lamps, full of some form of animal fat. Wooden shovels would have been used to clear the sandy topsoil and red deer antlers were used as picks. The flint nodules and the earth were transported to the surface and the waste used to fill in exhausted shafts. The flints were used to make axes and knives, providing the best sharp-cutting edges available. There is an exhibition in the Ancient House Museum, Thetford, which explains the process and the many uses of flint, which continued to be mined in this area until the Second World War. (Norwich Castle Museum has a panorama of the site and the famous fertility good-luck figure discovered in one of the galleries can be seen in the British Museum.) It was not until 1868–70 that the true function of the pits as mines became known, and this was not widely accepted until the twentieth century.

North Elmham Cathedral and Earthworks

NORFOLK

North Elham is currently the subject of archaeological debate. Are the remains of the cathedral pre- or post- Conquest? Indeed, are they in fact the remains of a cathedral, or of a bishop's chapel? For a cathedral, the site seems rather small, yet for a chapel the plan is rather lavish. It is known for certain that the see of the Bishops of East Anglia existed before the Conquest, and that it was located in North Elmham, the central point of the diocese. The Norman policy was for the bishoprics to be located in large towns and to this end the bishop removed briefly to Thetford, and in the 1090s settled in Norwich. The foundations of the church at North Elmham are somewhat obscured by its conversion to a fortified dwelling in the late fourteenth century, but the plan of west tower, nave, transept with angle towers and apse can be clearly seen. It seems extraordinary that in the Middle Ages

Cow Tower beside the River Wensum, Norwich

it was possible to convert a church into a dwelling but the instigator, Hugh le Despencer, was an extraordinary man, and Bishop of Norwich as well. Hugh appears to be one of those people, like King John, about whom history can find nothing good to say. Indeed by all accounts he was thoroughly bad. His main delight seems to have been in killing people, whether in support of the existing social order or in the name of religion. He brutally quashed various outbreaks of the Peasants Revolt and when England became too peaceful, extended his activities abroad. On the flimsy pretext that the French King was supporting the anti-Pope, he led an unsuccessful expedition into Flanders, notable for its savagery even by fourteenth century standards. At North Elmham he raised the earthworks that we see today and created the bailey, now obscured by later buildings. The church was rebuilt on the upper storey and converted into what was really a small shooting lodge, so he could indulge his passion for hunting. Archaeological excavations have revealed that a great deal of eating and drinking took place during his occupation. Subsequent bishops refused to have anything to do with the building and it fell into decay.

Cow Tower, Norwich

NORFOLK

Cow Tower is part of the city walls that encircled Norwich in the twelfth century, except on the west side where the River Wensum formed the defensive boundary. The walls were rebuilt in the late thirteenth to early fourteenth centuries, though Cow Tower is thought to date from the 1370s. It is circular in plan with thick brick walls, about fifty feet high, that still bear the remains of crenellations. The interior is empty and it stands alone in a landscaped riverside walk. More extensive remains of the city walls (not in the guardianship of English Heritage) can be seen on the south-west side of the city centre in Chapelfield Gardens, running southeast to the bus station. The City Museum and Art Gallery, housed in the splendid Norman castle, contains further information on the town's defences.

St Olave's Priory

NORFOLK

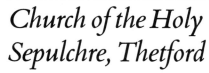

Most of the thirteen churches dedicated to St Olave are to be found in Norfolk. He was a Scandinavian King whose crusading message 'Baptism or death' converted many, though not all. He was murdered in 1030. The Augustinian priory dedicated to him was founded some 200 years later and largely destroyed at the Reformation. Little is known of its history; some of the buildings were dismantled to provide materials for the private house that now stands between the foundations of the church and the road. The main feature that survives today is the early fourteenth-century undercroft of the refectory, with circular piers forming two aisles of six bays each and a good example of the early use of brick vaulting. It was restored in 1904. The nearby River Waveney that provided the water supply and drainage for the priory was no doubt also the source of the bricks which would have come from the Low Counties as ships' ballast.

Church of the Holy Sepulchre, Thetford

NORFOLK

It is rare to find a church in England dedicated to the Holy Sepulchre. The remains of this church in Thetford belonged to the community of Augustinian canons, founded here in 1139. The founder was William de Warenne, 3rd Earl of Surrey, whose father had founded *Castle Acre Priory*, and whose vast family estates in Sussex, Yorkshire and East Anglia, included *Conisbrough* and the castle at *Castle Acre*. The dedication of the canons' church recalls that of the famous church of the Holy Sepulchre in Jerusalem, built by the crusaders over the cave when Christ was reputedly interred after the Crucifixion, and where the Resurrection took place. William de Warenne was a crusader knight who died on the Second Crusade, killed in Laodicea in Greece in 1148. (His only child Isabel married the son of King Stephen.) Not a great deal is known of the community at Thetford, which was never very large. It may have been colonised from the Augustinian house at Warwick, founded some twenty years before. The priory church consisted of an aisleless nave and chancel, of which the latter has disappeared: of the nave, the west end wall is the

ABOVE: St Olave's Priory looking across the cloister garth to the refectory

best-preserved part. Nothing remains of the claustral buildings and in the early nineteenth century the church was used as a barn.

Thetford Priory

NORFOLK

Visitors to the area would find it rewarding to first examine the more complete remains of another great Cluniac priory, *Castle Acre*, before attempting to unravel the ruins at Thetford. Thetford was begun about ten years after *Castle Acre*, in 1107,

having been founded 1103-04 by Roger Bigod. During the eleventh to fourteenth centuries Thetford was a large and prosperous town, and the priory covered a considerable area. A miraculous statue of the Virgin was one of the priory's most important treasures and pilgrims' contributions helped finance an extensive building programme in the thirteenth century. Much of this has disappeared and the ruins of the church are eroded pillars of flintwork, like the cliffs at Etretat in Northern France so popular with Impressionist painters. The foundations of the cloister buildings, including the infirmary range with its cobbled courtyard, can be distinguished, but the prior's lodgings are the best preserved, having been converted into cottages after the Dissolution. The priory was notable also as the burial place of the descendants of the Bigods, the Dukes of Norfolk. These tombs have either been destroyed or transferred to the parish church beside their castle at *Framlingham* (Suffolk). Some distance to the north of the site a well-preserved fourteenth-century gatehouse stands surrounded by twentieth-century housing. The Ancient House Museum, White Hart Street, Thetford, has some interesting drawings of the priory made in the seventeenth and eighteenth centuries when much more of it survived. Many other items of local interest, including information on *Grime's Graves*, are to be found in this fine fifteenth-century half-timbered house.

Remains of the prior's lodgings at Thetford Priory

Weeting Castle
NORFOLK

A circle of trees in the flat landscape marks the site of this fortified manor house. The ruins stand in a field beside the church, enclosed by a shallow moat. This can only be described as a token fortification given the nature of the terrain, so the word castle is inappropriate here. The ruins that we see today are of a stone manor house built *c.*1180 by Ralph de Plais. This consisted of an aisled hall with a two-storey service end to the east, and the solar range to the west in a three-storey tower. Both the solar and the service end were vaulted on the ground floor. This has been deduced from archaeological investigations, for the knobbly chunks of wall that survive today are not very forthcoming. The solar tower end is certainly identifiable, and the foundations of the hall and east end have been marked out.

Thetford Warren Lodge
NORFOLK

This was the fifteenth-century home of the abbot of Thetford's gamekeeper. Judging by the fortified aspect of the little tower house this was quite a hazardous job. Even today it has a rather solitary air in its sylvan setting, although it is only a couple of minutes from the carpark beside the road. Accommodation was on the first floor with a fireplace and garderobe (WC), with a gap above the ground-floor entrance for dropping stones and rubbish on to unwelcome visitors. Originally there was access to the roof by the spiral stair set in the angle of the wall, giving a good view of the surrounding countryside, but there is now a twentieth-century flat roof following an extensive fire in 1935. Only the walls survive and the interior is not accessible, though it is readily visible through the partially blocked entrance.

ABOVE: Weeting Castle

RIGHT: Thetford Warren Lodge

Bury St Edmunds Abbey

SUFFOLK

The two gatehouses are the best-preserved remains of this great Benedictine abbey of St Edmunds Bury, but the foundations of part of the church and claustral buildings, not all in the care of English Heritage, can be identified. The body of St Edmund, King and martyr, killed by the Danes, attracted both pilgrims and royal patronage to the abbey which was founded in 1020 on the site of a religious settlement dating from the seventh century. The first Norman Abbot, Baldwin, laid out the town on a grid system and throughout the Middle Ages relations between the abbey and its offspring were difficult and often violent. Other towns dominated by a monastery, such as Abingdon, had similar problems, but the riots of 1327 in Bury when the townspeople sacked the abbey were particularly bad, and again in 1381 when the prior was murdered and the King outlawed the whole town, fining it 2,000 marks. Standing beneath the remarkably-complete Norman gateway, built 1120-48, the visitor is looking at the centre of what was the 246 foot long frontage of the church; roughly a third longer than either Ely or Norwich. There was a very tall central spire over this west end

and octagonal towers with spires flanked the aisles. The buildings that face one today are a medley built into and out of the façade. To the east can be seen the foundations of part of the church which was 505 foot long. Continuing north along the west front of the precinct, one comes to the Great Gate, built after the riots of 1327 and completed after 1353. It is an excellent example of mid fourteenth-century design and is complete externally apart from the tops of the two octagonal stair turrets. This gave access to the Great Court, looking across to the King's lodgings and Abbot's palace. At the Dissolution the abbey was sold and stripped for building materials, becoming a quarry for the local people who built houses amongst the ruins. One marvellous relic of the abbey that has come down to us is *The Book of Jocelin of Brakelond*, a wonderful, gossipy twelfth-century account of life in the abbey at the time of Abbot Samson. Here we learn of the sacristan who had been pawning the holy seals, the fire in the sanctuary and the quite opposite interpretations of God's Will that the abbot and monks put upon it, the guests who were so badly behaved that the abbot excommunicated them ... it is an unique insight into twelfth-century monastic life. Some of the finds from the abbey can be seen in the Moyses Hall Museum, an interesting twelfth-century building, possibly built by a relative of the same Benedict to whom the sacristan had pawned the holy seals.

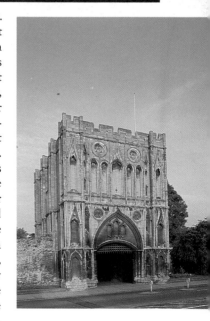

TOP: *the north transept of Bury St Edmunds Abbey church with the treasury in the foreground*

ABOVE: *the Great Gate*

Leiston Abbey
SUFFOLK

Pronounced 'Layston', this is one of the most extensive monastic remains in Suffolk. The Premonstratensian abbey was originally founded some two miles away, nearer the sea, in 1182. Repeated damage from flooding caused its removal to the present site in 1363, so the buildings are all late fourteenth-century, or later. There is an attractive variety of materials to be seen: flushwork, thatch, Tudor brick. The lady chapel was restored as a house of prayer in the early twentieth century and has recently been rethatched and refitted. Its east end wall has flushwork decoration, knapped flint and ashlar stone in a chequerboard pattern. Adjoining it to the south, the walls of the choir still stand, and beyond, the south transept wall rises almost to full height. A Georgian house now occupies part of the nave and cloister. To the west there is the octagonal brick turret of the external cloister gatehouse, which is early sixteenth-century. On the southern side of the cloister, the gable end of the refectory has a splendid pointed window.

The east end of the abbey church at Leiston

Landguard Fort, Felixstowe
SUFFOLK

Situated about a mile south of Felixstowe, near the docks, this site was first fortified by Henry VIII in the 1540s. It has undergone many alterations and what survives today is an eighteenth-century brick exterior, with a late nineteenth-century brick interior partly obscured by twentieth-century concrete additions. The fort was in use until just after the Second World War. In area it is about the size of *Tilbury Fort*; in plan it is polygonal with angle bastions, while the parade ground courtyard is segmental and dates from 1875, as does the entrance. Today the occupants of the fort scan the horizon for migrating birds rather than Dutch men o' war or German ironclads, for the Suffolk Trust for Nature Conservation has a bird observatory there.

St James's Chapel, Lindsey
SUFFOLK

This little thirteenth-century chapel, built of random rubble flint, has a late fifteenth-century or early sixteenth-century roof covered with thatch. The interior is empty, but there is a thirteenth-century piscina at the chancel end. The building is divided into two bays by the hollow-chamfered tie beam, held by curved braces springing from plain corbels. The door surround at the west end is of Tudor brickwork. The chapel probably had some connection with the nearby Lindsey Castle (not English Heritage), of which only the outline of the earthwork now remains.

Moulton Packhorse Bridge
SUFFOLK

This fifteenth-century packhorse bridge over the River Kennet lies on the old road from Cambridge to Bury St Edmunds. It has a four-arch span with pointed cutwaters and a rebuilt parapet. A concrete road now runs at water level beside the bridge, and the river is piped beneath it. To the south is another fifteenth-century bridge, constructed of flint. Medieval packhorse bridges are found in areas where roads were not sufficiently good for wheeled vehicles. Goods, and people, could therefore only be transported on the backs of animals, hence the narrow packhorse bridge. Bridges across broad rivers often had recesses above the cutwaters to give shelter to pedestrians when a string of animals was crossing, and also to provide the drover with a vantage point from which to shout encouragement to his animals.

Framlingham Castle
SUFFOLK

From the exterior Framlingham looks almost as it was built in 1190. Best approached from the Dennington road, it is a magnificent example of a curtain wall castle with thirteen square towers and no keep, one of the finest castles in England showing the influences of the Crusader castles of the Holy Land. Built by Roger Bigod, Earl of Norfolk, it passed in the fourteenth century to the Mowbrays, Dukes of Norfolk, and later to the Howards, who carried out some alterations including the present gateway and numerous decorative brick chimneys (which are almost all dummies). The alterations by the latter in the sixteenth century are easily distinguished because they are in brick, notably the entrance gateway. In 1635 the castle was sold to Sir Robert Hitcham who bequeathed it to Pembroke College, Cambridge, on condition that it be demolished and a poor house erected in its place. This unusual bequest led to the demolition of all the internal buildings of the castle, but the curtain walls were left. The poor house was built on the site of Roger Bigod's Great Hall, part of which survives in the north wing. The south wing was built in 1664 and the centre block in 1729; it now contains a museum. The castle has seen many exciting events: shortly after completion, King John successfully besieged it in 1215; Mary Tudor was living here when her brother Edward VI died, and it was here that supporters rallied to her when Lady Jane Grey was proclaimed Queen. After the execution of the Roman Catholic Duke of Norfolk in 1572, Elizabeth with rather heavy-handed irony turned the castle into a prison for recusant priests. Visitors to the castle must also see the parish church which contains an outstanding collection of sixteenth-century monuments to the Howards, one of whom married the Duke of Richmond, a natural son of Henry VIII. The Duke's tomb was originally at *Thetford Priory*, Norfolk, which was also founded by Roger Bigod, the builder of Framlingham.

Aerial view of Framlingham Castle

Orford Castle

SUFFOLK

Orford Castle keep has a unique plan, is remarkably well preserved, and has the additional interest of being the first castle for which the building accounts exist. The keep was completed within three years for Henry II, 1165-67, and the now demolished curtain wall with towers was finished by 1173. Orford was then a flourishing port and the castle immediately proved its stategic importance during the rebellion of 1173-74. In 1217 it was taken by the French and during the troubled reign of Henry III changed hands many times. Standing over ninety feet high the keep is circular internally and polygonal externally. There are three rectangular buttress towers, one of which is enlarged at the lower levels to form the forebuilding with chapel above and prison below. Above the basement there is a lower and an upper hall, both roofed with many small rooms in the towers. The upper hall roof, now flat, was originally conical, the painted ribs rising from the corbels which still remain. Little imagination is needed either in the chapel or as one ascends the spiral stair, to think oneself back in the twelfth century. From the roof there are splendid views across Orford and the Suffolk marshes, while in the basement there is a small exhibition on the castle's building and subsequent history.

RIGHT: Orford Castle

OPPOSITE: Saxtead Green Post Mill with the fantail in the foreground

BELOW: the middle floor of the Post Mill roundhouse showing two pairs of millstones in casings and a dressing machine

Saxtead Green Post Mill

SUFFOLK

The post mill is the oldest form of windmill and the post mills of East Suffolk are among the finest in the world. There has been a corn mill on this site in Saxtead since at least the fourteenth century, but the earliest reference to the one that we see today was in 1796. She ceased production in 1947 and since then has been fully restored. The principle of a post mill is that the 'buck' or body of the mill revolves on a post, so as to take advantage of the change in the wind's direction. The 'fantail', an eighteenth-century innovation, enables this to be done automatically. (There is a wonderful and complex vocabulary for describing windmills and their machinery that has grown up over the centuries.) The 'buck' stands above a solid brick roundhouse which has been raised three times over the years. When originally built, the round house was between eight and nine feet high at the eaves, and the sails swung near enough to the ground to hit a pig. There are four sails. Visitors can get a very good idea of how a corn mill functioned from a visit to the interior, which is full of fascinating machinery.

IN AND AROUND LONDON

Bedfordshire · Berkshire
Hertfordshire · London
Surrey

Bushmead Priory

BEDFORDSHIRE

This is a rare instance of a medieval monastic refectory surviving with its original roof more or less intact. At Bushmead, an Augustinian priory founded 1195, a mid thirteenth-century crown post roof remains and there is a small exhibition explaining timber constructional methods. From the facade of the building one can read much of its history. Firstly there is the steep pitch of the original roof, then there are the remains of the weather-moulding on the left-hand portion where the lean-to roof of the cloister ran. Thus visitors realise they are standing in the garth, or centre, of the cloister. The blocked arch of the lavatorium recess where the monks washed their hands before

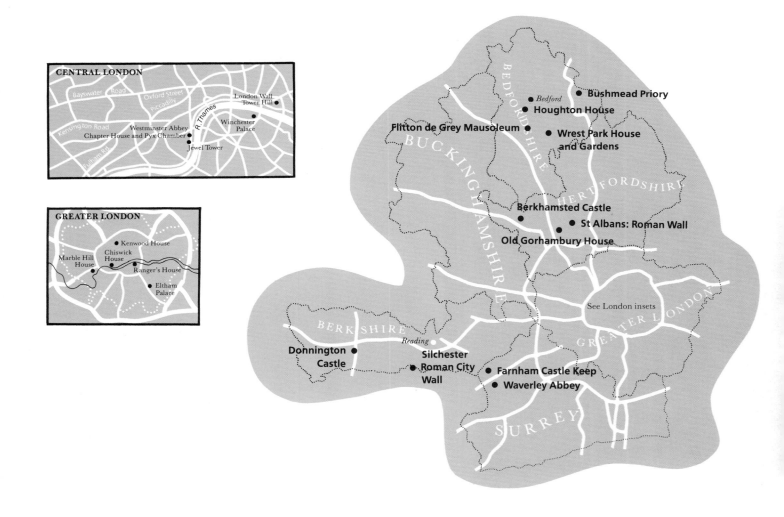

CENTRAL LONDON

Bayswater Road
Oxford Street
Piccadilly
Kensington Road
R. Thames
Fulham Rd
London Wall
Tower Hill
Winchester Palace
Westminster Abbey
Chapter House and Pyx Chamber
Jewel Tower

GREATER LONDON

Kenwood House
Chiswick House
Marble Hill House
Ranger's House
Eltham Palace

Bedford
Bushmead Priory
Houghton House
Flitton de Grey Mausoleum
Wrest Park House and Gardens
BUCKINGHAMSHIRE
HERTFORDSHIRE
Berkhamsted Castle
St Albans: Roman Wall
Old Gorhambury House
See London insets
GREATER LONDON
BERKSHIRE
Reading
Donnington Castle
Silchester Roman City Wall
Farnham Castle Keep
Waverley Abbey
SURREY

meals, and a blocked doorway adjoining, indicate that this was the refectory. (At the rear of the building to the north can be seen one of the large fire-places in the kitchen, with a massive stone lintel.) The ground-floor windows date from about 1500 when a floor was inserted in the refectory hall, whilst the larger first-floor windows are post-Dissolution. The priory was dissolved in 1536 and like many monasteries it was converted into a private dwelling. A rebuilt part of the house (not English Heritage) adjoins to the right. On the interior, the right-hand portion of the refectory has been left as two-storey, but to the left the floor has been removed so visitors can admire the roof, the same one that the monks were looking at when Edward I was King. Remnants of painted decoration can be seen in the reveals of the gable end window, and a blocked serving-hatch in the rear wall gave access to the kitchen. All of the other priory buildings have long since disappeared.

Flitton: De Grey Mausoleum

BEDFORDSHIRE

Tucked away behind the parish church of St John the Baptist, Flitton, is a remarkable treasure-house of sculpture, the mausoleum of the de Grey family. The de Greys, the family of the Earls of Kent, lived nearby at *Wrest Park*. The mausoleum consists of three rooms opening off the chancel of the church and entered through a fine eighteenth-century

wrought-iron gate. The mausoleum was begun for Henry, fifth Earl of Kent (died 1614), and the latest additions date from the mid-nineteenth century. This is a wonderful collection of funeral sculpture. The finest is the tomb to Henry de Grey, created Duke of Kent (died 1740), for whom Leoni re-modelled *Wrest Park* and Archer created the garden pavilion that still survives. The Duke's effigy is attributed to Rysbrack.

TOP: the refectory at Bushmead Priory

LEFT: the North Chapel of the de Grey Mausoleum where Anthony de Grey, died 1723, contemplates two of the children of Henry Duke of Kent: Henrietta who died in 1716 at the age of fourteen, and her brother Henry who died the following year aged twenty-one

Wrest Park House and Gardens

BEDFORDSHIRE

The appearance of this large eighteenth-century French-style mansion in Bedfordshire comes as something of a surprise. It was designed by its owner, Earl de Grey, and built 1834–39 on the site of an earlier mansion belonging to the family. Earl de Grey had inherited the estate from his aunt in 1833 and the following year he became President of the newly-founded RIBA, a post he held until his death in 1859. He demonstrated a wide knowledge of architecture and independent taste by choosing eighteenth-century French models for his house, notably Blondel's publication of 1737 *Maisons de Plaisance* for the garden front and orangery, and the Hotel de Matignon by Courtonne for the façade. The imposing walls concealing the kitchen garden with their fine gateway that greet visitors upon their arrival were inspired by Vanbrugh's work at Claremont. Inside the house the staircase hall has a double staircase with wrought-iron balustrade, and the principal rooms on the garden front are decorated in an elegant rococo. Half the reception rooms were in fact intended as his library, a function they still fulfil, for the building is occupied by an agricultural research institute. With the gardens at Wrest Park, Earl de Grey inherited a beautiful landscape garden evolved during the eighteenth century and one which he largely maintained intact. The main axis down the garden front centres on a canal terminating in Thomas Archer's Pavilion of 1711–12 with its painted interior. On either side of this formality lies natural landscape where the visitor is surprised and charmed by garden buildings from the eighteenth and nineteenth centuries. The early eighteenth-century Bowling Green House with its stucco decoration, the rustic bath house with pebble pavement and knucklebone floor, a Chinese Bridge, a pagan altar ... there is no end to the delights. Under the aegis of the agricultural research institute, 'an historically correct grass cutting regime' has been initiated which will be of interest to all gardeners, whereby the different periods of the gardens are mowed according to their original heights. This would have received Earl de Grey's full support.

The Orangery

TOP: *the garden front of Wrest Park*

LEFT: *the interior of Archer's Pavilion*

ABOVE: *the interior of the Bowling Green House*

The west front of Houghton House

Houghton House, Ampthill

BEDFORDSHIRE

Is this the 'House Beautiful' that Bunyan had in mind when he wrote *Pilgrim's Progress*? Many people think so, and even though only a gutted shell now remains on a hilltop, gazing far and away beyond the brickfields below, it is not difficult to believe them right. The house was built soon after 1615 for Mary, Dowager Countess of Pembroke. From old engravings it is known that the brick house had shaped gables and concave pyramid-roofed corner turrets, a fairly traditional design for the early seventeenth century, but it is of particular interest for the two classical centrepieces on the main (north) elevation, and on the narrower west front. The classical design of the ashlar-stone centrepieces has been attributed to the hand of Inigo Jones. The two-storey arcaded loggia on the main elevation, which had a pedimented top with volutes and obelisks, would have been highly novel, but the right return with columns carrying a straight entablature was quite unique. In the early eighteenth century the Houghton estate was acquired by the Russells at Woburn, but it was to have tragic associations for them. In 1764 it was occupied by the Marquis of Tavistock, heir of the fourth Duke of Bedford, on his marriage to Elizabeth Keppel. They had been married only three years when the Marquis was killed in a hunting accident. His wife, who was carrying their third child, was devastated and never really recovered. She died some months after the birth of the child the following year. Houghton was dismantled by their eldest son, the fifth Duke, in 1794 after the death of his grandmother. Why he chose to do so is not known. He had never lived at Houghton but had been brought up by his grandparents at Woburn. His neighbours were appalled to see the destruction of the beautiful house, and Lord Torrington, riding by, spoke with the overseer who told him of wallpaintings destroyed and panelling ripped out 'with the delight of a butcher killing a sheep'.

Donnington Castle gatehouse

Donnington Castle

BERKSHIRE

Only the gatehouse of this late fourteenth-century castle remains complete, the rest having been destroyed during one of the longest sieges of the Civil War. The castle was roughly D-plan in shape, with circular towers at the four corners, square ones on the north and south sides, and on the east, the gatehouse projecting. It was built by Richard de Abberbury, guardian of Richard II during his minority, and belonged briefly to descendants of Geoffrey Chaucer. The natural defensive properties of the site were strengthened during the Civil War by an impressive earthwork. In the continental manner, the embanked earthwork had star-shaped bastions with gun emplacements that could rake the surounding area with deadly fire. The position overlooking the Newbury-London road was of considerable strategic importance to the Royalists whose headquarters were at Oxford, and the castle was garrisoned at the beginning of the war under Captain Boys. In 1644 it was besieged by Parliament who destroyed three of the towers after twelve days' continuous artillery fire. At the approach of the Royalist army they withdrew and the garrison commander was knighted. After the second battle of Newbury, the Royalist heavy artillery was left at Donnington which was again besieged, this time by Sir William Waller who declared that he would not leave one stone standing upon another. To this the commander replied they would then fight for the ground upon which they stood. Faced with this determined resistance the Parliamentarians poisoned one of the castle wells. However, they regretted this action and told the garrison who were able to clean the well. Artillery bombardment recommenced, destroying a fourth tower. Again the castle was relieved and the winter was spent repairing the earthwork fortifications. Once again the castle was under attack but by the spring of 1646 the King's cause was lost. Boys was sent to the King for instructions and was told to get the best terms he could. Thus twenty months after the first demand Donnington finally surrendered.

Berkhamsted Castle

HERTFORDSHIRE

Berkhamsted is a fine example of a motte and bailey with an unusual double ditch. These three features are clearly distinguishable though the buildings have more or less disappeared. Its strategic position on Akeman Street, the old Roman road to London, meant that it was held either by the King or by those close to him; Thomas à Becket when Chancellor was one. Indeed it was here at Berkhamsted, before the castle was built, that William the Conqueror waited after the Battle of Hastings to discover whether he would have to take London by force or if the English earls would capitulate. The castle was begun soon afterwards with the earthworks that we see today, augmented in the thirteenth to fourteenth centuries. The buildings underwent many changes and were largely dismantled in the sixteenth century to provide building materials. One of the most dramatic events in the castle's history occurred in 1216 when it was besieged by the French. The garrison surrendered after being bombarded for a fortnight by mangonels. It is thought that the mounds between the beech trees on the north and eastern side of the outer ditch were the platforms for these evil-sounding machines. Berkhamsted, like *Farnham* and *Orford*, was one of the many castles captured by the French in the period 1216-17. The French had arrived by invitation; the barons opposing King John after he had revoked his promises made in Magna Carta invited Louis, Dauphin of France, to take the English throne. Louis had a tenuous claim through his wife Blanche of Castile. The appearance of the French inevitably forced the uncommitted to side with the King, who did his best to alienate all except his foreign mercenaries by laying waste the countryside. This unhappy state of affairs was only brought to an end by John's death.

Roman Wall, St Albans

HERTFORDSHIRE

An eight to ten foot high section of the town walls, with the remains of bastions and including the foundations of the London Gate, can be seen in the park in St Albans. The walls were built AD *c.*265-70, of flint and bonded tile, faced with dressed stone. In common with other Roman town walls, the facing stone has been stolen for other buildings, but the strength of the Roman mortar has preserved the core. The walls enclosed an area of 200 acres, twice the size of *Silchester*. Verulamium was the third largest town in Britain but probably the most important since it was the only one known defin-

itely to have achieved the status of a municipium. The site of the Roman town lies to the west of present-day St Albans and is bisected by Bluehouse Hill Road. The wealth of the town is indicated by the fine collection of exhibits in the Verulamium Museum (not English Heritage), including mosaics and painted wall plaster, as well as models of the town walls and gates. A few minutes' walk away to the west, across Bluehouse Hill Road, stand the remains of the theatre, the only Roman theatre in Britain open to the public. In general terms theatres were associated with temples and stood inside the town walls, as distinct from amphitheatres which provided more popular entertainments and stood outside the walls. Less than fifty years after the town walls were built the first Christian martyr in Britain, St Alban, was executed on a hill across the valley, where St Albans Abbey now stands.

Old Gorhambury House

HERTFORDSHIRE

Only the porch and empty shell of the Great Hall of Sir Nicholas Bacon's sixteenth-century house remain today. Every summer Queen Elizabeth and her court travelled around the country, staying with the more favoured members of the aristocracy and government. Woe betide those whose hospitality was thought deficient. Many of the great sixteenth-century houses were built mainly with her entertainment in mind, and thus she saved the cost of maintaining a summer palace. At Gorhambury the Queen was sadly disappointed in the accommodation provided, and she did not hesitate to tell Sir Nicholas Bacon so. He had begun the house in 1563 but hastily extended it in the 1570s. From the fine detail of the porch, it must have been a handsome building. The hall was set within a courtyard, like *Kirby Hall*, extended by various ranges of buildings of which unfortunately little is known. The house was dismantled in the 1770s when the new Gorhambury House was built. Sir Nicholas, Lord Keeper of the Privy Seal, was something of a hard liner; at the time of the St Bartholomew Day Massacre in France he advocated the expulsion of all French citizens from England, irrespective of their beliefs. He had a number of sons including the celebrated Sir Francis, Chancellor to James I, a philosopher with wide-ranging interests. At Gorhambury he created an elaborate water garden with islands, one of which was large enough to have a house on it. (All of this has vanished.) After Sir Francis Bacon's impeachment, he retired here to revise his famous *Essays*. He died in 1626

from a chill, caught while conducting one of the earliest experiments into the advantages of frozen food. The memorial to him in St Michael's Church, St Albans, conveys something of his personality, and is an outstanding piece of seventeenth-century sculpture.

The porch at Old Gorhambury House

Chiswick House

LONDON

Richard Boyle, the 3rd Earl of Burlington (1694–1753) and the builder of Chiswick House, was a remarkable patron of the arts. Not only was he a supporter of musicians, poets and philosophers, including Handel and Pope, but he also encouraged artists and landscape designers, at the same time endeavouring to reform the state of British architecture. He was one of the first noblemen to make the 'Grand Tour', absorbing classical culture in Italy and bringing back artists and ideas, as well as merely collecting works of art. Palladio and Inigo Jones were his two heroes and at his house in Chiswick he endeavoured to synthesise their ideas in a work of architecture of his own. Designed and built *c.*1723-29, Burlington modelled the house on Palladio's Villa Capra, with references to similar

concealed in the obelisks on the roof. The villa that we see today housed Lord Burlington's library and works of art, while the more mundane occupations of dining and sleeping were carried on in the existing Jacobean house which stood to the north linked by a corridor. This house was demolished in 1788 by Lord Burlington's heirs, the Dukes of Devonshire, who later leased the villa out as a private lunatic asylum. The ground floor now houses a collection of plans and drawings relating to Lord Burlington and the Palladian movement, while the main floor or piano nobile has been restored as nearly as possible to its condition in the early eighteenth century. William Kent was also involved in the gardens which initiated a freer, more picturesque style of landscaping, advocated in prose and

verse by Pope and others. Serpentine paths divide the grounds and there are a number of garden buildings and landscape features to surprise and delight the eye. 'The first essay of his lordship's happy invention' — the Bagnio, erected when he was twenty three — has been demolished but there is an obelisk and temple, an exedra with statues and a natural amphitheatre designed to be set with orange trees in tubs. The classical bridge across the river canal belongs to the alterations made by James Wyatt in 1788 for Georgiana, Duchess of Devonshire, who once again made the villa a popular resort for men of letters.

villas by Palladio's follower, Scamozzi. The interior is largely the work of an artist-turned-designer and architect whom Burlington had met in Rome, William Kent. Some minor concessions had to be made to the English climate such as the chimneys

ABOVE: the Ionic Temple

*LEFT: the Red Velvet Room
looking towards the Gallery*

fifteenth-century bridge, and see to the right the foundations of the chapel and the Royal Apartments that ran along the east end of the Great Hall. Adjoining the west end of the hall is the mansion built in the 1930s by Seeley and Paget for Stephen Courtauld who had rescued the Great Hall from its ignominious usage as a barn. He extensively restored the building and his house is now the headquarters of the Army Education Corps. Nothing remains of the mass of the buildings that stood on the south side of the Great Hall and which were demolished for building materials when the palace was sold after the Civil War. Inside the Great Hall, the screen with musicians' gallery and the panelling at the dais end have been added to give some idea of the building in use. Originally there was a central hearth, and remains of the smoke louvre can be seen in the centre of the hammer-

beam roof. The oriel bays that flank the dais end contain the blocked doorways that once gave access to the Royal Apartments. Erasmus dined here in 1500 and has left us an entertaining account of his visit.

Eltham Palace Great Hall

LONDON

The Great Hall at Eltham with its splendid hammerbeam roof was built in 1480 by Edward IV. Here he kept Christmas in 1482, 2,000 people feeding at his expense. The palace had already seen many royal Christmas feasts for it was the medieval practice for the King to hold Christmas in public, and Eltham, set in good hunting country, had been a favourite royal palace since the early fourteenth century. Henry VIII held Christmas here in 1527 but he preferred Greenwich, as did his successors. The palace stood on an irregular rectangular site surrounded by a broad moat, now largely gardens, approached through an outer court with gatehouse. The latter has gone but the much-restored Chancellor's Lodgings, rebuilt by Henry VIII, still stand in the north corner, while the houses adjoining are eighteenth-century refrontings of the former buttery and spicery. Visitors cross the moat by the

ABOVE: the dais end of the Great Hall at Eltham Palace

RIGHT: detail of the apex of the Great Hall roof, showing the decorative traceried lights inserted between the moulded collar beams

Kenwood

LONDON

The picture collection, the library designed by Adam and the eighteenth-century landscaped park are three first-class reasons for visiting Kenwood. There was a house on this site in the sixteenth century but the house we see today is largely a remodelling by Adam of an early eighteenth-century house. The estate was acquired in 1754 by William Murray, the future first Lord Mansfield, the famous orator and judge, in the year that he became the Attorney-General. He employed Adam,

LEFT: the garden front of Kenwood House

BELOW: detail of the Library ceiling at Kenwood

a fellow Scotsman, to redesign the house as his country retreat, from 1764 to 1774. Adam was responsible for the exterior of the central block with its grand portico on the entrance front and delicate stucco decoration above a rusticated basement overlooking the garden. The low wings of the orangery, a remodelling, and the library, a new creation, completed the composition. The dining room and music room on the entrance front were added by the second Lord Mansfield in the 1790s. Adam's library is one of his finest rooms to survive and it has recently been restored to its original splendour. Lord Mansfield intended this as the main reception room of the house and the other rooms are modest by comparison. The bulk of Lord Mansfield's collection of books was destroyed when his town house in Bloomsbury was burnt out by rioters in 1780. His refusal to keep his judgements in line with popular anti-Roman Catholic feeling made him a target for public hostility and he and his wife were lucky to escape with their lives. The preservation of Kenwood is a well-known story: the rioters had paused at the Spaniards Inn for refreshment after their tiring walk from Bloomsbury and the landlord served them so liberally that they lost all interest in burning down Lord Mansfield's second house, and settled down to getting drunk instead. The famous collection of eighteenth-century pictures at Kenwood including Romney's of Lady Hamilton, works by Gainsborough, Reynolds, Lawrence and Van Dyke, as well as Dutch scenes and works by Rembrandt and Vermeer, was formed by Lord Iveagh who presented the collection and the house to the nation in 1928. The Adam furnishings and fittings had

already been dispersed at auction in 1922 by the 6th Lord Mansfield, but some of the furniture has since found its way back to the house through donations. The landscaped gardens were created by the 1st Lord Mansfield and his successor who consulted Repton. It was the latter who resited the old Highgate-Hampstead road which had hitherto lain close to the north side of the house, separated from it only by a forecourt.

Marble Hill

LONDON

Marble Hill is a perfect example of the English Palladian villa. It was built between 1724 and 1729 for George II's mistress, Henrietta Howard, later the Countess of Suffolk, and has survived largely unaltered. The simple white villa set in green parkland on the edge of the Thames seems chaste by any standards, but particularly when one thinks of the house of the French king's mistress Madame de Pompadour. The liaison had begun when George II was still Prince of Wales and Mrs Howard was already separated from her highly unsatisfactory husband, whose main achievement seems to have been succeeding to the title of the Earl of Suffolk and dying soon afterwards. Lord Hervey remarked

ABOVE: *Marble Hill*

RIGHT: *the Staircase Hall*

of the relationship that the Prince 'seemed to look upon a mistress rather as a necessary appurtenance to his grandeur as a Prince, rather than an addition to his pleasures as a man'. The Prince's residence was then the Lodge in Richmond Old Park and the royal family were often at *Hampton Court*, very convenient by boat for Richmond and Twickenham where there were already a number of delightful villas before Marble Hill was built. The design was provided by Colen Campbell and executed in a simplified form by Roger Morris. Lord Herbert offered advice and the interior shows the influence of Inigo Jones, the earlier architect of part of Lord Herbert's own magnificent house at Wilton. The Great Room at Marble Hill, like the gallery at Lord

Burlington's *Chiswick Villa*, shows how the English Palladians, taking Jones as their guide, were able to create rooms of noble proportions within very small spaces. The recent regilding of this white and gold room has restored its original beauty. Paintings and furniture of the period have been assembled in the house and the upper floor has recently been re-opened to the public. The original bedroom wall-papers have been carefully reconstructed in colours that may seem alarmingly bright to the modern eye. However, it is the same with the original strong gouache colours on eighteenth-century prints. We are so used to faded eighteenth-century elegance that the robust colours and heavy gilding that covered the strongly moulded details of the earlier

part of the century, come as something of a shock. The gardens at Marble Hill were laid out by Mrs Howard's friend and neighbour, the poet Alexander Pope, assisted by Charles Bridgeman, and restor-ation of one of the grottos is currently underway. The gardens combined picturesque landscaping down to the river with the practical functions of supplying Mrs Howard's town house with produce. For a short period in the 1790s, the house was again occupied by another royal mistress, Mrs Fitzherbert and in 1902 Marble Hill was purchased jointly by the London County Council, Surrey County Council and Richmond Corporation in order to save the house and the surrounding parkland from redevel-opment.

London Wall, Tower Hill
LONDON

Various sections of the Roman wall enclosing London turn up in unexpected places, like the section preserved in London Wall underground carpark, or in the courtyard behind Midland House, 8-10 Coopers Row. However, the best-preserved piece stands opposite the Tower of London and can be viewed from the terrace near Tower Hill underground station. The wall was erected around AD 200 and bastions and river defences were added in the fourth century. (A section of the latter can be seen inside the Tower of London.) In the Middle Ages the walls were heightened, as can be seen at Tower Hill by the change in masonry. A visit to the Museum of London provides the best introduction to Roman London and its city walls.

Jewel Tower, Westminster
LONDON

This is one of those buildings that people see but don't notice, for it stands in the shadow of the Victoria Tower at the southern end of the Houses of Parliament, close by Westminster Abbey. Until 1965 it was obscured by buildings in Abingdon Street but since their demolition this interesting remnant of the medieval Palace of Westminister has been once again revealed. It was built in 1365-66 by Henry de Yevele, one of the most famous medieval masons, to house the personal treasure and regalia of the King, Edward III. The tower stood at the south-west corner of the palace and part of the moat has been excavated. The treasure was guarded on the upper floor of the three-storey tower while the principal rooms were on the ground floor with its stone-vault roof. The tower continued as the King's Jewel House until the death of Henry VIII. An inventory taken at his death reveals him as a great hoarder — an extraordinary quantity of items had found their way into his private treasury including one of Princess Elizabeth's dolls-houses. The ground-floor rooms were then used as kitchens for an adjoining building and Parliamentary papers were stored on the upper two floors. The building achieved its external appearance in the early eighteenth century when the round-headed window openings with Portland stone dressings were inserted and the other medieval features such as gargoyles and crenellations

Medieval wall-paintings in the Chapter House depicting scenes from the apocryphal life of St John

were stripped away. In 1869 the building took on a new function as the Weights and Measures Office, for its immensely thick walls made it immune from vibration. This function ceased in 1938. Evidence of these varied uses can be seen in the small exhibition contained within the tower.

Westminster Abbey Chapter House and Pyx Chamber
LONDON

Despite the 'hard-edge' finish of the Victorian work, the chapter house has been faithfully restored to its medieval appearance. Begun by Henry III in 1246, here is the first example of the use of bar tracery in England. It was completed by 1259, while the flying buttresses on the exterior were added in 1377 when the walls were decorated with paintings. The medieval sculpture that survives, particularly the Annunciation figures, are some of the finest English work to be seen. The novel design of the

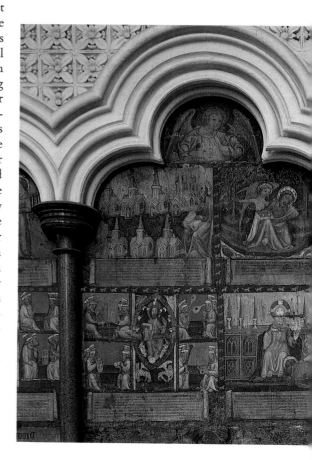

chapter house, an octagonal building with a central column, was much copied by other monastic foundations, for instance at *Thornton*, Humberside. From its conception, the building was intended to have a secular as well as a religious function, for Henry planned to use the undercroft as a treasury. Thus began the sequence of events that placed the chapter house in the care of English Heritage, rather than with the Dean and Chapter of Westminster. As a treasury the crypt did not prove very satisfactory for it was broken into in 1303. The chapter house itself was already providing a meeting-place for the 'commons' of the nascent Parliament, a function it fulfilled regularly in the latter part of the fourteenth century, much to the monks' disgust. This was not a use that Henry III had envisaged either and the monks finally removed the commons in 1395 with complaints that all the jumping up and down was ruining the floor. This floor of glazed tiles still survives today, one of the finest examples of its type. Between 1856 and 1872, the chapter house was thoroughly restored by Sir Gilbert Scott after the building had been much altered in the eighteenth century to form a record office. The vaulted roof had been demolished in 1744 so the one that we now see is Scott's rebuilding. Some extra sculpture was also added. Following bomb damage in the Second World War, the building was again restored. The Pyx Chamber, which adjoins the outer vestibule of

the chapter house on the south side, is the older of the two buildings. It was formed from the undercroft of the monks' dormitory and was divided in the twelfth century, part of it later forming the sacristy. The treasury was transferred here after the chapter house undercroft had been burgled, and from the fourteenth to early nineteenth centuries this was the strongroom of the Exchequer. This little room was famous for the Trial of the Pyx — a public demonstration of the true metal content of the coinage which continues to this day, now held in Goldsmiths' Hall in the City. 'Pyx' means box and the name comes from the 'pyx' in which the coins were kept for assay during the Middle Ages. Today the room contains some cope chests and a great chest dated 1545, and a Roman sarcophagus found during nineteenth-century excavations in the Abbey precincts.

The vault of the Chapter House

Ranger's House
LONDON

'I am now, for the first time in my life, impatient for summer, that I may go and hide myself at Blackheath and converse with my vegetables,' wrote Lord Chesterfield to a friend in 1753. His little country house at Blackheath is now also noted as the home of the Suffolk collection of sixteenth and seventeenth-century portraits and the Dolmetsch Collection of early musical instruments. Only in 1815 did it become known as the Ranger's House when the Princess Sophia Matilda, who held the title of Ranger of the Royal Park, acquired the property. The house was erected *c.*1700 and was one of a group of three houses set close together with splendid views across Greenwich Park. General Wolfe later occupied the other surviving house, but Montagu House, the home of Queen Caroline, was demolished by George IV. Despite these illustrious residents, Greenwich and the Thames to the east of London never achieved the fashionable status of Twickenham or the lands to the west, a fact already lamented by Lord Chesterfield when he acquired the property by inheritance in 1748. He refrained from selling it for fear of losing money and instead used it as his country retreat, erecting a remarkably splendid town house instead with elegant rococo decoration (since demolished). In this he was at variance with most of the English aristocracy whose residences tended to be modest in town and magnificent in the country. In many ways, however, the statesman and letter writer was unusual. His letters to his son, published posthumously in 1774, were in fact addressed to his illegitimate son whom he had fathered in 1732 while ambassador to The Hague. For nearly twenty years he wrote almost daily to the boy after he was five

years old; letters, that Dr Johnson claimed, 'taught the morals of a whore and the manners of a dancing master'. Lord Chesterfield had indeed failed to perceive the importance of Dr Johnson's Dictionary for the future of English literature, an error of judgement which may perhaps have influenced the latter's assessment of Lord Chesterfield's abilities as a moral philosopher. It was Mr Hulse, a later resident at the Ranger's House, who added the north wing to balance Lord Chesterfield's south gallery with bay window, for his marriage to Petronilla Melusina von der Schulenburg, an illegitimate daughter of George I, was without issue. The gallery now houses the splendid collection of full-length sixteenth and early seventeenth-century portraits, many by William Larkin, showing Elizabethan costume at its most opulent.

Winchester Palace
LONDON

Just west of Southwark Cathedral stand the remains of the Bishop of Winchester's London residence, or palace. Winchester was the richest see in England and before the Reformation the Bishop had eight residences, including *Wolvesey, Bishop's Waltham* and *Farnham Castle*. The London palace functioned in much the same way that Lambeth Palace still does today for the Archbishop of Canterbury, with the exception of the prison, the notorious Clink at Southwark which gave the word to the English language. The site was purchased in the 1140s from Orgar the Rich and others by that indefatigable builder, Henry of Blois. The last bishop of Winchester to occupy the palace died here in 1626 and after the Civil War the buildings were broken up. Much of it was destroyed by fire in 1814. The remains today are modest, only the foundations of the undercroft to the Great Hall and the west gable end with its early fourteenth-century window survive. The window design is unusual and the tracery has eroded to resemble bleached knucklebones. The Great Hall stood at the northern edge of the palace looking across Clink Street to the wharf beside the river. The rest of the palace was ranged around two courtyards to the south, with a large garden on the west side running to Park Street. The whole was enclosed by a wall and the main entrances were on the east side in what is now Cathedral Street. The prison buildlings stood in the southern courtyard and accommodated women, laymen and clerks. The bishop exercised legal jurisdiction over lands belonging to the see of Winchester, while those in holy orders (collectively termed clerks) claimed ecclesiastical exemption from the king's law. Many abuses resulted and these legal distinctions were abolished at the Reformation. Stow's *Survey of London* (1603 edition) records the existence of licensed brothels in the Middle Ages on the land to the west, and with the prison adjoining to the south, the palace can hardly have been a very congenial residence for the bishop. Fortunately, the see had many other episcopal residences, the remains of which are now mostly in the care of English Heritage. Today Winchester Palace forms part of a lively new riverside development at Pickfords Wharf, where the juxtaposition of old and new is highly successful. There is a riverside terrace and pub on the site of the bishop's wharf with a West Country top sail schooner of *c.*1900, *The Kathleen and May*, docked alongside at St Mary Overy's. Fine views are to be had up and down river.

ABOVE: the west gable end of the Great Hall, Winchester Palace

LEFT: part of the Dolmetsch Collection at Ranger's House

OPPOSITE: *Farnham Castle keep*

BELOW: *Farnham Castle, the gatehouse seen from the keep*

Farnham Castle Keep
SURREY

Farnham is rare among English Heritage properties in that the site has been in continuous occupation since it was built in the twelfth century. Only the keep is open to the public, but from here a large part of the castle can be seen and one gets something more of the feeling of what castles were like when in use. It was begun in 1138 during the anarchy of Stephen's reign by Henry of Blois, Bishop of Winchester (who was in fact Stephen's brother), and remained part of the see of Winchester until 1927. The site overlooking the town has natural defensive properties and here he raised a high tower with the motte banked up around its lower section. Certain differences of opinion between the Bishop and Stephen's successor, Henry II, led the King to take the opportunity of the Bishop's absence abroad to demolish this tower. It was not rebuilt but the basement area below the level of the motte still survives today. It is accessible to visitors and was probably used as a prison, for it has a very unsympathetic atmosphere. In the late twelfth century a shell keep was erected around the perimeter of the motte, rather than on top of it as was normal, and the top flattened off, like cake with a ribbon round it. Despite the castle's inauspicious beginning, it flourished. Standing mid-way between London and Winchester it was frequently used by the bishops who often had to entertain the monarch on his or her journeys. They were all accommodated in the buildings erected in the bailey below the keep. A story is told of Queen Elizabeth I on one of her visits to the castle. She had invited the Duke of Norfolk to dine, who, being a widower, was at that time rumoured to be contemplating a dangerous matrimonial alliance with Mary Queen of Scots. Rising from the table, the Queen informed him, 'pleasantly,' so we are told, 'to be careful upon what pillow he laid his head'. This enigmatic warning did not have the desired effect. Two years later he was arraigned for treasonable communications with Mary Queen of Scots and beheaded, still unwed.

Waverley Abbey
SURREY

Founded in 1128 by William Gifford, Bishop of Winchester, Waverley was the first Cistercian house in England. Sixty years later it had seventy monks and 120 lay brothers, which places it among the largest of the English monastic foundations. Time has not destroyed the tranquillity of the site, nor its separateness 'from the comings and goings of the people', which was so important to the founders. Only an eighteenth-century mansion (altered in the nineteenth century and not English Heritage) intrudes upon the wooded hillside that encircles the flood plain of the River Wey. The broad river, filled with cress and mallow, a home for swans, flows slowly in a loop around the site. The ruins are not extensive but they are spread over a large area amongst some fine oak trees. The south transept of the church with the chapter house adjoining can be distinguished, and the vaulted cellars beneath the lay brothers' dormitory, as well as the gable end wall of the mid thirteenth-century monks' dormitory. All Cistercian houses were great landowners and the abbey's chronicles reveal the usual monastic preoccupation with property, and its economic exploitation. They also record that the River Wey often flooded causing great distress to the monks. It was the publication of these *Annales Waverlienses* that gave Walter Scott the title for his first novel, begun in 1805 and published in 1827.

SOUTH EAST
ENGLAND

Hampshire
Isle of Wight · Kent
Sussex

Bishop's Waltham Palace

HAMPSHIRE

The last bishop to reside at Bishop's Waltham left in a dung cart disguised as a farm labourer. That was in April 1644 and the palace had been unsuccessfully defended by the Royalists against the Parliamentarians. Waltham had belonged to the Bishops of Winchester since Saxon times but nothing had been built here until *c.*1135 when the ebullient Henry of Blois began to build a palace. In this same year he acknowledged his brother Stephen as King of England. It was largely demolished by Henry II, whose mother Matilda's legal claim to the throne had been overlooked by the Bishop. (Henry also demolished the castle that the bishop had built himself at *Farnham*.) Most of the ruins that one sees today date from the fifteenth century. The site is rectangular, surrounded by a ditch with the main range of buildings surviving on the west side. These include the ruins of the Great Hall which stands on the foundations of the earlier one. The remains of the three-storey tower in the south-west corner date from the 1160-80 rebuilding, begun by Henry of Blois, nothing if not energetic. Of the Bishop's private apartments on the south side, little remains. Restoration is now complete on the later north-east guest range which is partly roofed and provides an exhibition area. Remains of a brick wall that encircled the palace *c.*1500 can still be seen, including an intriguing little brick gazebo (not in the care of English Heritage).

Calshot Castle

HAMPSHIRE

Beset by reminders of its recent past, this little fortress offers some fine views out to sea. Calshot belongs to the group of forts built during Henry VIII's reign in response to the threat of a French and Spanish invasion following his break with Rome. Stone from some of the dissolved monasteries was used, in this case from Beaulieu Abbey. The plan is satisfyingly simple — a circle within a circle, a keep closely surrounded by a curtain wall. Completed 1539-40, it was repaired after a fire in 1584. In 1774 the gatehouse was raised and extended laterally along the perimeter wall which was lowered elsewhere. Otherwise it has undergone little alteration. Its position on a spit of land commanding the mouth of Southampton Water has been put to a variety of uses. In the eighteenth and nineteenth centuries it was a base for the coastguard revenue cutter, the bane of smugglers. In time of war a boom could be laid across the Sound to the site of Bungalow Battery on the east bank. In 1913 it became one of the first Royal Naval seaplane bases, and in 1918 was renamed RAF Calshot. The seaplane connection continued between the Wars when Calshot Castle was a favourite place from which to view the famous Schneider Trophy races. The RAF hangars (now an activities centre) remain from this period, and a modern coastguard tower dominates the castle to the east.

OPPOSITE: Bishop's Waltham Palace

BELOW: the gatehouse at Calshot Castle

Fort Brockhurst

HAMPSHIRE

An outstanding piece of brickwork, Fort Brockhurst is a good example of a well-preserved nineteenth-century fort. Advances in the power, range and accuracy of artillery in the mid nineteenth century meant that for the first time in 300 years fortress building had to be radically revised. Brockhurst, as part of a chain of landward forts defending Gosport and Portsmouth, was one of the first of these new forts. In fact the armaments race

Fort Brockhurst, looking from the **keep along the moat**

was so rapid that Brockhurst was more or less obsolete by the time it was completed in 1862. The feared French invasion that had prompted the Prime Minister to build these forts fortunately never materialised, and they were consequently known as 'Palmerston's Folly'. If the French had invaded they would doubtless be known by another name, but defence spending is never popular in peacetime. One of the main consequences of the bigger guns was that a solid defensive wall was no longer practical, and separate forts now provided a wall of artillery fire, more flexible than a solid wall for the calibre and range of guns was continually increasing. Another development was a change in the planning of forts. The arrowheaded bastions

they are eight courses of brickwork thick. The whole is enclosed by a moat giving a rather romantic appearance. The former Regimental Institute, built inside the fort *c.* 1900, now contains an interesting exhibition on Portsmouth's defences.

The interior of the keep, Fort Brockhurst

Flowerdown Barrows

HAMPSHIRE

A hole and a hump stand in a field off the main road through the village of Littleton. This is how Flowerdown Barrows may appear to the ordinary visitor, but the archaeologist sees a Bronze Age disc barrow with a diameter of 178 feet. There is a ditch that is nineteen feet wide surrounded by an outer bank twenty-three feet wide and two feet high. Two mounds stand inside the circular platform, one of which also rises to two feet. This is a Bronze Age burial site dating from 1700-1200 BC, and one that can be recommended to those who find themselves in Littleton.

introduced in the sixteenth century had provided a limited number of protected enclosures for artillery, but the introduction of a polygonal plan gave long stretches of ramparts along which the guns could be deployed where needed, using rails for the bigger guns. This was a more flexible arrangement and one that enabled the garrison to switch from defence to offence more easily. Brockhurst has a hexagonal plan with a circular keep built into one angle. The walls are backed by brick-vaulted casements which absorb the effects of artillery fire much better than earthen ramps, and also provided accommodation for the men. The strength of the casements can be seen where Second World War bomb damage has been left unrepaired, showing

The Grange, Northington

HAMPSHIRE

One of the most important neo-Classical houses surviving in Europe, the Grange is largely the work of William Wilkins for the banker Henry Drummond, 1805-09. The later extensions by Cockerell and Smirke have been demolished and only the original block with an attendant temple (the picture gallery of the 1880s) remain. Wilkins was, in fact, remodelling an existing seventeenth-century red-brick house, one wall of which is now exposed on the south-west front. In his choice of this austere Greek temple style, his client was probably influenced by neighbouring Stratton Park, the home of another banking family, the Barings. Their neo-Classical house had a portico front, but was a very modest affair, hardly comparable with the complete Doric temple built for Drummond. The design, which Wilkins seems to have borrowed from a Scottish architect, Robert Mitchell, makes no concessions to early nineteenth-century living. The entrance is on the north-west front but the noble portico and steps on the garden front to the left invite the visitor to approach. Yet the height of the steps is so great that female visitors in the early nineteenth century — even those clad in the most generously draped of empire-style gowns — would have had to raise their skirts indecorously high in order to ascend. In 1816 Drummond tired of his house and sold it to Alexander Baring, later Lord Ashburton, who extended it to the south-west with the dining room and 'ladies wing', terminating in a conservatory. The picture gallery stands on the site of the latter, including the conservatory portico — a rare feature — but the rest has been demolished. It is interesting to speculate why this austere style appealed mainly to bankers in the early nineteenth century. The chief proponent of the neo-Classical, Thomas Hope, himself came from a banking family. At the Grange an austere exterior contrasted with an opulent interior, 'magnificent to death' as one of Lord Ashburton's visitors, Jane Carlyle, described it. Neither the interior of the house nor that of the picture gallery are at present open to the public.

The Grange and the Picture Gallery, formerly linked by buildings to form one continuous range

Old Bishop's Palace, Wolvesey

HAMPSHIRE

Visitors have to be prepared to concentrate at Wolvesey. Recently the scene of intense archaeological investigations, this small site contains the ruins of the twelfth-century fortified palace of the bishops of Winchester, subsequently much altered, which in turn stands upon the foundations of the Anglo-Saxon episcopal palace. Such gems as the foundations of the sideboard that held the dishes at the marriage feast of Mary Tudor and Philip of Spain have been uncovered. It was here in the East Hall that they gazed apprehensively at each other across the wedding breakfast, an occasion no doubt full of rather forced gaiety since the couple had met for the first time only two days before. The bishops of Winchester, occupants of the richest see in England, played an important role in medieval political and religious life. Perhaps the most famous was Henry of Blois, brother of King Stephen, bishop from 1129 to 1171, who was responsible for much of what we see today at Wolvesey. Set around a courtyard, the palace consisted of two great halls facing each other with ancillary buildings, a gateway to the north over remains of the Anglo-Saxon palace, and the west front extended with Wymonds Tower and the 'keep' (in fact kitchens), which forms the best exterior view seen from across the playing fields. The chapel, still used by the bishop and not in the care of English Heritage, was rebuilt between 1442 and 1447 on the site of the earlier Norman chapel. A whole range of buildings stood to the south, swept away when the bishop's palace was rebuilt in the seventeenth century. Wolvesey was besieged and threatened on various occasions, but strangely enough survived the Civil War unscathed, unlike nearby *Bishop's Waltham*. However, in the 1680s Bishop George Morley decided to rebuild the palace and he demolished the medieval buildings for their materials. Visitors approach the ruins across the site of this large Baroque palace, designed by Sir Thomas Fitch on a scale comparable with those of continental bishops' palaces. Only the west wing now remains, adjoining the chapel, for the east wing and long south front were demolished in 1786, having been little used. In the 1920s following the division of the see of Winchester, this south wing became the bishop's palace once again, and the ruins of the medieval palace were restored by W.D. Caroe. He inserted the red tile arches and quoins into the flint and ashlar ruins, cheerful if historically inaccurate.

Hurst Castle

HAMPSHIRE

Set on a spit of shingle, Hurst is one of Henry VIII's castles of the early 1540s, but one which was transformed in the mid nineteenth century into a glowering fortress commanding the narrow west entrance to the Solent. This was one of the last Henrician castles, with a twelve-sided tower surrounded by three semicircular bastions, and it is known to have been built by Thomas Bertie, who also worked at Netley Abbey. It was surrounded by a moat, filled in 1861 when the enormous wing batteries were begun. They almost completely conceal the earlier castle, and only the landward

LEFT: Hurst Castle looking from Henry VIII's Castle across the east wing battery to the Solent

BELOW: the interior of Henry VIII's Castle, the vaults inserted 1803–06 to carry the weight of the armaments on the roof

bastion survives in its original form. Finally completed in 1874, these long, low wings are pierced by casement openings protected by iron shields. They were designed for thirty heavy guns and a railway track was laid to enable ammunition and stores to be moved around the castle. Large numbers of guns were needed because the length of time necessary to reload these monstrous weapons meant that enemy steam-powered vessels might well be through the Needles Passage before the guns could get off a second shot. A few of these guns survive. Hurst continued to play an active part in the defence of the Solent up to, and including, the Second World War. The 1860s batteries were in fact replacing batteries added as recently as the previous decade, when a defensive strategy for the whole area was evolved under the threat of a French invasion. Hurst was linked with two new forts opposite on the Isle of Wight, Forts Albert and Victoria; the

former still survives. The sixteenth-century core of Hurst and part of the west wing are open to the public, and there is an exhibition about the castle and its history. Visitors can reach the fort either by ferry from Keyhaven, or by a two-and-a-half mile walk along the shingle spit.

Portchester Castle

HAMPSHIRE

Portchester is one of the most interesting and impressive castles in southern England, as well as having one of the longest histories of occupation. The Roman fort was built AD 285-90, one of the Saxon Shore Forts (and subsequently a Saxon burh), into which a Norman castle and priory were inserted. A residence of kings, the Normans used it as their port of departure for visiting their lands in Normandy, and here Henry V addressed his troops before they departed for their victories at Crècy and Agincourt. Indeed Portchester might have become a very important town had the harbour been better. Between the seventeenth and nineteenth centuries the castle was used to house Dutch and French prisoners-of-war, up to 5,000 at one time. The Roman fort stands four-square at the water's edge with fourteen of its original twenty D-shaped towers, or bastions, intact. The walls are said to be the best preserved Roman fortifications in Europe. The land and sea gates were rebuilt on a smaller scale in the Middle Ages and in the north-west corner stands the early twelfth-century keep of Henry I, to which Henry II added two extra storeys. The keep, particularly impressive from the exterior, is approached via an inner bailey containing the ruins of Richard II's palace of 1396-99, partly rebuilt in 1608, and the Constable's House of 1376-81 which includes Assheton's Tower. A moat separates the castle from the rest of the Roman fort which forms the outer bailey. In the south-east corner stands the parish church of St Mary, built as part of the Augustinian priory founded 1133. Some twenty years later it moved to Southwick. The west front is especially fine and the interior with its delightful font has hardly been altered, apart from the chancel. The view from the keep takes in the whole panorama of Portsmouth harbour with the masts of HMS *Victory* in the distance.

Netley Abbey

HAMPSHIRE

'Beinge of large buyldinge scituate uopon the ryuage of the sees is to the kings subgietts and straungiers trauelinge the same sees great releef and comforte', so Henry VIII's commissioners described Netley on the eve of the Dissolution.

Despite this recommendation the Cistercian abbey was dissolved in 1536, and some of the dismantled stone work was used to build Henry VIII's fort at *Calshot*. The abbey remains are extensive and evidence survives of the house that Sir William Paulet built out of the nave with the entrance range set in the south side of the cloister — the opposite to what happened at *Titchfield*. As one of the commissioners in charge of the defence of the area he also built Netley Castle at his own expense, but unfortunately it disappeared after the Civil War. The Cistercian Abbey was founded *c.* 1238 by Peter des Roches, Bishop of Winchester, but it soon became a royal foundation and the church was built *c.* 1245-1300, probably using masons who had worked on Westminster Abbey. The fine East window is remin-

iscent of the work at the *Chapter House, Westminster*. The abbey was little altered thereafter and what survives is imposing. The shell of the rooms on the east side of the cloister remain, the reredorter (latrine block) set at an angle over the stream. The south side of the cloister, which contained the kitchen and warming house, has a sixteenth-century entrance cut through on the site of the refectory. To the east lies the small guesthouse, a detached U-plan building with a vaulted lower storey. Netley was admired early in the eighteenth century for the picturesque qualities of its location, the ruins set among fine old trees by the seashore. It has been the scene of many pleasant excursions; Lord Peterborough and Alexander Pope spent an enjoyable day here in 1734 having sailed across from the Isle of Wight — they ate their lunch amidst the ruins and did a little sketching.

OPPOSITE: *the view from the keep at Portchester Castle*

LEFT: *the east end of Netley Abbey church*

Portsmouth: King James's Gate and Landport Gate

HAMPSHIRE

These two gateways now form the entrance to the services' playing fields; King James's gate is the officers' entrance, Landport Gate for other ranks. They were built as gates in the fortifications encircling Portsmouth which were demolished in the 1870s. Landport Gate was at first the only gate on the landward side and it still stands in the original position. It was rebuilt in 1760 in the form we see today and the playing fields cover the site of the adjoining earthwork and moat that were part of the seventeenth-century ramparts. King James's Gate, however, has been moved twice, losing various pieces of masonry in the process, including its pediment. As built in 1687 it stood across Broad Street, between Old Portsmouth and the Point. In the late nineteenth century it was re-erected in the Royal Naval Barracks and arrived at the sports ground in the twentieth century. The design was probably by Sir Thomas Fitch, who took over the supervision of the fortifications after the death of Sir Bernard de Gomme in 1685. As Engineer-in-Chief of the King's fortifications, Gomme had created a very complex arrangement of ramparts with arrowhead bastions and moats; a more elaborate version of his fortifications at *Tilbury* which can still be seen. Portsmouth's defences were amplified in the mid eighteenth century and destroyed in the 1870s.

Southampton: 58 French Street

HAMPSHIRE

This late thirteenth-century merchant's house is the finest example of its type to survive in England and it was opened to the public in 1987 after a very long and careful restoration programme, befitting the importance of the building. Excavations revealed many of the original medieval features which have been copied in replica, for instance the ridge tiles and louvres on the roof, and no features have been restored that cannot be fully substantiated. The house stands over a stone barrel-vaulted undercroft; three of the exterior walls are of stone and the façade — the gable end wall — is timber-framed, as are all the internal partitions. The house was altered in the early fourteenth century, possibly after damage sustained during the French raids on Southampton, and a fireplace remains from this period. The interior of the house has been restored and furnished as a wine merchant's house and shop of the fourteenth century.

ABOVE: Landport Gate

RIGHT: King James's Gate

Silchester Roman City Wall

HAMPSHIRE

Calleva (Silchester), the tribal capital of the Atrebates, is the most fully excavated Roman town in Britain. A great deal is known, therefore, about the layout of the town, but these excavations have been backfilled, and now only the town walls and the amphitheatre are visible. These are the best-preserved Roman town walls in Britain. Visitors would do well to orientate themselves by first visiting the little site museum, which is maintained by voluntary contributions. The town was settled before the Roman Conquest, but by the end of the first century it had been laid out on the grid system with public buildings and the other facilities of a tribal capital. The ditch and earth rampart of the second century was replaced between 260 and 280 by a stone wall enclosing the hundred-acre site. The best sections of wall survive by the south gate, south-west of the church, and are visible from the road. Standing outside the town walls, as always, are the remains of the amphitheatre. This circular earthen enclosure would have seated 4,000 people fairly comfortably on wooden benches. It lies north-north-east of the church. Apart from the parish church which stands on the site of the temple, Manor Farm is the only other post-Roman building within the town walls. Silchester was known from the sixteenth century as a Roman town, but the first major excavation took place between 1864 and 1878 under the patronage of the Duke of Wellington on whose land it stands. A good mosaic floor from Silchester can be seen at Stratfield Saye, the Duke's nearby residence. The systematic excavations of 1890-1909 followed, and many of these finds can be seen in Reading Museum which has an excellent collection of Roman material. The amphitheatre has recently been excavated.

The Roman walls of Silchester near the South Gate, St Mary's Church to the north-east

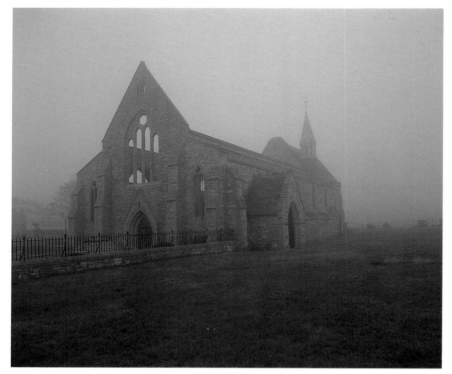

Portsmouth Garrison Church

HAMPSHIRE

Only the chancel now remains of the Garrison Church, entered through the shell of the nave, restored after being gutted by fire bombs in 1941. The church was built 1212–14 as a hospice for pilgrims who had landed in Portsmouth, en route for the shrines of southern England. The building consisted of a large hall, the nave, with the chapel (now the chancel) attached. The aisles may have been divided by wooden partitions into cubicles, and there were originally twelve brethren: six brothers and six sisters and a Master or Warden. After the Dissolution of the Monasteries it was briefly used as an armoury and then became the church for the garrison. Little attention was paid to the fabric of the building until the 1860s when it was restored by G.E. Street, the architect of the Law Courts in London. He rebuilt the west end of the nave and restored the aisle walls externally but the vault of the chancel is original, as are the east lancet windows. The decoration of the chancel is Street's and some of his stained-glass windows survive. The carved choir stalls are particularly noteworthy, each with a commemorative brass, and there is also a display of documents relating to the church and the garrison.

ABOVE: the Garrison Church, Portsmouth, seen from the south-west

OPPOSITE: Titchfield Abbey, the gatehouse seen from the cloister

Titchfield Abbey

HAMPSHIRE

The shell of a bold Elizabethan gatehouse range survives at Titchfield, part of the mansion once known as Place House, where possibly some of Shakespeare's plays received their first performances. The gatehouse range was created out of the nave of Titchfield Abbey, founded in 1232 for the Premonstratension canons. Here they erected their cloisters to the north of the church, rather than as was more normal to the south, thus providing the 1st Earl of Southampton with an uninterrupted south prospect for his mansion. The nave was aisleless, as in most of the canons' early churches, which also facilitated the conversion completed by 1542. The refectory on the north side of the cloister became the Great Hall with a fine porch addition, and the west range was retained, but the east end of the church and the adjoining claustral buildings were demolished. The architect of these alterations was Thomas Bertie, who also worked on some of Henry VIII's castles, including *Hurst*. His client, Thomas Wriorthesley, the 1st Earl of Southampton, was an ambitious and unscrupulous associate of Thomas Cromwell, acquiring considerable lands at the Dissolution which included Beaulieu Abbey and part of the Isle of Wight. In the 1590s the tutor to the 3rd Earl, his grandson, was a friend of Shakespeare's. Shakespeare composed some of his *Passionate Pilgrim* collection here, and a theory has been put forward that the young Earl was the Dark Lady of the Sonnets. Incontrovertible, however, is the evidence that the Earl encouraged economic activity in the area. For instance, in 1611 he created one of the first canals in the country by blocking the silted-up estuary of the River Meon and dredging it. In the seventeenth century the proximity of the house to the coast led to several royal visits; Charles I reputedly spent his last night of freedom here in 1647. On the death of the 4th Earl the estates were divided between heiresses: Beaulieu went to the Montagus and Titchfield to the Noels, who sold it. The house was largely demolished in 1781. Evidence of the abbey walls re-emerged in the gutted shell of the gatehouse range, and in the courtyard at the rear a few medieval tiles from the cloister survive *in situ*.

Appuldurcombe House

ISLE OF WIGHT

The bleached shell of this fine house, roofless and empty, stands amidst the rolling green landscape of Keat's 'primrose island'. It was mostly built *c.* 1701–13 by John James for Sir Robert Worsley, but was not completely finished until the 1780s. There is an early nineteenth-century *porte cochere* on the west front. The carved details on the east front are worthy of note, and, being a Baroque building, the animation of the façade creates an interesting ruin, though not in this case a romantic one. Taste in ruins is however rather a personal matter. The entrance drive to the house originally ran to the north via the handsome Freemantle Gate, possibly designed by James Wyatt. Sir Richard formed a very important collection of Greek marbles and antique gems at Appuldurcombe, but he is unfortunately better remembered for his disastrous marriage. In 1775 he married the eighteen-year-old Dorothy Fleming, 'for love and £80,000' according to

Gibbon. Seven years later the marriage ended in a spectacular divorce case. Reynolds' portrait of Lady Worsley *c.* 1780 shows her with an insouciant, rather tight-lipped smile, wearing a scarlet dress modelled on the uniform of her husband's regiment. It was for 'criminal conversation' with officers of this regiment that her husband sought a divorce. Despite her frank acknowledgement in court of twenty-seven lovers, Sir Richard only received a shilling damages on the grounds of connivance. Aristocratic morals were somewhat lax in the late eighteenth century but Lady Worsley's cavalier disregard for public opinion occasioned much adverse comment.

Appuldurcombe House, the south loggia and remains of the porte cochère on the west front

Carisbrooke Castle

ISLE OF WIGHT

Carisbrooke has always been the most important castle on the Isle of Wight. Lordship of the island went with the castle during the Middle Ages and later the captains of the castle were Crown appointees. From the sixteenth century they were known as governors and though latterly this has become an honorary title, the castle has always been kept in good repair for their occasional occupation. A motte and bailey castle was founded here in the 1070s, possibly on the site of a Saxon burh, or fortified town. In the early twelfth century a shell keep replaced the timber palisade and the bailey was enclosed with a curtain wall. A fine gatehouse was built in 1335 and the upper storey with gunports, like inverted keyholes, was added in the late fifteenth century. Of the buildings inside the bailey, apart from the keep, the ruins of the sixteenth-century governor's house can be seen adjoining the twelfth-century great hall and chamber which are now the Isle of Wight Museum. The buildings have undergone various alterations and were restored in the nineteenth century. To the east lies the well house, one of the main attractions at Carisbrooke. The well was dug in the twelfth century and the surviving well house is a sixteenth-century building containing a treadwheel. Donkeys now work the treadmill and this is one of the very few places where a donkey wheel can be seen in operation. To the south lies the chapel of St Nicholas which was rebuilt between 1904 and 1929 and has a good

interior. The castle is surrounded by the earthwork artillery defences of the 1590s. On the east side they were partially levelled in the mid seventeenth century to form a bowling green to divert the imprisoned Charles I. The King's captivity was a sorry mistake that need never have happened. He had fled voluntarily to the island in 1647 thinking that the governor, the brother of his chaplain, would assist him. This put the governor in a very difficult position and he felt obliged to follow orders from Parliament and detain the King. Three attempted escapes were planned, the most promising one foiled when the King found himself too large to get between the bars of his window.

Osborne House

ISLE OF WIGHT

'A place of one's own, quiet and retired', this was what Queen Victoria sought and found at Osborne. Here she and Prince Albert and their children could enjoy the pleasures of family life by the seaside, away from the restraints of court ceremonial. The house was designed by Prince Albert and built by Thomas Cubitt with Professor Grunner of Dresden advising on the interior decoration and gardens. The family moved in during 1846. The Queen's private suite of rooms have been left unaltered since she died and the house is both a testimonial of her love for Prince Albert and a wonderful monument to Victorian family life. There is the billiard table designed by Prince Albert, the birthday presents that Victoria gave him, and the miniature dining table for their nine children, all set amidst mementoes of all the ruling houses of Europe. In the gardens are the children's area, suitably far away from the house, with the Swiss chalet where they learnt cooking and gardening. They each had their own miniature gardening tools, including wheelbarrows, inscribed with their names. The Swiss Cottage Museum contains the splendidly eclectic collection of items made by the children including dried mosses from Scotland carefully arranged by the Princess Victoria (later Empress Frederick of Germany) and 'Mugger' a stuffed crocodile shot by Prince Arthur. Queen Victoria's bathing machine stands nearby. Osborne continued to grow over the years with a major addition in 1890 of a large room for state receptions — the Durbar Room. Every surface is covered with intricate plaster work, designed by Bhai Ram Singh and J. Lockwood Kipling in the Indian style, an unhappy example of cultural miscegenation. The room contains many of the gifts that Victoria received as Empress of India and in the adjoining corridor there is a very interesting collection of portraits of Indian rulers and subjects, the latter by Rudolf Swobada. Indeed the corridors are full of an extraordinary variety of gifts that the Queen received from all over the world. Resplendent after a recent restoration and regilding, the interior of Osborne may not be to everyone's taste but it is certainly an experience.

OPPOSITE: the Clock Tower seen from the terrace overlooking the Italian Garden

ABOVE: Osborne House from the Italian Garden

Yarmouth Castle
ISLE OF WIGHT

Finished in 1547, Yarmouth looks very different from the other forts built by Henry VIII. It is square in plan with a rectangular range of buildings fronted by an embanked platform overlooking the sea. In one corner on the landward side is a projecting bastion, arrowhead shaped in plan, and the earliest of this type to survive in England. Hitherto Henry VIII had used semicircular bastions, as at *Walmer Castle* for instance, but Italian developments had shown that other designs were more effective. The arrowhead bastion offered less of a target, and provided greater flexibility by creating a wider field of fire. Hence the star-shaped forts of the late sixteenth and seventeenth centuries of which Yarmouth is the tentative beginning. The castle is best seen from the sea, perhaps from the Lymington Ferry which docks beneath its walls. The town has rather smothered the castle on the landward side since the moat that linked it to the sea was filled up in the seventeenth century. The original entrance with the royal coat-of-arms on the east side now overlooks a tea garden, with visitors enter the castle furtively through an alley that leads to a postern gate inserted in the seventeenth century. Once

St Catherine's Oratory
ISLE OF WIGHT

Affectionately known as the Pepperpot, this fourteenth-century lighthouse stands at the south end of the downs above Niton on the highest point of the island, and commands panoramic views. It is octagonal with buttresses and an eight-sided roof. Medieval lighthouses or beacons are very rare, and they were usually religious foundations. This one was tended by a priest who lived nearby, and who also had charge of the oratory chapel of St Catherine beside it. These buildings have long since disappeared and the old lighthouse keeps the name of the oratory, while the new St Catherine's lighthouse stands below the cliffs at Niton. The carpark is a fifteen to twenty minute walk from the oratory, which can form the prelude to a bracing walk along the Downs.

ABOVE: St Catherine's Oratory

RIGHT: Yarmouth Castle, the base court and stairway to the gun platform

inside, however, one gets a good idea of what a small fort must have been like; rather cramped and confusing and fairly chaotic if ever under fire, which luckily it wasn't. The changes of level within the castle that give it a cheerfully unplanned air are the result of seventeenth-century alterations. Originally the gunports were just above sea level but the platform was raised to its present height in the seventeenth century. The master gunner's house dates from 1609 and the long room, 1632. The brick-lined powder magazines were inserted below the latter in the early eighteenth century. Sadly it was an accident with gunpowder that killed the two sons of the main promoter of the castle, the captain of the local militia, Richard Worsley.

Dymchurch Martello Tower from the sea-wall

Chatham Dockyard Timber Seasoning Sheds
KENT

These are the only two survivors of a humble type of building which was once vital to the well-being of the British navy — the timber seasoning shed. The Royal Navy had experienced problems throughout its history when the demands of wartime repairs created a shortage of properly seasoned timber, just at a time when the supply of foreign timber was difficult. The use of green wood meant that the ships very soon rotted. An instance of this was the sad case of the *Royal George* when the bottom fell out of the ship. In the 1770s firm action was at last taken, and the result was an interesting, early example of pre-fabricated construction. The Navy Board had calculated that to hold a three-year supply of seasoned timber, about 150 sheds would have to be built, costing the rough equivalent of building and equipping a seventy-four gun man o'war. In the event, only sufficient sheds for a year's supply of timber were constructed, and here at Chatham are two of them. Oak for the ships' frames was the main wood seasoned, coming from Britain whenever possible, or the Adriatic. North American and Baltic oak was not so popular but was used for underwater planking, together with beech, while elm was considered essential for the keels. Pine was used for planking on the ships' decks. However, only very small amounts of pine, elm and beech were stored in the timber seasoning sheds for the British Navy was 90 per cent oak. These sheds were restored in the 1970s, and one now holds timber used for restoration work by English Heritage.

Dymchurch Martello Tower No 24
KENT

In the opening years of the nineteenth century the threat of a Napoleonic invasion seemed very real, and a defensive chain of seventy-four small forts was erected along the coast from Folkestone to Seaford. Known as Martello Towers, the forts could be supplied by the Royal Military Canal which was dug on the north of Romney Marshes. About thirty feet high and built of brick, the forts had six feet thick walls and were designed to carry their main armament on the roof. A number of derelict towers survive along the coastline, but No 24 has been fully restored and contains an exhibition about the towers and the coastal defences. Visitors enter at first-floor level via a ladder into the living quarters, set above stores which contained food and ammunition. The fort's full complement was twenty-four men, though this would have been very cramped, and the company was not kept up to full strength except in emergencies. On the roof is one of the original muzzle-loading twenty-four-pounder guns, set up on a reproduction traversing carriage. By a twist of fate the design for the Martello Towers originated from Napoleon's home of Corsica. A tower of this type had held off two British warships at Capo Mortello in 1794, and finally had only been taken by a land assault. Fortunately the English Martello Towers were never tested. It can be seen in retrospect that the naval victories of 1805 at Trafalgar and Finisterre made a French invasion impossible, so most of the towers were in fact obsolete before they were built.

Dover Castle

KENT

Dover is one of the largest castles in England or Wales and there is much to see here, spanning almost 2,000 years of British history. The site has great natural defensive properties and its position commanding the shortest Channel crossing is the reason for its continuing importance. The castle is in a fine state of preservation, having been in military use up until 1956, and has of necessity undergone a number of changes. It is almost a history of fortification in itself, though some periods are more picturesque than others. The *Roman Pharos*, adjoining the Saxon church of St Mary-in-Castro, survives from the Roman occupation of the site, and the later Saxon burh which was built over by William the Conqueror. The earliest identifiable fortifications, however, date from the reign of Henry II when a comprehensive rebuilding programme took place, providing Dover with some of the earliest concentric fortifications in Europe. The rectangular keep, also built in the 1180s, is one of the best examples of its type and it is fully accessible with floors and ceilings. Amidst the curtain walls and towers it is interesting to observe the evolution of the gatehouse in the late twelfth century — two mural towers closely spaced, an unconscious return to the Roman design. Further work was done during the reign of King John when Dover featured in a dramatic siege. The castle was valiently defended by John's Justiciar, Hugh de

Burgh, against Prince Louis of France, who employed the same method of attack against Dover that John had used earlier against *Rochester*. In this case luck was with the defenders, for although the mines brought down part of the castle walls, the death of King John caused Louis to withdraw before he had pressed home his advantage. The imposing Constable's Tower was built to replace the north gate so heavily breached in the siege. It was part of further improvements that took place under Henry III. The eighteenth century saw the most radical alterations to the castle when nearly all the towers were reduced in height to provide a clear field of fire for the new batteries, and the medieval domestic buildings were transformed into a barracks. Further alterations took place in the nineteenth century, the most dramatic being the rebuilding of the medieval underground fortifications, parts of which are on view to the public. Among the many items of interest in the castle,

visitors should not miss seeing an unusual piece of ordnance, Queen Elizabeth's pocket pistol. This is a twelve-pounder brass Basilisk with an extraordinarily long barrel, highly ornamented, which was made in Utrecht in 1544. Contrary to appearances this is a lethal weapon, said to have a range of seven miles, which has been in the castle since 1613.

Roman Pharos, Dover

KENT

In the centre of *Dover Castle*, beside the church of St Mary-in-Castrar, stands the only surviving example of a Roman lighthouse in Britain. The word 'pharos' comes from an island off Alexandria where King Ptolemy Philadelphus II erected a lighthouse tower during the second century BC. One of the Seven Wonders of the World, it was said to stand 600 feet high, but this may be Egyptian propaganda. The Dover pharos probably stood about 80 feet high when built some 350 years later. It was matched with another pharos on Western Heights, still standing in the seventeenth century but which has now all but disappeared into the nineteenth century Drop Redoubt. Today the Dover pharos stands 62 feet high but the upper 19 feet are of medieval construction. In plan it is a square internally and an octagon externally. Much of the facing stone has gone but some good Roman masonry can still be seen at ground level. The pharos would have sent up a column of smoke by day, and at night a bright flame. Dover, or Dubris, was the headquarters of the Roman British fleet with another large naval base at Boulogne, where there was also a lighthouse.

ABOVE: Dover castle from the west

LEFT: the Roman Pharos: the keep of Dover Castle can be seen to the north-west

Deal Castle

KENT

Deal is one of the finest of the great series of castles built by Henry VIII, 1539-44. After many years of successfully playing-off France against Spain, Henry's diplomatic policy floundered with his failure to obtain a divorce from Catherine of Aragon, the aunt of the Spanish Emperor. He broke with Rome by declaring himself head of the English Church, and the Pope succeeded in uniting the French and Spanish powers against him. Henry was excommunicated in December 1538, and a Holy Crusade against England was preached. Henry's response was typically bluff and belligerent; he executed all major claimants to the throne and set about building a series of fortresses from Hull to Milford Haven. Stone from the demolished monasteries was used in many of them. Their novel design

was dictated by artillery warfare; no longer the proud towers of the medieval castle, but rather squat and menacing fortresses spread out their semicircular bastions across the beaches. These curved walls were to deflect shot, and bastions gave the defenders a wider field of fire. Though the general design may have originated in Bohemia or Southern Germany, there are no similar castles to be seen in Europe. Abroad, the angle bastion was preferred. Apart from a tentative appearance at *Yarmouth* and *Portsmouth* (now demolished), angle bastions were not seen in England until the fortifications at Berwick, twenty years later. Deal is a particularly fine Henrician castle with its circular tower and two tiers of concentric semicircular bastions. Crenellations and a straight parapet have replaced the original embrasures, such as can still be seen at *Calshot Castle*, but other alterations have been stripped away, revealing the castle in its original form. Deal, with *Walmer* and the vanished Sandown, were the 'three castles that keep the Downs'. The Downs, the stretch of channel protected by the Goodwin Sands, were the main anchorage along the east coast after the medieval harbours of the Cinque Ports began to silt up. Deal Castle contains an exhibition concerning its history, including the Civil War period, which was the most exciting.

Eynsford Castle
KENT

Tucked away down a lane off the main street lie the ruins of Eynsford Castle. The River Darent meanders round the north side and floods occasionally to fill part of the moat. It is hard to imagine how dramatic this castle must have appeared in the eleventh century, rising above the gentle landscape, one of the first stone fortifications built by the Normans. This earliest structure, dating from about 1088, was a very low motte enclosed by a curtain wall. The wall was raised and a hall and solar built in the twelfth century. Remains of the detached kitchen can be seen and the gate tower that marks the site of the bridge across the moat. The castle was held by vassals of the Archbishop of Canterbury until the Reformation, but it was derelict long before then. In 1312 the manor was part of a contested inheritance and while vacant one of the litigants, Criol, took the opportunity to hold a riotous party here for his supporters. Matters seem to have got rather out of hand and excavation has shown that amidst the proverbial drunken revelry, the doors and furniture were largely taken to pieces. It was patched up later so that the manorial court could still be held here, but was never again considered fit for human occupation.

Horne's Place Chapel, Appledore
KENT

This little chapel was built around 1366, when William Horne obtained a licence to hold Divine Service at his home. He was a man of considerable importance in fourteenth-century Kent and his house, which still adjoins the chapel, albeit in a much altered form, was one of those attacked and pillaged during Wat Tyler's rebellion in 1381. The chapel stands over a brick, tunnel-vaulted undercroft, and contains some finely carved details of unusual design, notably the rear arches to the windows. The arch-braced roof is carried on stone corbels carved with Catherine wheels, so a dedication to St Catherine is assumed. There is evidence of a gallery at the west end. The chapel was admired by Sir George Gilbert Scott in the last century, who identified the flower of the lesser celandine and its leaves as a source of inspiration to the masons who carved the decoration here. In the 1950s the chapel was thoroughly restored. It is very rare to find a chapel attached to a private house surviving from the fourteenth century, particularly one with this high quality of detail, and in such a beautiful setting.

ABOVE: the chapel at Horne's Place from the south-west

LEFT: Eynsford Castle from the west

Knights Templar Church, Dover

KENT

Standing on Western Heights, across the valley from the castle, are the foundations of the Knights Templar Church. Only the outline of this little building can be seen, a circular nave with a square chancel. The circular plan was employed by the Knights for their churches in emulation of the Holy Sepulchre in Jerusalem, which they were sworn to defend. Their most complete church surviving, though much restored, is the Temple Church in the City of London. This military order was founded in the twelfth century to defend both the pilgrims en route to the Holy Land and the holy places themselves. A truly international body, they were rich and influential, both respected and feared. Their wealth attracted the envy of the French king who was their debtor, and between 1307 and 1314 the order was disbanded, unjustly condemned of black magic and deviant sexual practices. Stories of the Templar treasure abound, especially in France, and at Dover there is a legend concerning a stolen crown of England.

Kit's Coty House and Lower Kit's Coty

KENT

No residence for the living but the remains of a Neolithic chambered tomb. The origin of the name is unknown but it is thought to derive from the Celtic Ked-quoit, tomb in the woods. Many legends and stories have grown up around the tomb which was one of the first to excite antiquarian interest in the early eighteenth century. The mound, aligned east-west, that covered the stones disappeared in the seventeenth century, and a single stone that stood to the west was destroyed in 1867. The three stones supporting the giant capstone are either a false portal to a lateral chambered tomb, similar to *Belas Knap*, Gloucestershire, or the centre of a single chambered tomb like *Trethevy Stone Quoit*, Cornwall. About 450 yards to the south are the jumbled remains of another tomb, Lower Kit's Coty, also known as Countless Stones from the reputed impossibility of quantifying them. There are about twenty heaped up beneath a tree, surrounded by railings. Kit's Coty House is also railed off so it is no longer possible to try out one of the more futile magic properties attributed to a Prehistoric site. It was said that if a piece of personal property was placed on top of the capstone at the time of the full moon, and its owner walked three times around the stones, the object would then disappear.

Lullingstone Roman Villa
KENT

Lullingstone is renowned for its mosaics, but it is even more famous as the site of one of the earliest private Christian chapels in Western Europe, and the only one known in England that was part of a villa. The site was first excavated in 1949 and it does not conform to any of the usual villa plans. The Roman occupation began AD *c*. 80-90 with a modest thatched dwelling which was totally transformed in the late second century into a luxury residence, possibly the summer home of some wealthy Roman official. A bath suite, a tiled roof, and a sanctuary to a local water nymph were among the many refinements, while the decoration included two fine Roman busts. Around AD 200 this 'house of pleasure', as the archaeologists have described it, was inexplicably abandoned, obviously in great haste for the busts were left behind. Copies are on view at Lullingstone while the originals are in the British Museum. For sixty to seventy years the house lay uninhabited and then came back into continuous occupation until the fifth century when it was destroyed by fire. Most of the remains that we see today date from the fourth century rebuilding by its prosperous yet rather more provincial occupants. The mosaics date from the mid fourth century: the dining room couches were arranged around the panel of Europa and the Bull, while Bellerophon riding Pegasus decorated the floor of the main reception room. At the Roman equivalent of cocktail parties, mosaics must have been a great boon to shy guests who didn't know anybody, for they could always wander round gazing intently at the floors. Around AD 370 the owners of Lullingstone converted to Christianity and installed a chapel in one of their rooms. Strangely enough it seems that a pagan shrine continued to be used beneath it. Painted wall plaster from the chapel and anteroom was recovered in thousands of fragments and this has been reconstructed in the British Museum. There is a reproduction at Lullingstone but it is a pale copy of the striking frieze of figures set between decorative columns to be seen in London. The Christian symbol of Chi-Rho was also recovered. Other finds from the site, which are preserved at Lullingstone, include a lead coffin with scallop shell decoration, peculiar to the Thames valley, and grave goods from the late third-century mausoleum of a young couple that was discovered behind the villa. The mausoleum is no longer visible.

The dining room mosaic floor at Lullingstone; Europa and the bull are in the foreground

St John's Commandery, Swingfield
KENT

This thirteenth-century chapel, later converted into a farmhouse, is a rare survival of a building belonging to a Knights Hospitaller, the ancestors of the St John Ambulance Brigade. As one of the military orders formed in the twelfth century to care for and protect pilgrims to the Holy Land, their main unit of organisation was the commandery. Here a group of knights and serjeants lived together under the rule of a commander, administering the properties with which the commandery was endowed in the same way as a monastery. Their main aim was the care of the sick pilgrims, particularly in the Holy Land. Thus the commandery would have included similar accommodation to that found in a monastery but the revenues from the commanderies helped to fund the hospitals abroad. Nothing is known of the other buildings on the site and only the chapel remains. The church has a two-storey porch at the north-west corner indicating that the west end always had an upper floor. A chimney stack was inserted in the sixteenth century and surviving beams and features belong to this period, though there is a thirteenth-century pointed arch opening to the room above the porch. The church at the east end has a crown post roof and three lancet windows in the east wall. A cellar has been dug at this end. It is known that before 1180 the site was occupied by the sisters of the Order of St John of Jerusalem.

Maison Dieu, Ospringe

KENT

Situated on the south side of the A2 (Watling Street) in Ospringe is an L-shaped early sixteenth-century building incorporating part of the thirteenth-century Maison Dieu. The building has been much altered over the years and recently restored. The 'maison dieu' of the Middle Ages can loosely be described as the forerunner of the hospital, but it also operated as an almshouse and home for the elderly. The benefactors of a hospital would have the right to nominate people to live there and it formed a way of pensioning-off employees. For instance, a former maid of Queen Eleanor lived at Ospringe for the last twenty years of her life, for it was a royal foundation, founded in 1234 by Eleanor's husband, Henry III. The main group of buildings stood on the opposite side of the road and included a chapel, hall, outbuildings and a special suite of rooms to accommodate the king and his retinue, all of which has now vanished. The London-Canterbury road was one of the most important pilgrimage routes in the Middle Ages and it led on to Dover and the continent. The many visitors, royal and otherwise, who sought hospitality were a severe strain on the hospital's resources and it was continually dogged by financial problems, partly caused by inefficient administration. The foundation was finally dissolved in 1516 and the revenues went to St John's College, Oxford. The chantry priests who served in the chapel continued on until the Reformation and they may have occupied the house we see today. It can be dated to around 1520 and contains some moulded beams, a little plasterwork and a king post roof in the upper chamber. Here on the upper floor is an exhibition devoted to Ospringe and the surrounding area in the time of the Romans. The ground floor is used for temporary local exhibitions.

ABOVE: Maison Dieu from the east

Old Soar Manor

KENT

Tucked away in the depths of the Kent countryside are the remains of a medieval manor house, built around 1290. It is rare to find a domestic building dating from this early period. The manor belonged to the Colepepper family, who became one of the largest landowning families in Kent and Sussex,

reputedly through a policy of kidnapping heiresses and marrying them. Only the two-storey solar end remains — the lord's private chamber where he withdrew from the communal life of the hall. At Old Soar the medieval aisled hall has been rebuilt and forms a separate dwelling, not open to the public. The solar has a privy chamber opening off it to the north with a garderobe. (The arched opening visible at ground level on the exterior is where the garderobe pit was cleaned out.) There is a chapel set in the angle of the east side of the solar, which originally was also accessible by an external stair.

Visitors enter at ground-floor level below the solar into a stone-vaulted room that provided a safe storage space. In later manor houses this ground-floor room would become a parlour opening off the hall; today it contains an exhibition of old photographs of the area. For the lord and his family, access to the solar was via a door from the hall that opened into the spiral staircase set in the thickness of the wall, and which also opened directly into the basement. The solar was always heated, though the hood is missing from the chimneypiece. Part of the original king post roof remains and there is evidence that the windows were originally shuttered, not glazed. The chapel window, however, was always glazed.

Milton Chantry, Gravesend

KENT

Until the nineteenth century Milton was a village quite separate from the port of Gravesend. Here in 1322 Aymer de Valence founded a chantry chapel, which still survives today, 650 years later, albeit in a much altered form. A chantry chapel was endowed so that the priests' sole employment was to say masses for the souls of the departed. The chapels were all dissolved at the time of the Reformation. Apart from the east gable end wall the exterior has been encased in brick and the alterations to the interior are a challenge to the architectural detective. Remains of the chapel's fourteenth-century roof can be seen, as can the sixteenth-century fireplace in the chimney stack, added in the centre of the building when an upper storey was inserted after the Reformation. The staircase, with its decorative newel posts, dates from the seventeenth century when the building became a tavern. The chapel now stands in a public park created in 1932 on the site of the New Tavern Fort (not English Heritage), in use from 1780 to 1918. This fort in fact took its name from the chapel, or New Tavern, which then became part of the barracks. The fort commands fine views up and down river and looks across to *Tilbury Fort* with which it was linked. The ramparts with gun emplacements and the magazine date mainly from the extensive remodelling carried out 1868-71, under the direction of Captain Gordon, later famous for his defence of Khartoum. Some guns still stand in the gun emplacements, and a light anti-aircraft gun from the Second World War when the fort was once again armed.

LEFT: Old Soar Manor, the solar with king post roof and the unblocked doorway to the chapel

Britain' was symbolised by a great triumphal arch eighty feet high, faced with Carrara marble and ornamented with bronze statues. Only the foundations can be seen today. In the mid third century it was converted into a watch tower and soon after dismantled when the Saxon Shore Fort was constructed. Three walls of this impressive fortification survive, and some of the buildings within the fort have been excavated. The museum contains finds from the port, once famous throughout the Roman world for the excellence of its oysters. Building materials, jewellery, pottery, even a gaming board with a loaded dice give glimpses into the life of this important settlement. The amphitheatre is rather less enlightening, having filled up with sand over the centuries so as to be barely visible. It stands in a field on the west side of the road, just before the turn off down the track to Richborough Castle.

Reculver Towers and Roman Fort

KENT

From the top of one of these towers you can see the Isles of Sheppey and Thanet, and two Second World War forts. Otherwise only the two gaunt twelfth-century towers themselves and mutilated west end of the minster church are to be seen at Reculver. The sea has taken most of the Roman fort, and the mother of the rector in 1809 caused the church to be demolished, leaving only the towers as a landmark for shipping. The Roman fort was the earliest of the Saxon Shore Forts built AD 210-30, a simple rectangle enclosing seven-and-a-half acres, with rounded corners and internally ramped-up walls. It originally stood at the

Richborough Castle and Roman Amphitheatre

KENT

ABOVE: the towers of the minster church at Reculver, set within the Roman fort

RIGHT: remains of the Saxon Shore Fort at Richborough

It was very likely at Richborough that the Roman invasion first landed in AD 43. Here can be seen the earliest Roman remains in Britain, the ditches that were dug to defend the encampment on the promontory. Though the ditches are still here the promontory has gone, and the landscape has altered radically. In Roman times, Thanet to the north was still an island, and Richborough a promontory on the mainland. The Roman army's main supply depot was quickly established here at Rutupiae, as Richborough was called, and the 'gateway to

northern entrance of the Wantsum channel between Thanet and the mainland, with Richborough to the south, guarding the main shipping route. The fort was abandoned in about 360. Some 300 years later King Egbert gave the land to Bassa to found a minster church. It was largely built of reused Roman materials and the foundations can still be seen. The original building had an aisleless nave, side chapels and an apsidal end with a continuous bench where the monks and abbot sat behind the altar. A sizeable village grew up around the church but by the early nineteenth century the sea had reached its present shore line. The erosion could easily have been halted with groynes, as it was soon after, but the rector, under the influence of his mother, persuaded the parishioners to demolish the old church and build a new one at Hillsborough, about a mile inland. No doubt she acted from the best of intentions, but what a tragic loss. This new church was replaced by another after only seventy years, whereas the previous one had stood for over a thousand.

Rochester Castle

KENT

One of the finest surviving examples of a Norman castle keep, Rochester is an excellent castle where the ample remains make both its purpose and how it functioned quite clear to the visitor. Dominating the Medway, it stands by the river crossing that had been in use long before the Romans built Watling Street. A section of the Roman city walls are incorporated into the curtain wall, which is part of the first stone fortifications that the Normans erected. Gundulf, Bishop of Rochester and builder of the White Tower, was responsible, though little remains of his work since the curtain walls of the oval bailey were largely rebuilt in the thirteenth century. However, the 100 foot high keep that we admire today is the work of another Norman cleric, Archbishop William of Corbeuil, between 1127 and 1139. The plan is square with pilaster buttresses and square corner turrets, the south-east one rebuilt in a circular form. The ruined forebuilding against the north wall contained the stairs over the dungeon, with the chapel above. The present entrance is at basement level and was cut in 1872. (Visitors should imagine something similar to the forebuilding at *Castle Riding*, which is almost contemporary.) Internally the castle is divided in half, top to bottom, by a cross wall. The stairs rise in the north-east corner through seven levels and within the thickness of the walls are galleries and small chambers. The Archbishop's formal suite occupied the third and fourth floors and here the cross wall becomes an arcade with scalloped capitals. The large fireplaces that heated the hall still remain.

The castle was of great importance during its early days and the siege of 1216, which resulted in the demolition of the south-east tower, was the most important of the Civil War between King John and his barons — the same war that produced Magna Carta. This siege is a good example of the principal threat to castle defenders, after treachery and starvation, mining. King John was present throughout and no effort was spared. 'We command you,' he wrote to his Justiciar, Hugh de Burgh, 'that with all haste, by day and night, you send to us 40 bacon pigs of the fattest ...' Not that he hoped to drive the hungry garrison wild with the smell of roasting pork, rather he needed the fat to fire the mines. In the days before gunpowder, mining involved digging large tunnels supported by timber props beneath the angle of a tower. The timber props were then ignited and with luck brought down the masonry. This is what happened at Rochester, but thanks to the internal cross wall the garrison were able to withdraw into the northern half of the castle and continue their resistance. Starvation finally forced them to capitulate. The castle was besieged again in 1264 and 1381, but fell into disrepair later. It was dismantled in the early seventeenth century by the Weldon family who removed all the timber work for building materials, but the stone walls defeated them.

Rochester Castle keep from the north-west

tion of shrines and tombs was swept away and a new abbey church built 1070–1130 with a large claustral complex to the north. Of the latter, little can be seen today. Tombs of some of the saints and kings were saved. A large section of the eleventh century nave wall, however, forms a fine backdrop to the site, heightened with Tudor brickwork. At the Dissolution the abbot's hall and guest house, together with this part of the nave, were reconstructed to form the King's House, one of a group of posting houses set up along the Dover-London road to provide accommodation for the king and important travellers. This was a service that the monasteries had hitherto provided. The King's House survived into the seventeenth century but then fell into decay. The magnificent north-west tower of the nave survived until 1822. Later in the nineteenth century the remaining parts of the abbey buildings were incorporated by William Butterfield into A.J. Beresford-Hope's St Augustine's Missionary College. This lies to the north.

St Augustine's Abbey, Canterbury

KENT

Founded by St Augustine in 598, this site contains the remains of the most complete group of early monastic buildings outside Italy, overlaid by the foundations of a fine Norman church. It is fascinating to disentangle from the mass of masonry foundations the outline of the buildings superimposed one upon the other. Within the first twenty years of St Augustine's mission, four separate churches had been laid out in a line east to west, largely within the area later covered by the Norman church. (The reason for this arrangement is not clear but it occurred elsewhere, at Glastonbury for instance.) The purpose of this second foundation of St Augustine, following the priory that is now the cathedral, was to provide a burial place outside the city walls for the members of the Kentish royal family, and for distinguished churchmen, with a group of monks to pray for their souls. Later in the mid eleventh century, just before the Conquest, Abbot Wulfric built a fifth church to a unique circular plan which would have linked two of the existing churches together, but destroyed the lady chapel of one in the process. Begun in 1049, it was incomplete at his death, but substantial foundations can be seen. At the Conquest this important collec-

ABOVE: St Augustine's Abbey looking west to Canterbury Cathedral

RIGHT: St Leonard's Tower

St Augustine's Cross, Ebbsfleet

KENT

Ebbsfleet by Pegwell Bay is the traditional site of the landing of St Augustine in AD 597. In the long term his mission was the decisive factor in the conversion of England to Christianity, and the establishment of an Anglo-Saxon church. His mission was sponsored by Pope Gregory, inspired, it is said, by the sight of some beautiful fair-haired English slave boys for sale in Rome. On asking where they came from he was told they were from Deira, modern Yorkshire, and their King was Ælle. 'Not Angei but "angeli" (angels),' he cried, '"de ira" fleeing from wrath, and Ælle's people must sing Alleluia!' The Venerable Bede relates that 10,000 Kentish men had been converted to Christianity by Christmas of 597 following the lead of Ethelbert, their King, who was already married to a Christian princess. The cross, modelled on a Celtic design, was erected in the nineteenth century, just south of the railway line at Cliffs Ends. It also serves as a memorial to the airmen from the nearby Manston Aerodrome who died during the Second World War.

St Leonard's Tower, West Malling

KENT

This Norman tower keep stands in an orchard on the outskirts of West Malling. A later wall abuts one corner and it is pretty spot with no other evidence of fortification. It is thought to have been built by Gundulf, Bishop of Rochester, who died in 1102, having built the White Tower in London and the first castle at *Rochester*. West Malling is probably one of the earliest examples of the tower keep. Gundulf founded a Benedictine monastery in Rochester in 1089 and a nunnery at West Malling about the same time. St Leonard's Tower was built 1090-1100 and may have had some connection with the nunnery. (This same nunnery was refounded in the nineteenth century and continues today. It is not accessible to the public but the parish church of St Mary contains some Norman work and other interesting features.) The square tower has clasping buttresses, one of which is enlarged and contains a spiral stair. There is blind arcading typical of the period and round headed windows on the upper floor. The interior is not accessible and the tower is roofless with a straight parapet. To the modern eye fortifications are distinguished by crenellations, but they became common only in the early twelfth century, and the late nineteenth-century restorers of the tower endeavoured to maintain historical accuracy.

ABOVE: Stone Chapel, Faversham

Stone Chapel, Faversham

KENT

It may enliven journeys along the A2 if one remembers that this is the course of Watling Street, the old Roman road from Canterbury to London. Many settlements grew up beside this important route and one, Durolevum, was situated about a mile to the west of present-day Faversham, half a mile from Ospringe. Various finds from the area can be seen in *Maison Dieu*, Ospringe where there is a small exhibition on the Roman period. Durolevum is now under ploughed fields but remains of fourth-century Romano-Celtic mausoleum survive in the form of a few courses of masonry later incorporated into a chapel, the ruins of which can be seen on the north side of the A2, set against a backdrop of trees. It is not certain whether this single cell Roman building, 20 feet square internally, was a mausoleum or shrine, and it may even have been a Christian site from the very beginning. Alternating courses of bonding tile and dressed stone distinguish the Roman building forming the western half of the chancel, with a large stone slab marking the threshold of the mausoleum. The chapel was probably erected in the eighth century and never achieved the status of parish church. It had fallen into decay by the sixteenth century.

Temple Manor, Strood
KENT

Set in a green oasis in the desert wastelands of an industrial estate, is an attractive brick and stone building, once the property of the Knights Templar. They were given the manor in 1159 and held it until their dissolution in 1308. The stone-built hall over an undercroft dates from *c.*1240, and at either end are brick additions of the mid-seventeenth century. This building is all that remains of a much larger building that survived until the 1940s. The first-floor hall, which is reached by a reconstructed external staircase, stands over an undercroft or cellar of three bays. It was not a typical hall but was divided into an inner and outer chamber, the latter indicated by the arcade with stone seats. Here remains of thirteenth-century wall plaster, painted with red lines to imitate ashlar masonry, can still be seen, a common form of early medieval wall decoration. It is believed that the building's primary purpose was to provide accommodation for members of the order travelling between London and the continent. In the seventeenth century a fireplace was inserted into the hall, which still remains, and the eastern end was extended with a brick bay that gives a fine view across the Medway to *Rochester Castle*. The room below is now the ticket office. At the west end, a three-storey stair turret over a porch was added about the same time giving access to a single room on each floor. It is thought that the seventeenth-century additions were made by the Blakes, a local family whose prosperity was founded on ironmongery, or scrap metal. Cannon balls and miscellaneous bits of ironwork were found in a dump near the house when it was being restored. The Temple Manor Farm estate was sold off in the 1930s.

BELOW: the hall at Temple Manor showing the medieval arcades and the fireplace inserted in the sixteenth century

RIGHT: Upnor Castle with the barracks to the south-west seen from across the Medway

Upnor Castle
KENT

Upnor on the River Medway deserves to be better known, for it is a rare example of an Elizabethan gun-fort in a very pleasant setting. The little village beside it grew up to provide comforts for the castle garrison. The fort is well preserved, roofed, and contains an exhibition on the Medway defences. After Henry VIII's massive building programme, his daughter Elizabeth felt that with the exception of *Berwick*, there was little need to spend money on fortifications. However, the growing importance of the dockyard at Chatham as a major base for the British fleet led to the construction of a blockhouse at Upnor *c.*1559-64, enlarged and strengthened 1599-1601. This blockhouse forms the basis of the range that fronts the river today, and was probably designed by Sir Richard Lee who worked at *Berwick*. The angle bastion projecting into the river was added in the late sixteenth century when the fort

was enlarged with curtain walls and a gatehouse on the landward side. Upnor's first, and last, engagement took place in 1667, when the Dutch navy unexpectedly stormed up the Medway and destroyed much of the shipping at anchor at Chatham. Upnor valiantly if belatedly mounted an offensive, but was unable to stop the Dutch leaving with the Royal Navy's flagship, the *Royal Charles*. Following this humiliation, the Medway defences were radically reorganised and Upnor lost its importance, being demoted to a powder magazine and store. This involved the heightening of the buildings, mostly in brick, and the fort took on the form that we see today. The barracks at the entrance vie with *Ravensdowne*, Berwick-upon-Tweed, as being the earliest in the country. They were built *c.*1717-18, possibly by John Lambertus Romer, and look more like a private house than a barracks. Hitherto the garrison had largely been billeted in the village.

Walmer Castle

KENT

Walmer, with *Deal* and Sandown, were the three castles built by Henry VIII, 1539-40, to guard the anchorage in the Downs. Walmer and the now-vanished Sandown were identical in plan: a central circular keep surrounded by four semicircular bastions sporting three tiers of guns. The particular interest of Walmer, however, is the modification that it has undergone since the eighteenth century when the castle became the official residence of the Lords Warden of the Cinque Ports; a function it still has. Thus the interior, a pleasing mixture of oddly-shaped rooms, is furnished, and there are attractive gardens on the landward side. The role of Lord Warden was an honourary one by the eighteenth century. The Cinque Ports were an ancient organisation, dating back to before the Conquest, which organised the defence of the Channel coastline. Hythe, Hastings, Romney, Dover and Sandwich were the original five, but at least thirty other towns shared their responsibilities and privileges during the Middle Ages. The use made by the Lords Warden of their castle has varied considerably, and some have visited it rarely, but the Duke of Wellington is the one who is perhaps best remembered. He was very attached to the place and often entertained Queen Victoria, for whom he thoughtfully altered the window openings so she could better admire the view. It was here in 1852 that he died. His room has been preserved just as it was; the original Wellington boots can be seen, the simple

campaign bed in which he always slept, and the upright desk that he used — for he always worked on his papers standing up. There is also a collection of other mementoes and engravings relating to him and Queen Victoria. That these were preserved is thanks to a later Lord Warden, W.H. Smith (who owned the firm of the same name). In 1874 an extra range of rooms was built in the castellated style adjoining the gatehouse and these are still used by the present Lord Warden. The bastions form a fine terrace overlooking the sea and the vista to the pebble beach where Queen Victoria liked to walk is framed by pine trees. The gardens on the landward side were laid out by Lord Granville and Lady Hester Stanhope. The Duke, in keeping with his frugal habits, used the moat as a kitchen garden, but it has now been grassed over and forms part of the series of gardens that embellish this peaceful spot.

The south front of Walmer Castle, the entrance to the gardens

Battle Abbey

SUSSEX

A splendid fourteenth-century gatehouse guards the site of the most famous battle fought on English soil, the Battle of Hastings. The Benedictine Abbey was founded in 1070 by William the Conqueror at the instigation of the Pope, an act of atonement for the blood shed in the conquest of England. The high altar of the abbey church was sited on the ridgeway, marking the spot where King Harold died. After the Reformation parts of the abbey were converted into a dwelling by Sir Anthony Browne, later altered in the eighteenth and nineteenth centuries and now a school. Though not normally accessible to the public, the buildings are visible from the exterior and a fair amount of the abbey ruins remain. Most notable are the mid thirteenth-century monks' dormitories which stand astride the ridgeway slope, set over the vaulted undercrofts that were the monks' common rooms, and the fine fifteenth-century cloister arcade built into the wall of the school. The undercrofts, or cellars, of the thirteenth-century guest house, with its two sixteenth-century stair turrets can be seen adjoining the site of one of the abbey barns. The foundations of other buildings are marked out on the grass and the school occupies the site of the abbot's lodgings. The abbey church was demolished at the Reformation but a nineteenth-century memorial marks the site of Harold's death. Where he was buried is not certain — possibly at Waltham Abbey. Time has mellowed the site of his defeat. The battlefield is now a gentle valley, partially-wooded with streams on the south side of the abbey. The ground level has risen since 1066 reducing the gradient of the slope, and the marshy land that lay below the ridge has been drained. Harold arrived here on the evening of 13 October 1066, his army having marched the fifty-eight miles from London during the previous two days. He had hoped to surprise William as he had done Harold Hardrada three weeks earlier near

York, but in the event the reverse occurred. Luckily, however, Harold was occupying a strong defensive position on the ridgeway when the Normans appeared, a site that sloped quite gently to the south but which was protected on the flanks by steep spurs of ground. William ordered an advance at 9.30 am on 14 October — by dusk, victory was his. Display panels on site enable one to follow the course of the battle.

Bayham Abbey

SUSSEX

The ruins of this Premonstratensian abbey in the tranquil valley of the River Teise were among the first to be appreciated in the eighteenth century for their picturesque qualities. Here the landowner built himself a small house sometime before 1752, sited to obtain the best view of the ruins, which were slightly landscaped to enhance their qualities. Horace Walpole, doyen of the Gothick, came and was impressed. Later in the century the second Lord Camden enlarged this house to the north after seeking advice from Humphrey Repton. It is now known as the Dower House and is being restored to its eighteenth-century condition with period wall-papers and the original colours. The abbey that Lord Camden and his predecessor so admired was founded c. 1200 and has extensive remains, particularly of the church. It is built of the excellent local sandstone, a warm golden yellow, that carves into fine detail. Like so many churches, Bayham was built from east to west and no sooner was it finished than the east end was extended and rebuilt in a grander and more up-to-date manner. The crossing and the north and south transepts have some particularly good detailing, rebuilt in the late thirteenth century by master craftsmen. The south wall of the nave also rises to almost its full height, likewise rebuilt, here with large raking buttresses

ABOVE: the vaulted undercroft of the monks' common room

RIGHT: looking across the remains of the guest house north to the Great Gate

pierced by openings to allow perambulation around the cloister. The plan of the claustral buildings is easy to determine and there are various interesting features, such as the book cupboard with its cusped opening built into the wall of the old south transept that was used as a library. Standing on the Kent/Sussex boundary, the abbey had a gatehouse for each county. Only the Kent gate remains with its bridge over the River Teise. It was built in the fourteenth century but landscaped in the eighteenth century with the addition of columns from the chapter house forming a little loggia overlooking the lake. Above on the hillside to the northwest stands a large Victorian mansion built 1870-72 by David Brandon, for which Bayham became the Dower House, a much more dignified description than granny house.

Bramber Castle

SUSSEX

Part of the gatehouse and fragments of the curtain wall survive at Bramber, and the earthworks are well-preserved, embossed with a fine variety of trees, between which views of the Downs can be glimpsed. The motte and bailey castle was built soon after the Conquest by William de Braose, who also erected the delightful chapel that stands below the castle, now the parish church of St Nicholas. The motte is in fine shape and probably supported a wooden tower when first built. It stands within the bailey, the flat top of a natural knoll. The 76-foot-high wedge-shaped section of masonry that dominates the south side is the eleventh-century gateway that was heightened to become the keep, as at *Richmond* in Yorkshire. A new gateway was added to the west which has since disappeared. Sections of curtain wall remain. The de Braose family were among those opposed to King John in the early thirteenth century and he demanded hostages from them in the form of their two sons. Lady de Braose refused, declaring that she would not entrust her children to a man who had already murdered his own nephew, the unfortunate Prince Arthur. With this spirited, if rather rash declaration, the family decamped to Ireland. Unfortunately they were apprehended by King John's men, and Lady de Braose and her two sons were starved to death, the same unhappy fate that had overtaken Prince Arthur. The castle was seized by the King and some rebuilding is known to have taken place 1208-15. It never came under attack and though still in use in the fourteenth century, was derelict by the sixteenth century.

Pevensey Castle

SUSSEX

On the morning of 28 September 1066 Duke William of Normandy and his armada beached at Pevensey and occupied the Roman fort. The next day they moved on towards Hastings. This derelict castle on a spit of sand was the last of the Saxon Shore Forts built by the Romans sometime around AD 340. Unlike the earlier *Portchester* and *Burgh* in Norfolk which are rectangular, Pevensey is an irregular oval, with bastions, enclosing an area of about ten acres. A castle was added in the Middle Ages and the fort continued to have an eventful history. It was besieged in 1088, 1147, 1264-65, and in 1399. Important prisoners were kept here in the fifteenth century, including King James I of Scotland and Queen Joanna of Navarre who was accused by her stepson, Henry V, of being a witch. In the sixteenth century it fell into decay. The ruins were refortified in 1940 and gun emplacements were concealed among the old Roman bastions. Today the main road hugs the north and east sides of the fort, while to the south the walls that once looked down on the sea have disappeared, steep banks remain and meadows stretch away into the distance. In the east corner stands the stone keep of *c.*1100 with its apsidal towers incorporating part of the Roman walls. A fine mid thirteenth-century curtain wall with three D-shaped towers encloses the inner bailey with an early thirteenth-century gatehouse. The moat has been dammed to the north of the gatehouse and mirrors two sides of the curtain wall.

TOP: openings in the buttresses of the nave wall forming part of the cloister at Bayham Abbey

BELOW: the north front of the medieval castle erected inside the Roman fort at Pevensey

THE
SOUTH WEST

Avon · Cornwall
Isles of Scilly · Devon
Dorset · Somerset
Wiltshire

Temple Church, Bristol
AVON

There is no shortage of fine Perpendicular churches in Bristol, but Temple Church has one of the best towers. This large fifteenth-century church was gutted by bombing during the Second World War, but the exterior walls still stand to their full height and most of the window openings are complete with tracery. The handsome tower was finished in 1460 and is a disconcerting five feet four and a half inches out of vertical. Beside it, at the west end, is a good early eighteenth-century doorway. The nave arcades have disappeared and the foundations of the earlier church of the Knights Templar are known only from excavations. A bizarre concrete screen supports the chancel wall, marking the site of the rood screen. To the east, the two bay arcades to the north and south chapels survive, and there is a nineteenth-century vestry addition beyond. The graveyard has been turned into a public garden. The Knights Templars established themselves in Bristol around 1150 and owned large areas of land, including the area now known as Temple Meads where the railway station stands. They were disbanded in 1307 and visitors can trace the development of the area in the nearby museum of local history, located in St Nicholas's Church.

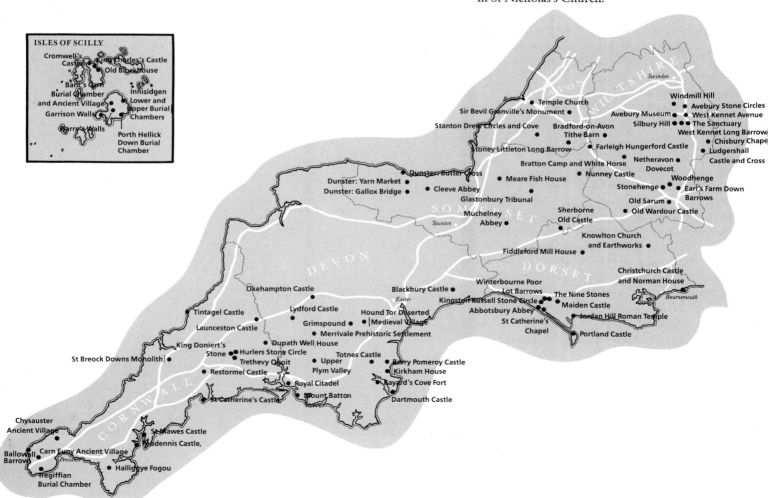

ISLES OF SCILLY

Cromwell's Castle
King Charles's Castle
Old Blockhouse
Bant's Carn
Burial Chamber
and Ancient Village
Innisidgen
Lower and
Upper Burial
Chambers
Garrison Walls
Harry's Walls
Porth Hellick
Down Burial
Chamber

Bristol · Temple Church
Sir Bevil Granville's Monument
Stanton Drew Circles and Cove
Windmill Hill
Avebury Stone Circles
Avebury Museum · West Kennet Avenue
Silbury Hill · The Sanctuary
West Kennet Long Barrow
Chisbury Chapel
Ludgershall
Castle and Cross
Bradford-on-Avon
Tithe Barn
Farleigh Hungerford Castle
Netheravon
Dovecot
Stoney Littleton Long Barrow
Bratton Camp and White Horse
Nunney Castle
Woodhenge
Earl's Farm Down
Barrows
Dunster: Butter Cross
Dunster: Yarn Market
Cleeve Abbey
Meare Fish House
Stonehenge
Dunster: Gallox Bridge
Glastonbury Tribunal
Sherborne
Old Castle
Old Sarum
Old Wardour Castle
Muchelney
Abbey
Knowlton Church
and Earthworks
Fiddleford Mill House
Christchurch Castle
and Norman House
Okehampton Castle
Blackbury Castle
Winterbourne Poor
Lot Barrows
The Nine Stones
Maiden Castle
Jordan Hill Roman Temple
Kingston Russell Stone Circle
Abbotsbury Abbey
St Catherine's
Chapel
Portland Castle
Lydford Castle
Hound Tor Deserted
Medieval Village
Grimspound
Merrivale Prehistoric Settlement
Tintagel Castle
Launceston Castle
King Doniert's
Stone
Dupath Well House
Hurlers Stone Circle
Totnes Castle
Upper
Plym Valley
Berry Pomeroy Castle
Kirkham House
St Breock Downs Monolith
Trethevy Quoit
Restormel Castle
Royal Citadel
Bayard's Cove Fort
Mount Batton
Tower
Dartmouth Castle
St Catherine's Castle
Chysauster
Ancient Village
St Mawes Castle
Pendennis Castle,
Ballowall
Barrow
Carn Euny Ancient Village
Halliggye Fogou
Tregiffian
Burial Chamber

Sir Bevil Granville's Monument, Charlcombe

AVON

From the aesthetic point-of-view, Sir Bevil's monument is disappointing. An overscale rusticated plinth supports a dado with a small eroded heraldic animal of indeterminate origins; one of the type that usually goes around in pairs and is to be found adopting an aggressive stance atop a gate pier. The monument stands on the edge of a spur looking across the narrow valley to Freezing Hill, and was erected around 1720 to commemorate the death, some eighty years before, of Sir Bevil Grenvile at the Battle of Landsdown. (His descendants altered their name to Granville in the late seventeenth century.) It is worth taking a closer look at the inscribed panels attached to the monument. Sir Bevil's work in Cornwall for the Royalist cause is extolled, and we learn that in him 'a brighter courage and a gentler disposition were never married together to make the more cheerful and innocent conversation'. Also, 'in this battle on the Kings part were more officers and gentlemen of quality killed than private men ...' It was July 1643 and the Royalists had determined upon an all-out attack upon the Parliamentarian forces in the West country. The armies were about equal, though the Royalists had more cavalry. The Parliamentarians under Sir William Waller were drawn up along Landsdown Hill, a very strong defensive position on either side of the monument, while the Royalists took up a position to the north at Freezing Hill. Assaults by the Royalist cavalry were unsuccessful. A combined assault was then attempted; flanked by parties of musketeers, Sir Bevil and the Cornish pikemen launched a frontal attack up the steep slope, supported by the cavalry. Visitors standing by the monument will appreciate the heroism of this action. The cavalry fell back under the hail of fire from above, but the Cornishmen doggedly fought their way up the hillside, and having gained the summit, maintained their position against cavalry charges by the Parliamentarians. It was here in the midst of the fighting that Sir Bevil Grenvile died. The Parliamentarians fell back a few hundred yards, and the Royalists gained the hill. But by now both sides were exhausted and running out of ammunition — both withdrew. Eight days later they met again at Roundway Down, near Devizes, where the Royalists achieved a decisive victory.

Temple Church looking west, the bases of the aisle piers visible in the foreground

Stanton Drew Stone Circles and Cove

AVON

The largest stone circle in Britain after *Avebury*, and a very important Neolithic religious site. Subsequent building in the area has not been very sympathetic, however. Standing in one field are the remains of the Great Circle and the Little Circle to the north-east, both with the remains of stone avenues opening to the east. Most of the stones are now recumbent. Two fields away to the south-west lies another circle of recumbent stones, and the 'cove' can be found in the carpark of the Druids Arms public house to the west. The original construction of the cove is not known for certain. There are two upright stones set about ten feet apart with a recumbent stone between them. Whether it originally lay on top of them as a capstone is not known. A line drawn through the centre of the south-west circle and the Great Circle would link up with the standing stone known as Hautville's Quoit, the other side of the River Chew, covering a distance of about fifty-five yards in all. The quoit stands on the south side of the B3130 road and is in private ownership. The field boundaries and later buildings mean that more imagination is needed here than at *Avebury*.

Stoney Littleton Long Barrow

AVON

This is perhaps the finest of the Neolithic long barrows of the Cotswold-Severn group, for it is almost intact and visitors can enter in. It is a good idea to bring a torch. The key can be obtained from Stoney Littleton Farm and the barrow is half a mile away across a patchwork of fields. Aligned north-

west/south-east, it is about 100 feet long and belongs to the transepted gallery type. However it is unusual in that three pairs of chambers open off the central gallery, rather than the normal two. Visitors should note the fine ammonite cast in the blue lias stone of the left door jamb at the south-east entrance. Inside, in the vestibule opening into the gallery, there is a tablet commemorating the restoration of the tomb in 1858. It reads, 'This tumulus — declared by competent judges to be the most perfect specimen of Celtic antiquity still existing in Great Britain — having been much injured by the lapse of time, or the carelessness of former proprietors, was restored in 1858 by Mr T.R. Joliffe, the

Lord of the Hundred; the design of the original structure being preserved, as far as possible, with scrupulous exactness.' The north-west end is a conjectural reconstruction, having been damaged by ploughing. The barrow had first been opened in 1760 and it is not now known how many bodies were originally interred here. Two skulls recovered from the tomb can be seen in the Bristol Museum, which has a very good display on the Prehistoric sites in the area, and a model of Stoney Littleton.

Part of the Cove at Stanton Drew

Carn Euny Ancient Village

CORNWALL

Though not as extensive as the Iron Age village at *Chysauster*, occupation at Carn Euny goes back much further into the Bronze Age, and the large fogou here is well preserved. The settlement of Bronze Age timber dwellings was replaced in the Iron Age by stone huts of the courtyard type, some of whose foundations still survive. The inhabitants were farmers and stockbreeders, and possibly traded in tin. A pit lined with china clay for storing grain was discovered in 1965, and pottery sherds have revealed something of the development of the settlement. However the purpose of the fogou, which stands in the middle of the site, in unclear. It is a curved underground passage about seventy feet long, created by digging a deep trench, lined and roofed with stone slabs, the latter projecting slightly above the surface of the ground. At Carn Euny it is unique in that it provides access to a circular stone-lined pit, like an underground room which is now open to the sky. One end of the fogou finishes by the foundations of a house, the other has a short lateral passage opening off it, called a creep, and used for storage. The village was occupied well into the Roman period and the fogou must have fulfilled a variety of functions over the centuries.

Carn Gloose (Ballowall Barrow)

CORNWALL

Dramatically sited at the cliff's edge looking towards Land's End, Carn Gloose is finely preserved, and a very unusual, middle Bronze Age cairn. Its complex plan seems to indicate a religious site connected with the underworld. In the centre of the seventy feet diameter cairn is a T-shaped pit dug into the earth, surrounded by double walls standing about twelve feet high. The outer wall is about twenty feet thick. Four urns containing ashes were discovered when the site was excavated in 1874. The cairn was originally covered with earth, now the dry stone walls are patterned with white pennywort. These same excavations also revealed that a ring of stone cists, probably originally covered by barrows, surrounded the cairn. Remains

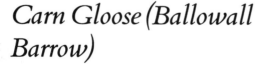

ABOVE: an opening in the fogou at Carn Euny

ABOVE RIGHT: looking west over Carn Gloose

RIGHT: Bronze Age houses at Chysauster

of one of these square stone slab graves can be identified amidst the bracken. The whole site was enclosed by a wall that has long since disappeared.

Chysauster Ancient Village

CORNWALL

Chysauster is a Bronze Age village consisting of a 'street' of eight well-preserved houses, their walls standing four to five feet high. The unexcavated remains of another two houses lie to the west and a partially excavated fogou to the south. The exact size of the settlement is unknown: the houses follow a roughly similar plan of a courtyard, or hall, with rooms opening off it; a round room, a rectangular room and a small round room. Entrances are on the east or north-east sides, away from the prevailing south-westerly wind. Remains of sleeping benches, post holes for the roof post, drainage channels and floor slabs can be identified. Each house had a terraced garden and there is one pair of

semi-detached dwellings. This was probably a mixed farming community that settled in the second to first century BC and dispersed in the third or fourth century AD. In the nineteenth century the site was sometimes used for Methodist meetings and it was known as the Chapels. Indeed it was not until 1849 that Chysauster was identified as a Prehistoric village. The site, a ten-minute walk from the carpark, lies on a windswept hillside looking to the sea — the haunt of many rare species of birds. In the summer the village is covered with wild flowers; foxgloves, honeysuckle, cornflowers, slipper orchids and pennywort.

Halliggye Fogou
CORNWALL

The fogou is something of a mystery, and Halliggye has the finest and most mysterious fogou in Cornwall. These underground passages, dating from the Iron Age, were associated with a vanished settlement, and seem to have been connected with a defensive system of ramparts. The plan is in general terms that of a curved, stone-lined passage, about fifty-four feet long lying east-west, joined at the eastern end by a north-south passage forming a T-junction. At the south-west corner there is a short side passage or creep. In the main passage, near the creep, there is a two foot high stumbling block for intruders, so visitors are therefore advised to bring a torch. The use of the fogou for storage has been suggested, but at Halliggye it does not seem very practical unless the passages were connected with storage pits that have now disappeared. As a refuge in time of war, the entrance to the fogou is rather too reminiscent of an open grave. However, visitors to the site may obtain some special insight, and the fogou is only to be found in Cornwall. It must be added that structures of a similar nature can be seen in Ireland and France where they are known as 'souterrains'.

Dupath Well, Callington
CORNWALL

This is an engaging little building that shows an interesting affinity with Breton architecture of the same period. The stone-built well house was constructed around 1500 by the canons of St Germans to protect a little spring, which was believed to have healing properties. It is built of the local granite with a stone-barrel vault and roof tiles, crocketed finials and a little bell turret with ornamental top. The stone trough remains inside, though the spring no longer tipples into it, preferring to remain outside in the thick grass by the stream.

ABOVE: Dupath Well House

LEFT: the interior of Halliggye Fogou

King Doniert's Stone

CORNWALL

Two pieces of a ninth-century commemorative cross stand in a semicircular walled enclosure beside the road. There is a fine view all around and a bench to sit upon. Some decorative carving in the form of interlocking shapes can be distinguished upon the larger piece, and one of the two is said to bear the inscription 'Doniert Rogavit Pro Anima' — pray for the soul of Doniert who caused this cross to be erected. The stone is very weatherworn. This is thought to commemorate Durngarth, King of Cornwall, who was drowned c.875. Whether Doniert's Stone has always stood here is not known, nor indeed is it certain whether these are two pieces of the same stone, or of two different stones.

Hurlers Stone Circle

CORNWALL

This area of Bodmin Moor is rich in Prehistoric remains and Hurlers Stone Circle is not one but three interconnected Bronze Age circles lying on an axis north-east/south-west. The central and largest stone circle is the best preserved with seventeen standing stones, while the northern one has thirteen and the southern one nine. (Legend has it that these are the petrified figures of those who 'hurled the ball' on the Sabbath — Sunday rugger players who were turned to stone.) Excavations have shown that there was a paved ceremonial way linking the circles, whose granite stones were dressed and buried so as to stand to a uniform height. This is fine walking country, a friendly landscape on a summer's day with unseen birds singing. Following the axis of the circles about quarter of a mile to the north-east lies Rillaton Barrow (not in the care of English Heritage), a Bronze Age barrow that yielded the famous Rillaton Gold Cup. The cup, with its accompanying dagger, can be seen in the British Museum. At least twenty other round barrows exist within a mile radius of the circles. The horizon is punctuated by later archaeological remains, the tall chimneys of abandoned tin mines.

Launceston Castle

CORNWALL

In the Middle Ages Launceston was the most important town in Cornwall, and until 1840 it was the administrative centre with the Assize courts and jail. It had great strategic importance controlling the country between Bodmin Moor and Dartmoor, and also the main route into the county, until the Tamar bridge was opened in 1859. William the Conqueror's half-brother, Robert Count of Mortain, made Launceston the centre of his vast estates and had erected a motte and bailey castle by the time the Domesday Book was compiled. This has been much altered over the years. The ruins now comprise a late twelfth-century shell keep with a mid thirteenth-century tower rising above it. The motte upon which they stand and the bailey were landscaped in the late eighteenth century and again

in the mid nineteenth century when it became a public park. The North Gate, which was the constable's lodgings and later the prison, was rebuilt in the thirteenth century when the south gateway was refaced and the Great Hall, whose foundations remain, was erected. This was the period of Richard, Earl of Cornwall, and was the most important in the castle's history. His heir made Lostwithiel the administrative centre of the estates in order to be nearer the main source of revenue,

the tin mines. During the Civil War the castle was captured twice by Parliament. In the eighteenth century the insanitary conditions of the prison in the north gatehouse and keep attracted the attention of John Howard, the prison reformer. George Fox, founder of the Quakers, was one of the most celebrated inmates. On no account should visitors miss the parish church of St Mary Magdalene, erected 1511-24, with its splendidly decorated exterior.

Pendennis Castle

CORNWALL

Pendennis is the most westerly of the chain of forts erected by Henry VIII between 1538 and 1543 in response to the threatened French and Spanish invasion following his break with Rome. Together with *St Mawes* it was built to guard the entrance to the anchorage at Carrick Roads. It was not until early in the following century that the town of Falmouth developed, promoted by the castle governors and local landowning family, the Killigrews. In the sixteenth century Falmouth was only a collection of fishermens' huts near the Killigrew's mansion of Arwenack, known as Pennycomequick. The castle at Pendennis is a circular keep sur-

rounded by a circular curtain wall, the two linked by the gatehouse range in the north-east corner with a handsome gateway. This in turns stands within the bastioned earthworks of the 1590s, with a ruined blockhouse, Little Dennis, on the shore below. Thus it is a much more formidable proposition than *St Mawes* opposite. Governors of the castle were frequently members of the colourful Killigrew family, all staunch Royalists. One of them, Lady Jane Killigrew, was tried at Launceston for piracy. She was accused of personally leading an assault on two ships from the Hanse ports that had sought refuge in the harbour. Maintenance of the garrison was at the governor's expense, for which he was later reimbursed by the Crown. Payments were often years, if not decades, in arrears and in 1627 Sir Robert Killigrew complained that the men had to sell their bedding in order to buy food and some had died of malnutrition. This is not as unlikely as

Pendennis Castle from the south

it sounds for the area was then very isolated and supplied by sea rather than land. During the Civil War the castle was bravely defended by the Royalist Colonel Arundell. Upon being asked to surrender in March 1646, the seventy-year-old Governor replied, 'I will here bury myself before I deliver up this castle.' He held out until August with a garrison of over 900 men. Royalist attempts to supply the castle by sea from St Malo were thwarted by a chain of boats and barges, and in August the fort capitulated, many of the men on the point of starvation.

Restormel Castle
CORNWALL

When asked to name their favourite castle in Cornwall many people will go for the romance of *Tintagel*, others the functionalism of *Pendennis*, but a good few will say Restormel as its symmetry and order are very pleasing. This motte and bailey castle was erected around 1100 by Baldwin Fitz Turstin in the middle of a deerpark. About a hundred years later the timber palisade on top of the motte was replaced by a crenellated shell keep. Against the inner wall were placed a two-storey range of domestic buildings in the late thirteenth century, including a chapel that projects out from the keep. One can still walk along the top of the parapet wall and gaze down into the ruins of the buildings below. The distance that the commander's voice could carry was one of the considerations in castle planning that we sometimes forget today. And again the distance that a horse could travel in a day limited the area that a castle could control, about a ten-mile radius. In 1299 Restormel became part of the Earldom, later the Duchy, of Cornwall, and remains so to this date. Though in ruins by the sixteenth century, it was garrisoned by Parliament during the Civil War and captured by the Royalists in 1644.

St Breock Downs Monolith
CORNWALL

This is a Prehistoric sacred standing stone, originally about sixteen feet high. Little is known about it, except that it is rather hard to find and OS map number 200 is needed. (The NGR reference is

SW968 683.) The stone stands in beautiful countryside which takes its name from the fifth century Welsh St Breock, who spent much of his time in France where he is known as St Brieux. In England he is called St Briavel, and has one church dedication in Gloucestershire, where the castle and village also share his name. These sacred stones or menhirs reappear in later cultures as the shafts of crosses, like King Doniert's, transformed again as medieval preaching crosses, then obelisks and columns.

ABOVE: the west front of Restormel Castle

BELOW: St Breock Downs Monolith

circular keep rises above three semicirclar bastions laid out in a clover-leaf pattern, approached on the landward side by a drawbridge over a moat. It has hardly been altered, and the carvings and Latin texts composed by the antiquarian Leland which adorn the string courses contribute to its fairytale atmosphere. The success of the design was never properly tested, for the first time it came under attack was during the Civil War, when it proved impossible to defend from a landward assault because of its

St Catherine's Castle, Fowey

CORNWALL

This little blockhouse was built during the reign of Henry VIII, but probably predates the splendid chain of fortifications of the 1538-43 period to which *Pendennis* and *St Mawes* belong. It was built to defend Fowey, then an important port, and commands fine views of the coastline. A ten-minute climb up the wooded slopes brings one to the blockhouse, a roofless ruin, flanked by retaining walls. On the hillside above there is a mysterious monument of rusticated masonry in the form of two intersecting arches, topped by a cross. It is dedicated to members of a well-known local family, notably William Rashleigh, died 1871, who lived nearby at Neptune Point, Readymoney Cove. Rashleigh had been MP for East Cornwall in the 1840s and published in 1844 *Stubborn facts from the factories by a Manchester operative. Published and directed to the working classes by an MP.*

St Mawes Castle

CORNWALL

ABOVE: St Mawes Castle guarding Carrick Roads

RIGHT: St Catherine's Castle and the river Fowey

Looking at the plans of some of Henry VIII's castles, of which St Mawes is one, the visitor may sometimes wonder whether the beauty of the geometric design overrode considerations of defence. Here the

position at the bottom of a hill. Otherwise the castle's history was uneventful. The garrison consisted of between sixteen and a hundred men during the sixteenth and seventeenth centuries, and from 1572 until the Reform Act of 1832 they had the right to elect a Member of Parliament. St Mawes faces *Pendennis* across the entry to Carrick Roads, the most westerly safe anchorage in the Channel and a very large one. In the sixteenth century British squadrons often assembled here,

and in the following century it was used as a packet station for Ireland and the near Continent, later the Americas and then the East Indies. In pre-wireless days, ships would call at Falmouth for 'orders', and between the Wars the last of the great square riggers would assemble here in the early summer before taking part in the grain race to Australia.

Tintagel Castle

CORNWALL

Despite excavations and the mass of legend that surround Tintagel, our knowledge of this dramatic and mysterious island site is almost as tenuous as the wisp of land that links it to the mainland. Remains of the twelfth to thirteenth castle of the Earls of Cornwall guard the isthmus but why they should choose this spot far removed from other habitation is something of a mystery. It was roofless in the fourteenth century and indeed it is not certain which of the Earls built the castle, nor

exactly when. It has been suggested that they were bolstering their newly-acquired authority by building upon a site already celebrated in myths dating back to the Dark Ages after the Romans left. In Cornish legends, Tintagel is the home of King Mark, whose nephew Tristan fell in love with his uncle's bride-to-be, Isolde. It was not until the nineteenth century that Tennyson made it the birthplace of King Arthur — found on the beach beside Merlin's cave. Both the island and the site of the parish church on the mainland are believed to have been occupied in Roman times and it was possibly the 'Fort of the Cornovii', known from documents as a capital of the native tribe of Cornwall, but as yet unlocated. Until quite recently it was thought that the island was the site of a

monastery during the Dark Ages. However, in 1983 a fire on the island revealed the foundations of buildings and a mass of imported pottery indicating a trade with the Mediterranean in luxury goods. Oil from Tunisia, fine dishes from Carthage, scents and spices, and even glass from the Near East were used in Tintagel from the fourth century to the eighth. More imported pottery has been found in Tintagel than in all other British and Irish sites put together. Yet who lived here is unknown. Probably tin was traded in exchange for these goods. The remains of the chapel of St Juliot on the island are later, dating from the tenth century, while the church on the mainland, dedicated to St Materiana, is twelfth century, accompanied by some very early Christian burials in slate graves. The church itself is strangely isolated from the village. On sunny days the archaeologists will continue their selective excavations, yet when the mist comes swirling through Merlin's Cave and the surf thunders against the cliffs, they may turn back to the writings of Geoffrey of Monmouth and the medieval poets.

Trethevy Stone Quoit, St Cleer
CORNWALL

Like a giant piece of sculpture, the remains of this Neolithic chamber tomb stand nine feet high in the landscape. Eight stones with a massive capstone form the tomb with antechamber. Of the barrow that originally covered them, nothing now remains. It dates from the period 3400–2400 BC and was possibly reused during the Bronze Age.

Tregiffian Barrow
CORNWALL

The remains of this chambered tomb truncated by the B3315 are not shown on the OS map. They stand in an area extraordinarily rich in Prehistoric sites (not English Heritage), which can be seen in the fields all round. The Merry Maidens, a Bronze Age stone circle with nineteen dressed, upright stones, is particularly impressive, while about a quarter of a mile to the north-east are two fifteen feet stones known as the Pipers.

ABOVE: Trethevy Stone Quoit

LEFT: Tregiffian Barrow

Cromwell's Castle, Tresco

ISLES OF SCILLY

Cromwell's Castle stands on a promontory guarding the lovely anchorage between Bryher and Tresco. It was built in 1651–52 after Parliament captured Tresco from the Royalists. Building materials were taken from *King Charles's Castle* on the ridgeway above — a position that had proved hard to defend. The castle consisted of a two-storey circular tower entered at first-floor level by an external stair. The main armament was carried on the roof and it was similar in design to *Mount Batten*, Devon. Around 1740 the castle was enlarged with a platform on the seaward side and visitors now enter by a stone stairway onto the platform. The interior is accessible and the first-floor room has a good stone vault. On the roof are two cannons.

King Charles's Castle, Tresco

ISLES OF SCILLY

Dramatically sited on the headland at the northern end of Tresco, this ruined castle commands spectacular views on all sides. It was built *c.*1550–54 by Henry VIII and is a rare survival of the blockhouses that he erected, mainly along the Thames estuary. The plan was that of a two-storey hexagonal block sporting armaments on two tiers to command the entrance to the channel between Tresco and Bryher. At the rear was a single-storey hall and kitchen with a small room opening off on each side. Walls stand to about six feet or so and remains of the doorways, window openings, and kitchen fireplace survive. The problem was that like *Harry's Walls*, the castle had been badly sited. It could not command a clear field of fire across the channel mouth, nor was it defensible from landward attack. During the Civil War when the Scilly Isles was one of the last Royalist strongholds, earthworks were constructed on the landward side, of which traces can still be seen. After Admiral Blake took the islands, King Charles's Castle was dismantled and the stone reused for *Cromwell's Castle*, sited below on the rocks. The castle is reached by a half-hour walk up through woodlands and across the heather-covered headland which is a nesting ground for terns. The coastal path is for the athletic.

Cromwell's Castle with King Charles's Castle on the headland above, Tresco

Harry's Walls, St Mary's
ISLES OF SCILLY

From here one gets a fine view overlooking St Mary's harbour with the *Garrison Walls* and Star Castle above. Harry's Walls are scanty pieces of masonry from a late sixteenth century castle that was never completed, probably because the builders realised that they had put it in the wrong place. The foundations of the two angled bastions linked by a section of wall can be seen and the original plan of the castle, recently discovered at Hatfield House, shows that a square plan with arrowhead-shaped bastions at each corner was intended. The design is too advanced for the reign of Henry VIII and dates from that of his daughter, Elizabeth.

Gunner, whose initials appear over the gateway, along with those of George II. The bastion on the town side was rebuilt and the site encircled with walls and bastions, except on the north-west side where a Royalist earthwork remained from the Civil War. A fine promenade can be taken around the ramparts, which needless to say offer beautiful views across the islands.

Garrison Walls, St Mary's
ISLES OF SCILLY

ABOVE: the harbour at Hugh Town seen from Harry's Walls

ABOVE RIGHT: The Old Blockhouse built to defend Old Grimsby, Tresco

RIGHT: a bastion on the Garrison Walls encircling the headland west of Hugh Town

Approaching St Mary's by boat, the fist of land that juts out protecting the harbour at Hugh Town is the first thing the visitor sees. It is crowned by Star Castle, now a hotel and not in the care of English Heritage, while the lower slopes are protected by the Garrison Walls and earthworks. The site was first fortified in the early 1590s when the narrow neck of land adjoining the town was fortified and the castle was built. The design of the castle is an eight-pointed star, already rather outdated by 1593, but it survives in a fine state of preservation. A major refortification took place between 1715 and 1746 under the charge of Abraham Tovey, Master

Old Blockhouse, Tresco

ISLES OF SCILLY

The remains of this little blockhouse overlook the white sandy bay at Old Grimsby. It dates from the 1550s, and at the time of the Civil War was the only defence on the eastern side of the island. It was here on this vulnerable flank that Admiral Blake chose to attack the Royalists in 1651, and they were not able to offer much resistance.

Porth Hellick Down Burial Chamber, St Mary's

ISLES OF SCILLY

This late Neolithic-early Bronze Age stone cairn is forty feet in diameter and stands about five feet high. The top is turfed over and is one of a group of

five in the eastern part of the island. The site is very exposed and open with high-hedged terrace gardens to the south. On the beach below, the body of Sir Cloudsley Shovell was found after the wreck of the *Association* in 1707. It is said that he was still alive when washed ashore, but was murdered by an elderly resident for his rings.

Innisidgen Lower and Upper Burial Chambers, St Mary's

ISLES OF SCILLY

These late Neolithic or early Bronze Age burial chambers lie on the northern side of the island looking towards St Martin. The upper burial chamber is probably the earlier and the lower one now lies almost on the sea shore. Pine trees and a swathe of bracken form the backdrop to the cairns.

ABOVE: Porth Hellick Down Burial Chamber, St Mary's

ABOVE LEFT: Innisidgen Upper Burial Chamber, St Mary's

Bant's Carn Burial Chamber and Ancient Village, St Mary's

ISLES OF SCILLY

The remains of this late Neolithic-early Bronze Age burial mound lie on the hillside above the ancient village site, looking across to Tresco and Bryher. The tomb was in use for about 500 years but had been sealed long before the Iron Age village was begun. It is probable that there was an earlier settlement here which has now vanished beneath the waves, the sea level having risen considerably. The Iron Age village was in use well into Roman times and the remains of at least four courtyard houses can be detected. As with the other archaeological sites in the Scillies, Bant's Carn enjoys a wonderful location.

RIGHT: Bant's Carn Burial Chamber

BELOW: Bant's Carn Ancient village looking towards Tresco and Samson

Bayard's Cove Fort, Dartmouth

DEVON

Situated at the end of Dartmouth quay is the low circular structure of Bayard's Cove Fort, punctuating the very picturesque line of gabled houses frequently seen on film and TV. Yet it was originally conceived as part of a carefully thought out defensive system for the town, one of the first based on the use of artillery power. The small fort was begun *c*. 1510 as a back-up for the main forts guarding the harbour entrance. Should any enemy ships break through the chain stretched between *Dartmouth Castle* and Kingswear, and survive the crossfire, then the town would be protected by the artillery fire from the eleven gunports of Bayard's Cove. The gunports were ranged in a straight line which gave a very restricted field of fire, a problem not at first appreciated in these early days of artillery fortifications, but a fact that emerged again during the Second World War when the fort was briefly used as a machine-gun post. The cobbled quay beside the fort has the date 1665 inset. It was here some forty-five years earlier that the *Speedwell* and the *Mayflower* had tied up and the Pilgrim Fathers waited anxiously while repairs were carried out.

Blackbury Castle

DEVON

Castle is something of a misnomer. This is an Iron Age site that seems to have been a stock pound and was never permanently occupied. Ramparts form an oval enclosure with a wedge-shaped outer enclosure fronting the entrance and covering about six acres in all. The plan is difficult to make out on the ground, as it is covered by trees. Part of the ramparts can be seen from the road that runs along the northern side and there is a carpark to the east. This is a pleasant place for a walk. The scanty finds from the site can be seen in the Rougemont House Museum, Exeter.

ABOVE: Bayard's Cove Fort and the river Dart

LEFT: the earthworks at Blackbury Castle

Dartmouth Castle

DEVON

Dartmouth Castle was begun in 1481 by the townspeople themselves in order to protect their port, one of the largest in England in the Later Middle Ages. The Castle is notable as the first English fortification constructed with artillery in mind. But to the visitor all this pales into insignificance beside the beauty of the Dart estuary and coastline. The castle on the rocky promontory began as a circular tower, but then the plan was changed and a square one added beside it. The gunports were in the basement just above the waterline and the openings were splayed internally to allow a certain degree of traverse for the guns, which at this time were strapped to wooden boards rather than mounted on carriages as they were in Henry VIII's forts of the 1540s. The Church of St Petrock beside the castle is a twelfth-century foundation rebuilt in 1641, and the whole makes a very attractive group. In 1491 another castle was begun across the estuary at Kingswear. A chain could be stretched between the two, stopping hostile ships from entering the estuary. Kingswear was abandoned in the 1640s and rebuilt as a private house in the nineteenth century. During the Civil War the castle was taken by the Royalists who built earthworks on the heights above. The castle continued in use, and in 1861 a battery was constructed on the site of one of these earthworks as part of the revision of coastal defences stimulated by the fear of a French invasion. Now known as the Old Battery, it was rearmed in 1940 and has recently been restored and opened to the public. Visitors can now follow the development of England's first artillery fort from the fifteenth to the twentieth century.

Berry Pomeroy Castle

DEVON

Berry Pomeroy is an impressive ruin surrounded by dense woods. On two fronts it rises sheer above the Gatcombe valley, with a little stream idling through the woods below. Bluebells in spring and the wild roses of early summer adorn the site. Regarding the ruins, the gatehouse and curtain wall linking St Margaret's tower survive dating from c.1300, but more extensive are the remains of the large house built by the Seymours in the mid sixteenth and early seventeenth centuries. A many-windowed

façade looks on to the courtyard of the castle, while the Great Hall and living quarters open on to an inner courtyard with a ground-floor loggia. The ruins of the kitchens and service range lie to the east. It was said to be a day's work for a servant to open and close all the casement windows at Berry Pomeroy, and the house has indeed almost swallowed the castle, rendering it, one would imagine, more or less impossible to fortify. The fate of the house is uncertain; it seems to have survived the Civil War and was intact in 1688 when Sir Edward Seymour was able to welcome William, Prince of Orange, to Berry in the month before his death. Some time between then and 1701 the house had become a ruin, one theory being that it was struck by lightning and burnt out. In the meantime, the Seymour family, latterly the Dukes of Somerset, had transferred their principal seat to Wiltshire and the castle was left to become an ivy-hung ruin, the haunt of ghosts. One ghostly sighting in the eighteenth century, recorded by a highly respected doctor who later became a royal physician, was that of a distraught woman who is said to have murdered her child, the result of an incestuous relationship. (She was reputed to be a member of the de la Pomerai family who held the castle from the time of the Conquest up to 1548.) The appearance of her richly-dressed figure was believed to signal the death of one of the inhabitants of the castle — in the case reported, that of the steward's wife. In the parish church nearby there is an entertaining memorial to the Seymours, as well as a very fine screen and some notable stained glass by Christopher Whall, the arts and crafts designer.

Merrivale Prehistoric Site

DEVON

The clouds cast great shadows like giant birds of prey across the moorland at Merrivale. It is very quiet. No birds sing. This Early Bronze Age religious site consists of two double rows of standing stones running east to west, 596 feet and 864 feet long respectively, with blocking stones at their eastern ends and a little stream oozing through the heather between them. There is a cairn in the centre of the southern row. A single line of standing stones to the south runs south-west/north-east terminating in a cairn at the north-east end. Evidence of other burials and a stone circle can be seen in the vicinity. The site is a few minutes' walk uphill from the lay-by on the south side of the road and it is also known as the Plague Market, or Potato Market, for a market was held here centuries ago when the plague was raging in Tavistock.

OPPOSITE: *looking west along the axis of one of the stone rows at Merrivale*

BELOW: *on the ramparts at Dartmouth Castle*

Grimspound, Dartmoor
DEVON

One of the most famous sites of Dartmoor, this Late Bronze Age settlement dates from *c.*1000–800 BC. A stone wall about four feet high encloses a circular site of about four acres. The wall was reconstructed when the site was excavated in the late nineteenth century, but the original massive entrance remains in the south-east side with a paved pathway. Remains of storage huts, cattle pens and circular living-huts can be seen. The latter are distinguished by hearths or cooking pits: sometimes raised sleeping benches can be identified, and also the post holes for the central roof post. Because of the acid soil no artefacts have survived. It was changes in the soil that brought about the abandonment of the village. Between 2500–1000 BC forest clearance and intensive farming took place on Dartmoor. Soil erosion and an increase in rainfall around 1000 BC meant that the nutrients were leeched out of the rich dark earth and blanket bogs quickly took their place. Settlements were abandoned and the area used for seasonal pasture only. Unlike *Hound Tor*, Grimspound was not reoccupied in the mid Saxon period, perhaps because the site is not very defensible as it is overlooked by tors. The stream nearby called Grim's Lake would have been a great advantage to the Bronze Age cattlemen, however. A ten-minute walk up a steepish track from the road brings the visitor to this rewarding Prehistoric site.

Hound Tor Medieval Village, Dartmoor
DEVON

This settlement on Dartmoor at Hound Tor was a hamlet rather than a village — a group of three or four farmsteads that were abandoned in the fourteenth century. The ruins were thoroughly investigated between 1960 and 1968 and this has been identified as a typical example of the hamlet settlement. (Hamlets rather than villages were the normal settlement in upland areas throughout Europe during the Middle Ages.) Hound Tor was first occupied in the Bronze Age and was abandoned, to be reoccupied in the mid Saxon period.

At first the occupation was probably seasonal, and only later became permanent. Although there is so much stone around, excavations have shown that the houses were built of turf until the twelfth century. The occupants of these hamlets were usually all related by blood or marriage, and Dartmoor was a well-populated area at this time. Looking down on the site, the foundations of the buildings, yards and paddocks can clearly be distinguished. Each farmstead consisted of a longhouse (a dwelling and stable combined), a little cottage, a barn and a circular corn-drying kiln; the latter to dry the corn for storage. This is upland farming, and at 1150 feet above sea level it is well above the present tree line. Evidence of ridge and furrow ploughing can be made out beside the settlement, and there was open grazing beyond the walls of the paddocks and gardens. The worsening climate and the decline in population in the fourteenth century would seem to be the reasons why the settlement was abandoned. The fall in population after the Black Death meant that it was no longer necessary to farm these less fertile upland areas. Set beneath the twisted form of Hound Tor, the ruins of the hamlet lie in a beautiful moorland setting, a healthy twenty-minute walk up from the carpark.

Kirkham House, Paignton

DEVON

Kirkham is an interesting example of a late fourteenth– early fifteenth-century town house, which was restored in the 1950s. The house may have been built for some official connected with the Bishop of Exeter's palace and deerpark at Paignton, which stood close by the church; or possibly it was for a chantry priest employed by the Kirkham family, who are buried in the church. In either case, the plan is not the normal one encountered in late medieval Devon houses. Visitors enter by the original screens passage and find to their left the parlour, instead of the normal pantry and buttery. A later addition opens out of the parlour with a stairway to the upper floor. To the right of the screens passage is the hall, which is partly open to the ceiling and partly filled with the first-floor room that is jettied out into it. There is a fireplace against the rear wall, and beyond a timber partition is an unheated storeroom or shop. This is another unusual feature. Both the hall and parlour originally had lavers, little stone washhand basin recesses, which were removed during the restoration through the mistaken belief that they were piscinas taken from churches. It is unusual to find such comforts in a small house, and this supports the theory that the house was connected with the bishop's palace. Upstairs there are three rooms, accessible from an external first-floor gallery. All rooms are empty of contents, and remains of the kitchen can be seen at the rear.

ABOVE: remains of the medieval farmsteads on Hound Tor

Mount Batten Tower

DEVON

There is not a great deal to see of Mount Batten, but from it, good views can be obtained across Plymouth Sound and north to the *Citadel*, Barbican and Sutton Harbour. The tower was probably erected in the 1650s under the Protectorate, and it predates the *Citadel*. Plymouth was then concentrated in the small area on the west side of Sutton Harbour, protected by walls with towers at the shoreline, part of which can still be seen as one descends from the *Citadel* to the old town. Mount Batten would therefore have acted as a lookout post to warn the port of ships approaching through the Sound, and probably had a beacon beside it. Timber gun emplacements had already been erected here during the 1590s. Visitors enter the tower by an external stair to the first floor room and from here there is access to the flat roof with its fine views and three old cannons. The design anticipates the martello towers of the early nineteenth century, for it was constructed to carry the main armaments on the roof, and is similar to *Cromwell's Castle* on Tresco in the Scilly Isles. The tower is now in the midst of the RAF station which grew out of the Royal Naval Air Squadron, set up here in 1916. After the First World War it became a 'care and maintenance' depot, and later two squadrons of flying boats were stationed here. Perhaps the most famous member of the squadron was the station commander's runner, Aircraftsman Shaw. He was already well-known as Lawrence of Arabia, but he had joined the RAF in 1922 under an assumed name in search of anonymity.

Lydford Castle, Banks and Fort

DEVON

Lydford was an important town before the Normans came. It was a Saxon burh, the most westerly town fortified by King Alfred in his kingdom of Wessex, and was one of the four boroughs of Devon, with a royal mint, in the early eleventh century. It stands on a wedge-shaped promontory above the lovely gorge of the River Lyd, with the Saxon town bank defending the eastern side. The Normans erected a fortification at the western tip of the promontory and the remains of the earth-

work can be seen in a field west of the parish church. The *Domesday Book* recorded that forty houses were laid waste, presumably to make room for the castle, and the Saxon town layout is still discernible. However, Lydford Castle as we know it today stands to the north — a stern, square keep up on a high mound. It is not in fact a motte and bailey castle and was begun on level ground *c.*1195. Later it was heightened and encircled by a deep ditch. The earth was banked up, burying the lower storey, which was filled in apart from a small cellar or pit. The aim was probably to convey the intimidating power of a castle, for it was around this time that the castle became the administrative centre of the Royal Forest of Dartmoor. The Crown had a particular interest in the area because of its right to a percentage of all mineral deposits found in the kingdom, and Dartmoor tin was an important source of revenue. A charter of 1201 confirmed the tinners' right to search anywhere, and they had their own courts, one of which was held here at Lydford. These survived until the early nineteenth century. Lydford law was proverbial:

ABOVE RIGHT: Lydford Castle

'I oft have heard of Lydford Law
How in the morn they hang and draw
And sit in judgment after'

So a sixteenth-century poet put it. However, he then went on to explain that this was done out of kindness by the judges, to spare the prisoners the extreme discomforts of Lydford Castle jail.

Royal Citadel, Plymouth

DEVON

The walls of this proud citadel remain largely intact, still guarding a military presence — an artillery regiment of the Commandos. The fortress at Plymouth was begun c.1670 with the two-fold purpose of defending the coastline from the Dutch and keeping a royal eye on the inhabitants of Plymouth, who had been strongly pro-Parliament during the Civil War. Known as Sutton in the fifteenth century, Plymouth only became an important port in the following century because of the war with Spain and trade with the New World. The citadel was designed by Charles II's Chief Engineer, Sir Bernard de Gomme, who was reponsible for *Tilbury Fort*. The plan was modified as building progressed to include the earlier fortification of the 1590s, later swept away. The plan was a pentagon with three arrowhead bastions on the landward side. The coastal side underwent many changes and the citadel was enlarged in the mid eighteenth century. In the late nineteenth century the surrounding earthworks were levelled and the moat was filled in. Madeira Road, which runs along the coastal side of the citadel, cuts through the site of these earlier fortifications. Plymouth cannot therefore rival *Tilbury* as a complete example of seventeenth-century fortifications, but it is bigger, and the situation is much more dramatic — the walls are seventy feet high in places and rise 200 feet above sea level. Visitors enter from the landward side by Sir Bernard's fine Baroque gateway dated 1670, which originally had a drawbridge over the moat. The barracks are still in use and are part of the nineteenth-century reorganisation. A statue of George III surveys the parade ground with an imperious eye to remind us of the eighteenth-century alterations that have now largely vanished. Beside him stands the chapel, a cruciform building erected in the 1670s to replace an earlier chapel dedicated to St Katherine. It has an unexpectedly elegant interior; galleries were added in 1845 and there is stencilled decoration. A good hour's walk can be taken around the ramparts which offer excellent views of Plymouth and the harbours, including *Mount Batten* to the south-east. In summer there are conducted tours of the Royal Citadel.

The ramparts of the Royal Citadel, Plymouth

Totnes Castle

DEVON

Most of the medieval town walls and gates are still intact at Totnes, which is a delightful hill town. Its strategic importance at the head of the River Dart becomes apparent when one ascends the castle to enjoy the view across the roof tops and down to the river. The castle was erected around 1080 and has the largest motte in the country. As with most mottes it was raised in two stages. The foundations of the original square timber keep can be seen, while the crenellated shell keep, rebuilt in the fourteenth century survives almost intact. Below are remains of the horseshoe-shaped bailey with part of its wall and ditch. The gardens of the houses have encroached upon the bailey and all is happily jumbled up together with the town walls. Totnes was one of the four Anglo-Saxon boroughs in Devon but unlike Exeter it did not put up any resistance to the Normans. The castle was erected by a Breton supporter of William's, Judhael, and had a singularly uneventful history. After the mid fourteenth century it was not of great importance to its owners and was in decay by the fifteenth century.

Upper Plym Valley

DEVON

Upper Plym Valley is unique amongst English Heritage properties in that there is not one site, but scores, scattered over an area of six square miles of Dartmoor. The area is exceptionally rich in Prehistoric remains, but it is also of interest to the naturalist, and indeed to anyone with a pair of walking shoes and an OS map. In the Bronze Age, Dartmoor was intensively farmed and densely populated. There were an average of twenty-three huts to the square mile, whereas the average for the country was only five. This has been accounted for by alluvial tin mining in the River Plym, which continued intermittently into the Early Middle Ages. Tin is not found elsewhere in Devon. A good Bronze Age settlement can be seen at Legis Tor NGR SX 569 652, where there are at least ten hut circles by a stock pound and a view south across the river to Trowlesworthy Warren. Here, at NGR SX 566 649, are the stone walls of another group of hut circles, and by ascending Trowlesworthy Tor, more fine views can be obtained. It may be possible to identify a series of pillow mounds running in a line

Remains of the keep, Okehampton Castle

from Trowlesworth Warren House north to the river. These cigar-shaped mounds, also known as buries, were medieval rabbit warrens which have been dated to the twelfth and thirteenth centuries. Rabbits, bred both for meat and fur, were caught with nets over the burrow openings after a ferret or similar animal had been introduced into the warren. There are also cross-shaped vermin traps to stop unplanned entries by ferrets into the warren area; however since they are only about a foot high, the traps are rather difficult to identify. Higher up the river on the north bank at Drizzlecombe is a Bronze Age religious site. There are two impressive rows of standing stones and a number of burial mounds including a stone cairn, the Giant's Basin, seven feet high and seventy-one feet in diameter. More Prehistoric sites await discovery by the visitor.

Okehampton Castle

DEVON

Okehampton is the only Devonshire castle mentioned in the *Domesday Book*. It was founded in open countryside by Baldwin de Meules and had a large deerpark attached. The borough of Okehampton grew up and around the castle which was almost completely rebuilt by the Courtenays in the early fourteenth century. The castle stands on a natural outcrop of stone with the motte raised at one end. The Courtenays enlarged Baldwin's eleventh-century stone keep at the rear, and the bailey was filled with a fine group of lodgings, Great Hall, kitchen and chapel. The gatehouse was protected by the barbican, whose distinctive feature is the long, slightly twisted tunnel-like corridor which would have trapped and confused any maraunders who broke through its gateway. In fact the castle was never besieged and served more as an opulent setting to demonstrate the wealth and influence of the Courtenays, Earls of Devon. The medieval aristocracy needed to give tangible evidence of their power and wealth to the surrounding countryside in order to maintain their supporters — otherwise, as one historian has put it, they would find themselves in the position of a modern bank when rumours begin to spread that they are no longer financially sound. The Courtenays were the greatest landowners in the West Country but friendship with Henry VIII and his daughter Mary was their undoing; Courtenays father and son lost their royal friends and their heads into the bargain. The castle was probably dismantled in the mid sixteenth century.

Abbotsbury Abbey Remains

DORSET

Abbotsbury is a charming village of stone and thatch cottages, lying to the north of the abbey remains. The Benedictine abbey from which the village takes its name was founded in 1044 by Orc, belived to have been a steward of King Canute. At the Dissolution the site was bought by Sir Giles Strangeways who built a house out of the abbey buildings, later destroyed during the Civil War when it was besieged by the Parliamentarians. The abbey church stood close to the south of the medieval parish church, but nothing survives except some foundations in the churchyard. The section in the care of English Heritage is a full-height gable end wall, with central buttress, that was part of one of the buildings on the east side of the cloister. It dates from c.1400, but the purpose of the building has yet to be discovered. Other fragments of the abbey such as the inner gatehouse have been incorporated into buildings (not in the care of English Heritage). About 200 yards to the south of the parish church, beside the village pond, stands the most spectacular of the abbey remains — the Great Barn; likewise not in the care of English Heritage but also visible from the road. Constructed around 1400, it is about 280 feet long and is partly used to store thatching materials for the village. A path to the south leads to the abbey fishponds and on to the swannery, for the Benedictine monks at Abbotsbury were famous for breeding delicious swans for the table. Swans were always a popular feature at any medieval banquet.

signposted from White Hill, about a mile away, but five footpaths in all converge on the site, most of which pass by Prehistoric sites, although they are not readily identifiable without a map. The OS map number 194 is particularly useful when visiting the many archaeological sites in this area.

Kingston Russell Stone Circle

DORSET

On Tenants Hill all the Kingston Russell stones lie buried in the grass and many have disappeared. This Bronze Age circle is roughly oval in plan, lying north–south, about ninety feet by eighty feet wide. The largest stone is about eight feet long. There is a clump of trees beside the circle, like a sacred grove set in the flat landscape, and a visit is something in the nature of a pilgrimage. The main footpath is

Kingston Russell Stone Circle

Fiddleford Mill House

DORSET

Not a mill house but a remarkable medieval interior greets the visitor to Fiddleford. The house was built 1374–80 for William Latimer, Sheriff of Somerset and Dorset, and it was altered in the early sixteenth century for the White family, who have thoughtfully initialled most of their alterations. Visitors enter the hall via the site of the screens passage: on the west wall are two richly carved doorways inserted in the sixteenth century and bearing the initials of Thomas and Anne White. A

gallery above, composed of the ceiling of the screens passage and seventeenth-century panelling, provides a good position from which to view the splendid fourteenth-century roof. Originally the hall extended further east and had a louvre to let the smoke out from the central hearth. In the sixteenth century a chimney stack was inserted, resited at the east gable end when the hall was shortened in the seventeenth century. The roof was also slightly altered in the sixteenth century when a plaster ceiling was added, which has since been removed. The room to the left of the screens passage was divided in the sixteenth century to become the pantry and buttery, whereas before it had been the store for valuable goods kept below the solar, as at *Old Soar*, Kent. The solar above also has a roof of the 1370s but it is finer than that in the hall for it has not been altered. Here is a three-bay arch-braced collar-beam roof with two tiers of cusped wind braces and extra horizontal and vertical windbracing — a carpenter's delight. The north wall still contains a fourteenth-century window, and there is a plasterwork overmantel to the fireplace bearing the initials of the White family. The building was extended north in the sixteenth century (not accessible to the public) and a west range was added in the seventeenth century which has since been demolished. The mill buildings lie to the north-west (not in the care of English Heritage).

ABOVE: the Hall at Fiddleford Mill House; the windows were inserted in the sixteenth century

LEFT: detail of the solar roof at Fiddleford showing the lavish windbracing

Poor Lot Barrows, Winterbourne Abbas

DORSET

This is an important Bronze Age cemetery consisting of forty-four barrows of different types, with two Neolithic long barrows immediately to the south-west. The site is bisected by the A35; the marjority of the barrows lying on the south side but the most informative view is to be obtained from a small hill lying to the north-east, where a disc barrow and a triple bowl barrow are located. These different types of barrows are named with reference to their shapes when seen in cross-section, but the significance of these different shapes is not yet clear to the archaeologists. These are individual burial sites as distinct from the group burials of the preceeding Neolithic period, and denote the rise of a hierarchical society. They are remnants of the brilliant Wessex culture that grew up on the important trade route between Ireland and Europe and lasted *c.*1800–1300 BC. About half the barrows in the cemetery are bowl barrows; six are disc barrows which are known from other sites to contain female burials, while bell barrows, of which there are seven here, are known to be male. These are the most prominent. There are also triple bowl and pond barrows to be seen, but ploughing and

The Nine Stones, Winterbourne Abbas

DORSET

The remains of this Bronze Age stone circle lie uncomfortably close to the south side of the A35, and it is difficult to find anywhere to park. The plan is roughly circular with a diameter of about twenty-eight feet maximum. On the northern side is a gap, although antiquarian accounts suggest that a tenth stone stood here. There are two large sarsens and seven small ones, and all the nine stones are still standing which is unusual.

ABOVE: the Nine Stones, Winterbourne Abbas

RIGHT: Portland Castle

other activities over the last 3,500 years have damaged some of the mounds. Only two of the forty-four have been excavated; they were pond barrows and did not contain any burials.

St Catherine's Chapel, Abbotsbury

DORSET

This sturdy little stone chapel, set on the hillside like a sentinel, dates from the same decade as Fiddleford Mill House, the 1370s. Here, too, there is a fine roof. In this case a stone barrel vault, of a type rarely seen in England, ribbed and ornamented with bosses and cinquefoil-headed panels. The chapel is about forty-two feet by fifteen feet internally, comprising a single space, and has walls over four foot thick. There are north and south porches and the damaged remains of a stair turret that gave access to the roof, possibly so that a beacon could be lit. The chapel was built by the abbey and one might note in passing the numerous dedications to St Catherine that stand on high ground; *St Catherine's Oratory* on the Isle of Wight is another example.

St Catherine's Chapel

Portland Castle

DORSET

One of the best preserved of Henry VIII's forts, built under the threat of a French and Spanish invasion. Between 1539-40 two forts were erected to protect Portland Harbour; Sandsfort Castle near Weymouth has crumbled, but Portland, at the north end of Portland Island beside the naval helicopter base, is in fine condition. It is built of Portland stone, which was not widely appreciated until the following century. The plan is a segment of a circle, fan-shaped, with the curved walls of the low keep flanked by wings in each corner. This was the accommodation for the governor and officers, while the soldiers' barracks were in the courtyard which was roofed over. The castle had an eventful time during the Civil War, changing hands on several occasions, once as the result of a rather cunning Royalist ploy. The castle was then in the hands of the Parliamentarians. A Royalist commander disguised half of his company as Parliamentarians and chased them up to the fort which opened to give them shelter. Too late they discovered their error.

Christchurch Castle keep

Christchurch Castle and Norman House

DORSET

Standing to the north of the magnificent priory church are the scanty remains of the castle keep. The motte and bailey castle was begun by the Redvers family *c.*1100, from whom it passed to the Crown in 1293, probably about the time that the keep was rebuilt. Only two walls remain, the castle having been slighted during the Civil War. The hall of the castle however is in a better state of preservation and dates from around 1160. It stood against the curtain wall of the bailey overlooking the River Avon, an area now part of the gardens of the Kings Arms Hotel. The rectangular block contained a first floor hall entered by an external stair on the bailey (west) side. The basement, or undercroft, had a wooden ceiling, not a stone vault like the almost contemporary *Burton Agnes*, Humberside, and so, like the roof, has not survived. The carved window in the north wall lit the dais or upper end of the hall; it had shutters, not glass. The hall window openings remain, as does one of the earliest chimneys in the country. In the thirteenth century a garderobe tower was added to the solar. This emptied into the river, as had the earlier privy, set above a buttress. One of the later occupants of the castle was Lady Margaret Pole, Countess of Salisbury, who caused the splendid Salisbury chantry chapel to be erected in the priory church. It still survives, though she herself is buried in the Tower of London.

Jordan Hill Roman Temple

DORSET

The foundations of this Romano-Celtic temple, enclosing an area about 240 feet square, are marked out with gravel. There is nothing else visible but excavations have discovered a sacrificial pit about five feet deep. It contained the burnt remains of birds (ravens, buzzards, starlings and crows), and coins, separated into layers by stone slabs. The coins date from the fourth and early fifth centuries. Situated on top of a hill, now part of the suburbs of Weymouth, this was possibly a shrine to a local

deity whose origin is unknown. The normal plan for these Romano-Celtic temples was a square tower-like structure surrounded by a veranda with a lean-to roof. The foundations of one such as this can be seen nearby at *Maiden Castle*. The outer (veranda) wall is missing at Jordan Hill and the stones were probably removed for building materials centuries ago. The Museum of London has a good section on religious practices in Roman Britain.

Maiden Castle

DORSET

The finest hill fort in Britain, Maiden Castle lies, as Thomas Hardy once described it, like a slumbering dinosaur in the landscape. The oval 100-acre site is enclosed by a series of ramparts with entrances at the east and west ends — the latter defended by a veritable maze of outworks to confuse the enemy. This splendid example of an Iron Age hill fort lies on the site of an earlier Neolithic camp of *c.*3000-2000 BC, which stood at the eastern end. At that time the area was still forested but by 350 BC, when the site was reoccupied, the forests had gone. Soon the fort was extended west, ramparts were added about 150 BC and strengthened *c.*75 BC. Even today, more than 2,000 years later, they are still very impressive and continue their original function not just to defend but to overawe as well. This was the tribal capital of the Durotiges, the fortress of their rulers, which acted as the place for tribal gatherings and offered refuge in time of war. Recent excavations have revealed a rich and sophisticated settlement, probably consisting of about 1,000 people. The data is still being analysed, but we know they drank wine from Spain and France and used pottery from many parts of southern England. A large complex of grain pits has been discovered, and backfilled, which are rather interesting. About six feet deep and three feet wide, the grain pits had a life span of about four to five years, after which they became too damp and were used as rubbish pits. In AD 43 this flourishing capital came to an abrupt end. The Roman invasion spearheaded a three-pronged attack across the country in the spring of that year and Maiden Castle was one of the twenty southern hill forts that fell to Vespasian and the Second Legion. What happened here that fateful spring? The dramatic picture of the east gate battle painted by Sir Mortimer Wheeler may have to be redrawn in the light of recent excavations. Sir Mortimer's pioneering work between the wars at Maiden Castle, which did so much to arouse public interest in archaeology, identified the famous 'war cemetery' at the eastern gate, but it seems that only fifteen out of the thirty-eight male burials so far investigated died violently. Still there is something very poignant about the thought of these huddled burials, each with his mug and parcel of food, such as a leg of lamb, to sustain him on the journey to the underworld. One of the twisted skeletons, with a bolt from a Roman ballista embedded in his spine, can be seen in Dorchester Museum. By AD 70 Maiden Castle had been abandoned and the Durotiges were resettled in the new Roman town of Durnovaria (Dorchester). The fort was briefly a religious site in the AD fourth century and the outlines of a Romano-Celtic temple can be seen. Motorists can obtain fine views of the site from the A35, A354 and B3159.

Aerial view of Maiden Castle from the east

Sherborne Old Castle

DORSET

TOP: *Knowlton Church*

BELOW: *remains of Sherborne Old Castle*

'A malicious and mischievous castle, like its owner', declared Cromwell when he laid siege to Sherborne in 1645. He was unaccustomed to finding Royalist castles in such excellent repair. The owner, Lord Digby, was in fact absent but his stepson, Sir Lewis Dyve, held out against Cromwell and Fairfax for sixteen days. Thereafter the castle was carefully dismantled. Today the ruined south-west gatehouse, the lower stages of the keep and north range with part of the curtain walls still survive. The plan is innovative: it was built between 1107 and 1135 by Roger Bishop of Salisbury, or Sarum as it then was, and the foundations of his palace at *Old Sarum* show marked similarities with the ruins at Sherborne. The keep is set in one corner of buildings ranged around four sides of the courtyard, with a covered way like a cloister all around. The curtain wall is even more interesting since it is octagonal, a rectangle with canted corners, more or less symmetrical, with corner towers and entrances on the north side and in the south-west corner. Here were features that the crusaders had seen in the Holy Land; canted corners were less susceptible to mining and projecting towers offered a wider field of fire. In 1592 Queen Elizabeth leased the property to Sir Walter Raleigh who set about converting it to a dwelling. However, he soon changed his mind and began the new building upon an eminence to the south, now known as Sherborne Castle. The two are separated by a tree-fringed lake, part of Capability Brown's beautiful landscaping of the 1750s and '70s, not in the care of English Heritage.

Knowlton Church and Earthworks

DORSET

Here is an example of the conscious adaptation of a pagan religious site to one for Christian worship, showing a continuity that archaeologists are now beginning to believe was much more common than was once thought. At Knowlton, the ruins of the church stand in the centre of a Neolithic henge monument, with henges on either side. The smaller North Circle, a D-shaped henge, has been obliterated by ploughing and the larger South Circle is bisected by the road; so only the Centre Circle with church is visible. The village of Knowlton, abandoned by the nineteenth century, stood in fact 600 yards to the north-west, away from the henges which the villagers apparently wished to keep inviolate. The remains of the church include the twelfth-century nave and chancel, fifteenth-century tower and eighteenth-century north aisle. The church was disused by the mid seventeenth century and an attempt was made to demolish it in 1659. However it underwent a revival in the 1730s when the north aisle was built. Unfortunately, later in the century, the roof collapsed. A clump of trees to the east marks the remains of the Great Barrow, surrounded by two crop-mark ditches, while on the opposite bank of the River Allen to the north-west is the site of another deserted village, Brockington.

range is thirteenth-century, apart from the eighteenth-century roof, and contains one of the finest dorters, or dormitories, surviving. So that they could rise quickly in the night to celebrate Matins and Prime, the monks always slept fully-clothed, though the Benedictine Rule forbade the monks to take their knives to bed with them lest they injured themselves. In the Later Middle Ages the dormitory was divided with partitions to form cubicles, and one can still see the window seats tailored to fit the individual monks. Beneath the dormitory are rooms which include the sacristy with cupboard recesses and piscinas, and the library — in most monasteries, part of the sacristy but here a separate room. Beneath the south range of the fifteenth-century frater are separate rooms for the monks, another example of the general trend towards greater privacy in the Later Middle Ages. The frater, or dining room, has a splendid mid fifteenth-century arch-braced roof with carved angels. The builders intended it to be ceiled to form a wagon roof of the type very popular in Somerset churches, but it was never completed. There are some wall-paintings in the room adjoining to the west, while to the south can be seen the tiled floor of the former frater dating from the thirteenth century. These tiles are very fine, but the later refectory was much more elegant and part of the general trend towards a more comfortable monastic life. A rare survival in the north wall of the cloister is the Collation Seat, to be found only in Cistercian monasteries. Here the abbot sat when he supervised a reading from the *Collationes* or *Conferences of the Hermits in the Egyptian desert*, heard before the evening service of Compline. The word also referred to the light meal taken afterwards, and later came to mean a light meal in general.

BELOW: the south front and the interior of the refectory at Cleeve Abbey

Cleeve Abbey

SOMERSET

At Cleeve Abbey is to be found one of the best-preserved group of cloister buildings in the country. The Cistercian abbey founded in 1198 was first known as Vallis Florida. Its history was uneventful, though one of the more colourful grants to the abbey was the right of shipwreck to coastlines bordering the monastery's estates. In 1468 there was a heated dispute between the abbot and sheriff of Devon over the wreck of the Bristol ship, the Raphaell. The church was destroyed soon after the Dissolution and the buildings around the cloister were turned into a house, and later a farm. The south and east ranges are complete with their roofs, while the north aisle wall of the church remains and part of the cloister of the west side. The east

The Buttercross, Gallox Bridge and Yarn Market, Dunster

SOMERSET

Somerset has many delightful villages and Dunster is deservedly one of the best known. It still has all the important ingredients of a medieval settlement: the proud castle dominating the village street; the old Benedictine priory church, now the parish church, nestling below; the medieval residence of the Abbots of Cleve opposite the Yarn Market and at the other end of the village, the old mill near the Gallox Bridge. The upkeep of roads and bridges in the Middle Ages was the responsibility of those who held the land tenure and while the monasteries were particularly active to help pilgrims and travellers, they also encouraged others to do likewise with generous indulgences. The Gallox Bridge was probably built by the priory in the fifteenth century. The Buttercross stands away from the centre of the village and is late fourteenth to early fifteenth century, possibly marking a boundary of the priory's property. Large numbers of medieval crosses survive in Somerset; they fulfilled many functions, as not only were they a site for preachers and an appropriate place from which to announce news, but they also acted as boundary markers, signposts and sometimes commemorated important

TOP LEFT: the Yarn Market in the main street of Dunster

TOP RIGHT: Gallox Bridge

BELOW: the Buttercross

religious events. At *Wetheral* in Cumbria for instance, another Benedictine priory, criminals could claim sanctuary for crimes committed outside the bounds of the priory and this area was marked out by six crosses. The priory at Dunster was founded in 1094 by the Mohuns who owned the castle, one of the two castles in Somerset mentioned in the *Domesday Book*. The Mohuns promoted the development of the village in the twelfth century by establishing a market and laying out the main street. Their successors, the Luttrells, continued to encourage trade and the Yarn Market was built as a covered market in the late sixteenth to early seventeenth centuries, extensively repaired in 1647.

Farleigh Hungerford Castle

SOMERSET

Had newspapers been published in the sixteenth century, the journalists of the popular press would have made many trips to Farleigh, for the happenings there were quite sensational. In 1523 the widow of Thomas de Hungerford was convicted of the murder of her first husband four years earlier. She was hung at Tyburn. Whether she had assisted

her second husband from the world is not known, but in his will he had left everything to her, excluding his son by his first marriage, Walter. This might have been because of Walter's notorious bad character. He buried two wives and the third he kept incarcerated in the south-west tower for three to four years with little sustenance save the ministrations of the chaplain whom she claimed was trying to poison her. In 1544 he was executed for treason and 'unnatural vice'. His own son, who married twice, accused his second wife of adultery and attempted poisoning. When the case was dismissed he chose to go to prison rather than pay her costs. At his death he left everything to his mistress and her children, but his wife later recovered the estate. Matters improved a little in the seventeenth century, but not much. The chapel, restored in the nineteenth century, is the best preserved part of the castle. The walls and towers of the 1370s castle built by Sir Thomas de Hungerford are in ruins, and the foundations of the earlier manor house enclosed by the rectangular curtain wall are scanty. In the 1420s the outer bailey was built, enclosing the parish church which then became the castle chapel. It contains a fine collection of tombs, including an outstanding pair of mid seventeenth-century marble effigies. The ceiling beams are painted with cherubs and there are some weapons and body armour from the Civil War on display. The reconstructed priest's house has an exhibition about the castle and the Hungerfords.

Glastonbury Tribunal

SOMERSET

This well-known building in the centre of Glastonbury was originally built in the fifteenth century as a courthouse. The Abbot of Glastonbury had judicial power over a large area, and here the king's itinerant judges lodged and heard the cases, as in the Assize courts. The façade was rebuilt c. 1500 to give more light to the courtroom on the first floor. At the Dissolution of the Monasteries the building became a dwelling and a kitchen wing was added at the rear. The plan is typical of a medieval town house and there are many original features surviving including fireplaces, stone doorframes and compartment ceilings with moulded beams. In the back room on the ground floor there is a plaster-work ceiling inserted in the sixteenth century. The kitchen wing now contains a small museum of miscellaneous items maintained by the Glastonbury Archaeological Society. Visitors are kept up to date with the Society's research project on the Somerset Levels. The excavations of the Prehistoric timber causeways, like the Sweet Track, that lay across the Somerset Levels are a major item. The stone façade of the Tribunal with its oriel and eight-light ground-floor window is a fine example of its period. Only a couple of doors down can be seen the splendid fifteenth-century façade of the hostel for pilgrims to the abbey, now the George Hotel.

TOP: the Glastonbury Tribunal

LEFT: Farleigh Hungerford Castle

The south front of Nunney Castle

windows on the second floor of the castle identify the Great Hall, below which were the servants' quarters with the kitchens on the ground floor. On the top floor were Sir John's private rooms. Some fireplaces still survive. In the early fourteenth century the castle passed through the female line to Sir John Poulet, died 1436, whose tomb can be seen in the parish church. During the Civil War the castle was held for the king but surrendered after the first artillery bombardment which damaged the north wall. It was not damaged further by the Parliamentarians, though the floors and ceilings were probably removed at this time. In 1910 the north wall finally collapsed as a result of the damage sustained over 250 years before.

Meare Fish House
SOMERSET

This little building standing in the middle of a field was the home of the chief fisherman to Glastonbury Abbey. The large mere or pool from which the village takes its name stood to the north, and also included a duck decoy. Medieval fishponds are often identifiable as depressions in the landscape with small hillocks — these were islands when the pools were full of water. Monastic dieticians made important distinctions between meat, fowl and fish; the former was in theory only for the sick, and the latter was most important for fast days. Some fowl were given fish status, like the barnacle goose which was thought to have been born in a barnacle on the sea shore, though this may have been a genuine error. (Only those who have eaten barnacle goose are in a position to judge!) The fish ponds served not only for breeding fish but also for storing those caught in the rivers until needed. The little two-storey stone house at Meare is thought to date from 1322 to 1335. It was gutted by fire in the nineteenth century and restored with a new roof in the twentieth century. There was originally an external stair to the first floor, as can be seen from the first floor blocked doorway. There is little to see on the interior (key obtainable from Meare Farm), and the floors have gone. Probably the ground floor was used for the storage of fishing equipment and the upper floor was the fisherman's dwelling. Later the building became a two-storey dwelling. The buttery and pantry were to the right of the entrance, a fireplace was inserted on the ground floor, and the staircase was resited internally.

Nunney Castle
SOMERSET

At Nunney survives the shell of a castle built in 1373, which has only undergone very minor alterations since. The plan is very unusual, possibly unique. It is a compact rectangle with circular corner towers set so close as to be almost touching on the shorter sides. When built by Sir John de la Mare the castle rose directly from the moat, but a terrace was later added and the moat now encircles it like a ribbon. The outer bailey is lost in the village surrounding the castle. The towers originally had conical roofs with attic windows and a machicolated parapet crowning the walls. (A machicolated parapet projects out from the walls carried on corbels giving a wider field of vision and fire.) The castle must have looked very similar to those seen in French illuminated manuscripts, like the Duc de Berry's *Riches Heures*. Although little is known of Sir John de la Mare's early life, it is thought that as a soldier he profited from the wars in Gascony. Large

Muchelney Abbey

SOMERSET

Muchelney means Big Island, and until recently the village was more or less an island surrounded by marshes. There was a religious site here in the ninth century, but it was destroyed by the Danes and refounded in the tenth century. Little survives of the Benedictine monastery except the refectory, abbot's lodging and the south cloister range. The latter two were rebuilt *c.* 1508. The cloisters are fan-vaulted in golden Ham stone, in emulation of Gloucester Cathedral cloisters, and above them are three rooms accessible by a broad stone stair from a room at the west end of the refectory. These were the abbot's lodgings. One room contains a very ornate chimneypiece and carved doorway, with a moulded compartment ceiling and two windows with ornate tracery. Another room has a wagon roof and a third the remains of some wallpaintings. Here one gets some idea of the luxurious surroundings that were the lot of many abbots on the eve of the Dissolution. Given the modest resources of the abbey, this building programme was probably rather unwise, and it is known that in the 1530s the abbey was heavily in debt. Two hundred years earlier the notes made on an episcopal visitation in 1335 give an insight into the life of the abbey; it was found that some monks had built themselves cubicles inside the dormitory for greater privacy, and others avoided the refectory, preferring to dine elsewhere in the abbey. Laymen, women and girls frequented both the refectory and the cloister. The partitioning of rooms in monasteries was probably more common than we can appreciate from studying the masonry remains, whilst the prevalence of women in monasteries is rather harder to evaluate objectively. The parish church stands hard by the foundations of the abbey church and contains some medieval tiles taken from the abbey, as well as a delightful painted ceiling covered with laughing angels. The Priest's House at Muchelney is a famous example of a fifteenth-century dwelling, built of stone with all the original traceried windows extant.

ABOVE: the cloisters at Muchelney Abbey

LEFT: the Fish House, Meare

to the third millenium, dating from *c.*3800–3000 BC, though it was in use for about a thousand years. *Silbury* is currently dated to *c.*2700 BC, some three centuries or so before work began on the great henge at *Avebury*. This was completed by 2000 BC when the arrival of the Beaker people, and the beginning of the Bronze Age, saw the creation of the *West Kennet Avenue* and the enlargement of the *Sanctuary*. The prosperous farming community that created these ceremonial sites benefited from its position on the great Prehistoric trade route, the Ridgeway. While *Stonehenge* continued to excite interest down the ages, Avebury was largely forgotten until the seventeenth century when it was rediscovered by John Aubrey. He felt it surpassed 'the much renowned Stonehenge, as a cathedral does a parish church'. The work of the antiquarian William Stukeley from 1719 to 1724 was of vital importance, for he published plans and drawings made on the spot. Many of the stones were being broken up even as he worked. For instance, of the thirty stones remaining of the Beckhampton Avenue that he plotted, not one remained in the 1920s. Avebury owes its appearance today to Alex-

Avebury Museum
WILTSHIRE

This museum, set beside the parish church in Avebury, contains displays of archaeological material relating to the sites in the great Neolithic and Bronze Age complex at Avebury. These constructions cover the period *c.*3800 BC to 1500 BC, a time span slightly shorter than that of the Iron Age to the present day, and despite radiocarbon dating the chronology is still vague. The oldest site is *Windmill Hill*, a settlement of early Neolithic farmers dating from *c.*3800–3500 BC. The burial site at *West Kennet Barrow* is also thought to belong

ABOVE: the stones at Avebury

RIGHT: Avebury Stone Circle

ander Keiller who, in the '20s and '30s, restored the henge and created the museum to display his finds. The heir to the Keiller marmalade fortune, he purchased the manor of Avebury (not in the care of English Heritage) and acquired much of the land around which he excavated with the most up-to-date methods. After his death, his widow gave the land to the National Trust and care of the monuments devolved upon the Ministry of Works, later English Heritage.

Avebury Stone Circles

WILTSHIRE

Unlike *Stonehenge* which stands proud in an open landscape, this henge enfolds the village at Avebury and has a more intimate and human scale. Indeed the stones seem almost to have personalities of their own, though many would disagree with this inter-

pretation. Dating from *c.* 2500–2200 BC, and earlier than the present structure at Stonehenge, the Avebury circle encloses an area of twentyeight-and-a-half acres bisected by four roads that follow the original entrances of the henge. A deep ditch originally thirty feet deep, encircles the area. The effect of the white chalk circle against the green grass must have been stunning when built. The western side of the outer circle is almost complete and inside the circle are remains of two smaller configurations, the northern circle with a central 'cove' and the southern circle with a central Z-shaped layout. Missing stones are marked by concrete blocks. In the Middle Ages there was a conscious attempt to 'murder' the stones. They were uprooted and carefully buried, while attempts were made to destroy others by burning them and then pouring cold water over the molten rock to crack it. Alexander Keiller was able to recover a number of the stones that had been buried in this way and beneath one was found the skeleton of a man that the stone had crushed as it fell.

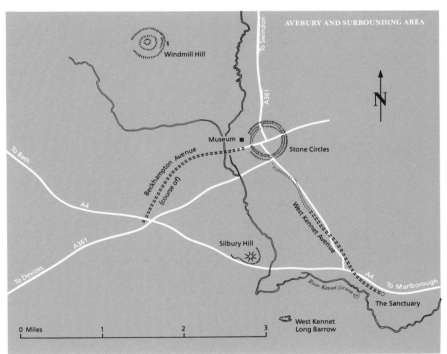

Silbury Hill

WILTSHIRE

Silbury Hill — the great enigma; a mound built by Prehistoric man but to what purpose? It is the largest Neolithic construction in Europe, dating from *c.*2700 BC, and containing a cubic capacity comparable with that of the smallest of the three pyramids at Giza, which is roughly contemporary. Excavations have shown that it was constructed in four stages, yet it does not seem to contain a burial. A shaft sunk through the centre of the hill in 1776 yielded nothing, and later, more scientific attempts have failed to produce any evidence of a grave. The effort involved in its construction is daunting. It contains an estimated eighteen million man hours, the equivalent of 500 people labouring for a decade, though one recent theory suggests that it was built within a two-year period. Another remarkable feature is that after 5,000 years the structure has hardly weathered at all. One possible explanation seems to be that the mound is a symbol of fertility, perhaps a great communal work celebrating life and regeneration, towering above the low burial mounds that the individual communities raised to cover their dead. This must be the product of an age of optimism and agricultural prosperity, and one with some centralised spiritual and political power. In order to preserve Silbury Hill from erosion, it can only be viewed from a distance.

Windmill Hill

WILTSHIRE

Although there is not a great deal to see at Windmill Hill, this is one of the largest and earliest Neolithic earthworks in Britain. It was possibly first occupied *c.*3700 BC and the earthworks begun *c.*500 years later. A small segment of the three concentric rings of ditches survives. These ditches, which enclosed an area of about twenty-one acres, were crossed by a number of causeways. During the later Neolithic period the banks were deliberately broken down to fill the ditches which were levelled off with rubbish, presumably because the site was no longer of importance. Perhaps it was superseded by the complex at *Avebury*. This was not a defensive unit, rather a regional focus for those living in the scattered communities around. Some Bronze Age barrows lie within the confines of the earthwork, which is at least a mile away from the road.

Silbury Hill from the south

Bradford-on-Avon Tithe Barn

WILTSHIRE

This fine medieval barn dating from the fourteenth century was part of a grange, or outlying farm, belonging to the great Benedictine nunnery at Shaftesbury. The farmhouse and a medieval granary are adjoining, but they are not in the care of English Heritage. The barn is stone built with many of the mason's marks still visible, and a stone slate roof. The building is fourteen bays long, in this case totalling 167 feet by 30 feet, with most of the original roof surviving. There are pairs of gabled porches on the north and south fronts. After the Second World War the building underwent a thorough restoration to a very high standard of craftmanship. For instance, the bolt holes have been countersunk and plugged with wood, the grain so carefully matched as to make them almost invisible. The interior space is most impressive and contains a collection of agricultural machinery lent by the Wiltshire Archaeological Society. The nunnery at Shaftesbury also had a grange at Tisbury where a similar, and dare one say it, even finer barn still exists.

West Kennet Avenue

WILTSHIRE

From the south entrance to the circle at *Avebury*, this avenue of stones ran in a sinuous curve south-south-east to the *Sanctuary*, about one-and-a-half miles away. The first 600 yards or so from the circle were excavated and restored by Keiller in the 1930s, but the rest is known only from excavation. There were originally 100 pairs of stones standing forty-nine feet apart with eighty feet between the pairs. Each pair consists of a relatively tall narrow stone and a shorter, broader one — thought to represent male and female symbols. Stretching away into the distance from the circle at *Avebury* they are an imposing sight. Another avenue running from the west entrance to the circle was recorded in the eighteenth century by Stukeley, but it was not until the 1960s that one of the sarsens was recovered. Known as Beckhampton Avenue, the stones ran south in a curve and then possibly continued west after crossing the site of the present A4.

The Sanctuary, Overton Hill

WILTSHIRE

The Sanctuary, its different building periods represented by concentric circles of low concrete posts, lies at the southern end of *West Kennet Avenue*. It is the site of a circular hut which was subsequently enlarged and surrounded by a stone circle. The building was begun *c.*3000 BC and the grave of a young man dating from *c.*2000 BC has been found inside the inner circle. It has been suggested that the bodies of those destined for burial in the chambered tombs, such as *West Kennet Long Barrow*, were kept here prior to burial. The site lies beside the Prehistoric route, the Ridgeway, at its junction with the A4.

The interior of Bradford-on-Avon Tithe Barn showing th fine fourteenth-century roof

West Kennet Long Barrow

WILTSHIRE

This is one of the largest of the Neolithic transepted gallery tombs of the Cotswold-Severn type, a great wedge-shaped mound 330 feet long, orientated east-west. The restored face of upright sarsens erected when the tomb was ceremonially closed is very impressive. Though most of the stones are local, some have been brought from up to twenty miles away. Visitors can enter inside the barrow to see the two pairs of tomb chambers opening off the central gallery with a terminal chamber to the west. For almost 1,000 years the tomb was in use, between 3700 and 3000 BC, and as with other tombs of this type, the bodies were defleshed elsewhere before interment. It is believed that these were collective graves in the Neolithic period, one for each community, without distinction of rank or age. (Thus they can be distinguished from Bronze Age burials which were only for people of importance.) West Kennet forms part of the great *Avebury* complex, lying due south of the henge and close to *Silbury Hill*. The tomb was opened in the seventeenth century but only one of the chambers was disturbed. In 1956 a thorough excavation and restoration was carried out and the remains of forty-six people ranging from babies to the elderly were discovered. All those over thirty has arthritis, some had spina bifida, and an elderly man found in the south-west chamber had a foot bunion and an arrow wound in his wind pipe which probably killed him. The bodies had been dismembered and certain parts, notably the skulls, were missing. Mixed with the bodies were pieces of pottery and other fragments which can be seen in the Devizes Museum. The barrow lies half a mile from the carpark.

The entrance to West Kennet Long Barrow

Bratton Camp and the White Horse

WILTSHIRE

The White Horse below the Iron Age hill fort at Bratton

Wonderful views are to be had from this Iron Age hill fort on top of Westbury Hill. Wedge-shaped in plan, the fort covers twenty-five acres with entrances on the south side and through the north-east corner via which the road now runs. A Neo-lithic long barrow, about 230 feet long, inside the camp, predates it by more than 2,000 years, though neither have been scientifically excavated. The White Horse to the west, a familiar sight to train travellers on the Westbury line, was recut in 1778. Before that date the horse faced in the opposite direction. His pedigree is uncertain. Possibly he was cut to celebrate King Alfred's great victory over the Danes at Ethandun in 878. The precise location of Ethandun is not known for certain either, but it was one of the major battles in British history. As a result Britain was saved from total Danish domin-ation and the country was divided between Alfred's kingdom of Wessex and the Danelaw, a complete change of fortune for Alfred who had spent the previous winter hiding in the marshes at Athelney, in fear of his life.

Netheravon Dovecot

WILTSHIRE

This little eighteenth-century brick dovecot, recently restored, stands in a pleasant orchard. Visitors can see the nesting boxes inside through a grill in the door. For medieval man, doves were an important source of fresh meat during the winter, but by the late eighteenth century they were merely ornamental. This dovecot belonged to Netheravon House, now a barracks, which was built in the eighteenth century and enlarged by Sir John Soane for William Hicks Beach. Mr Hicks Beach employed the Reverend Sydney Smith, the local curate, as tutor to his son. Smith, later famous as a wit and raconteur, did not greatly enjoy his time at Netheravon, for as he once remarked, 'I have no relish for the country; it is a kind of healthy grave'.

Chisbury Chapel

WILTSHIRE

This little thirteenth-century chapel has recently been rescued from use as a farmbuilding and restored. It forms part of Manor Farm (not in the care of English Heritage), which is in turn set within a large oval earthworks of uncertain date. One suggestion made is that this was one of the Saxon burhs, or fortified towns, established by King Alfred in the ninth century. These planned settlements were laid out within either new or existing earthworks and towns such as Lyford and Oxford owe their origins to Alfred's masterly response to the Danish invaders. In this way communications could be kept open and safe refuges provided for the country people in time of war. Train travellers to the West Country can see the earthworks as they pass through the agreeable countryside of the Kennet and Avon Canal between Little and Great Bedwyn, just south of Hungerford.

ABOVE: *Netheravon Dovecot*

BELOW: *Chisbury Chapel*

Ludgershall Castle and Cross

WILTSHIRE

There is not a great deal to see here apart from the remains of some modest eleventh-century earthworks and a bit of twelfth-century tower. Archaeological excavations, however, have revealed at least seven periods of building over a 200-year period, but these are not readily discernible. Who built the castle in the eleventh century is not known, but it belonged to the Crown by the reign of Henry I (1100–1135). Its main function was to provide accommodation for the King when hunting and an aisled Great Hall was erected by Henry II in 1244–45. The royal account books provide some interesting glimpses into the interior of the castle. For instance, the piers of the Great Hall were painted to imitate marble, the King and Queens' bedroom had wooden panelling, and in 1251 King Edward's son's room had two fireplaces and two privy chambers. The ovens were big enough to roast two or three oxen at one time. Leland described the castle as 'clene down' in the sixteenth century. The defaced remains of a cross can be found opposite the police station in Castle Street. Only the head has survived, surrounded by some mutilated Victorian railings. Earlier visitors were able to identify two of the four sculptured faces as depicting the Descent from the Cross and the Incredulity of St Thomas. Today one has to take this on trust. After this woebegone piece of masonry a visit to the parish church is called for to see the particularly fine sixteenth-century monument to Sir Charles Brydges, died 1558. His wife was a daughter of Sir William Spencer of Althorp.

Old Sarum

WILTSHIRE

Old Sarum is one of those interesting cases of history of 'what might have been'. For here in the twelfth century stood a walled city complete with castle, cathedral, bishop's palace and houses; a thirty-acre site set in an Iron Age hillfort. Where are they now? The cathedral and town are in New Sarum, Salisbury, only the foundations of the former survive, and the Norman castle, whose occupants were the main cause of the town's removal, stands not much higher. Although unoccupied, Old Sarum continued to return a Member of Parliament until 1832, by which time it was one of the most infamous of the 'rotten boroughs'. To appreciate the topography of the site, it is best seen from the west looking to the hillfort across the Avon valley from the A360. Fine views of the countryside can be had from the ramparts and the motte, and this is a popular spot for walks. The Iron Age hillfort had a single bank and ditch which was partly redug by the Normans. The site must have been important in Roman times as a number of Roman roads including Portway and Ackling Dyke converge here. There is some evidence that it was also occupied in Saxon times. The large motte dates from *c.*1078, while the curtain walls and gatehouse are twelfth century, as are the foundations of Bishop Roger's Palace that stands in the inner bailey on the motte. He also built Sherborne Old Castle. The cathedral, begun at the same time, was largely destroyed by a storm in 1092, five days after its

RIGHT: foundations of the Norman castle at Old Sarum

BELOW: the remains of Ludgershall Castle

consecration. By the beginning of the next century it had been rebuilt and stood for about 100 years. By 1226 it had been removed. Carved fragments from the cathedral can be seen in the exhibition on site and Salisbury Museum has a lot of interesting material.

Earl's Farm Down Barrows, Amesbury
WILTSHIRE

On the south side of the River Avon where it runs parallel with the A303 are four small Bronze Age round barrows. They are now to be seen against a backdrop of council housing, with army buildings much in evidence. The site was formerly known as Ratfyn Barrows.

Old Wardour Castle
WILTSHIRE

Old Wardour has always delighted visitors and owners alike, and the latter have shown it great respect from the consciously Gothic alterations of the late sixteenth century to the romantic landscaping of the eighteenth century. Begun in 1393 the castle has a unique plan which, like that of *Nunney*, derives from French castles seen during the Hundred Years War. Tall and compact, it is hexagonal, with the sixth side, the entrance front (north-east) distinguished by two square towers. The hexagonal interior courtyard was little more than a light well, though the effect is now lost since the south-west front was destroyed during the Civil War. Between 1576 and 1578 Robert Smythson, the architect of Longleat, enlarged the windows in an old-fashioned style so as to be in keeping with the building, at the same time creating a very up-to-date classical gateway with alcoves, and redecorating the interior, now unfortunately lost. He also erected the outer curtain wall which echoes the hexagonal plan of the castle. The damage done during the Civil War was the result of two heroic sieges. The first was when Lady Blanche Arundell held the castle against the Parliamentarians led by Sir Edward Hungerford, (whose fine tomb can be seen at *Farleigh Hungerford*). During the second and

much longer siege, Parliament defied Lord Arundell, who at length resorted to destroying part of his own home in order to dislodge them. That was a siege 'famous to posterity, both for active and passive valour to the utmost', as a contemporary put it. In the 1770s New Wardour Castle (now a school) was built to the north-west and the old castle and park landscaped. A delightful Gothic-style banqueting house, a suitable venue for the Hell Fire Club if they ever met this far west, was erected by the curtain wall overlooking the lake. It has recently been restored. On the other side of the castle, on the edge of the woodlands, is an extremely large grotto. It must be one of the largest eighteenth-century grottos to survive. What is all the more extraordinary is that it is built of plaster over brick with a minimum of stone. It was built by John Lane of Tisbury, a famous grotto builder, or grottoist; a trade that ought to be revived.

Old Wardour Castle

Stonehenge

WILTSHIRE

One piece of magic that never fails is the sight of Stonehenge appearing on the horizon as one travels west along the A303. Here is the finest Prehistoric monument in Europe, and one which every generation seems to find it necessary to reinterpret. Close to, Stonehenge may seem disappointingly small, for we are used to being dwarfed by modern buildings. But think of trying to move these megaliths with only the tools available to Neolithic man, and the perspective changes. The history of the building of Stonehenge still contains many mysteries but three building periods have been identified. The first stage c. 3100 BC was a bank and ditch forming a circle with an entrance in the north-east corner. The entrance is marked by the only unworked stone on the site, the 'heel stone'. Fifty-six small pits containing burials, known as Aubrey's Holes after the antiquarian, formed a circle within the bank: these are now marked by concrete posts. The second stage took place before 2100 BC and involved the transportation of the 'blue stones' from the Prescally Hills in Wales. This enormous undertaking seems only reasonable if these stones were considered 'holy' or prestigious. These eighty stones weighing up to four tons each were brought by water; they may have arrived along a ceremonial path leading to the 'heel stone'. The final stage that created the structure we see today was probably the work of an important local chieftain c. 2000 BC, one of those who lie buried in the Bronze Age barrows nearby. The blue stones were dismantled and naturally eroded sarsens from the Marlborough Downs weighing twenty to eighty tons were added. The construction of the outer circle is unique; the massive stone lintels are morticed-and-tenoned to the uprights upon which they rest, as well as being curved to follow the diameter of the circle. Despite the sophistication of its constructional details, Stonehenge is now seen as a traditional work, belonging in spirit to the earlier Neolithic period, and out of date when built. The Bronze Age used its human resources to create memorials to individual chieftains, rather than the communal works of the earlier more egalitarian society. But then this is merely an opinion of the 1980s and will no doubt go the way of Roman temples, Druids, space ship launch pads and Mycenean architects, all earlier interpretations.

Woodhenge

WILTSHIRE

Disrespectfully referred to as 'concrete henge' by some visitors, these are the foundations of a large circular timber building composed of six concentric rings of timber posts which have been marked out with low concrete piles. The posts would have supported a thatched conical roof and looked rather like an African tribal hut, though this is still a matter of debate among some archaeologists. It has been dated to c. 2300 BC. A henge is by definition a circular ceremonial site surrounded by a bank and a ditch, and while the most famous ones, *Stonehenge* and *Avebury*, have stone settings, others with timber superstructures have been discovered in the twentieth century by the use of aerial photography. Woodhenge and the adjoining Durrington Walls (not English Heritage) are two. The latter stands about 150 yards to the north of Woodhenge, about 550 yards across and thirty acres in area, its eastern corner bisected by the A345. It has been calculated that 900,000 man hours went into its creation, which pre-dates Woodhenge by a couple of centuries or so. Unfortunately it is difficult to appreciate at ground level, and its relationship to Woodhenge is easier to understand from the OS map, number 184. A glance at the map also shows the cursus to the west, a long narrow embanked area so named for its similarity to a racecourse. The purpose of these curcuses is unknown, but this one appears to be aligned with the long axis of the concentric oval rings at Woodhenge and points to the rising sun on Midsummer Day.

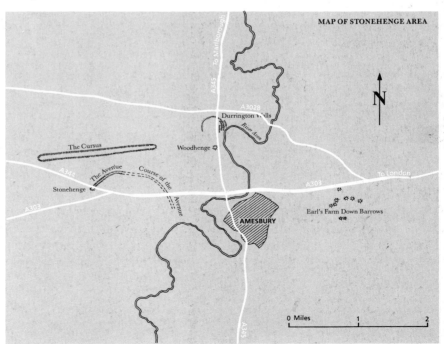

MAP OF STONEHENGE AREA

GLOSSARY

The illustrations below have been included to assist the visitor to English Heritage sites and as such are an impression rather than in all cases architecturally exact.

ABUTMENT
The solid part of a pier or wall which supports the thrust or lateral pressure of an arch.

APSE (noun)
APSIDAL (adj)
Semicircular or polygonal recess in a room or building, such as at the east end of a church. church.

ARCH BRACED ROOF

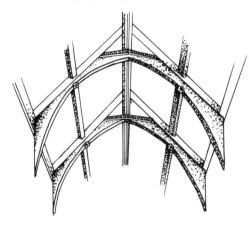

ASHLAR
Squared hewn stone laid in regular courses with fine vertical joints.

BAILEY
The defended courtyard of a castle. See MOTTE.

BARBICAN
Outwork or extension defending the entrance to a castle, often with two towers erected over a gate or bridge and linked by a narrow passage forming a potential death trap for attackers.

BARROW
Mound of earth and/or stones raised over a burial. Also known as TUMULUS. Long barrows mainly Neolithic, round barrows mainly Bronze Age. Round barrows sub-divided into different types named after their shape in cross section:

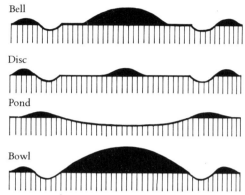

Bell

Disc

Pond

Bowl

BASTION
A projection from outer walls of fort or castle, enabling defenders to use flanking fire along the walls. Increasingly complex from mid sixteenth century and included earthwork bastions beyond the walls of the fort or castle. Named after that shape on plan, semicircular and angle are the two main types with arrowhead a refinement of the latter.

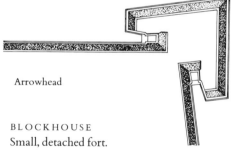

Arrowhead

BLOCKHOUSE
Small, detached fort.

BOSS
A knob or ornamented projection usually covering the intersection of ribs in a vault or ceiling.

BUTTERY
In a medieval dwelling, a small room opening off the SCREENS PASSAGE where ale and provisions were kept.

CAIRN
A heap or mound of stones. In prehistory usually covering a burial, although some were used for ceremonial purposes, while others were boundary markers.

CAMBERED
Slightly curved or arched.

CAPITAL
Head or crowning feature of a column or PILASTER. Examples in Gothic architecture:

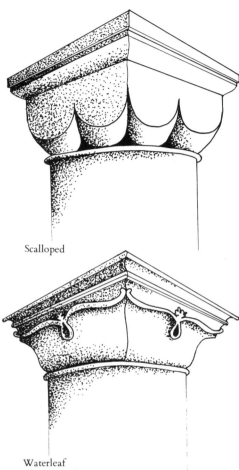

Scalloped

Waterleaf

CASTELLATED
Built in the style of a castle and decorated with battlements.

CHAMFER
The surface produced by planing off a square edge at 45°.

CHAPTER
A meeting of members of a religious house, held daily in a monastery to discuss business and hear a chapter of the monastic rule. Hence their meeting place, the CHAPTER HOUSE.

CINQUEFOIL
Five leaf, or foil-shape, often found in the head of an opening to a window, etc. in Gothic architecture.

Cinquefoil window

CLAUSTRAL (adj)
Pertaining to a CLOISTER — the covered walk or arcade enclosing the open court of a quadrangle; in a monastery, linking main buildings.

COLLAR BEAM ROOF

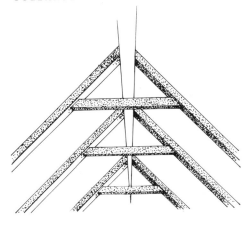

CORBEL
A block of stone or wood projecting out from a wall to support feature such as a roof timber.

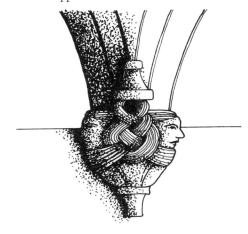

COVE
In archaeology, a U-shaped arrangement of standing stones, usually in or near a stone circle.

COVED CORNICE
Concave moulding in angle between wall and ceiling.

CRENELLATED (adj)
Furnished with battlements: a parapet pierced with openings known as EMBRASURES, the raised portions between being called merlons.

CROCKETED (adj)
In Gothic architecture, the small ornaments in the form of buds or curled leaves found on the edge of any sloping edge, eg a pinnacle.

CROWN POST ROOF

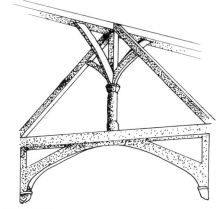

CUPMARKS
Circular indentations found on prehistoric stones — purpose unknown.

CUPOLA
A small circular or polygonal domed turret crowning a roof.

CUSPED (adj)
In Gothic architecture the cusp is the projecting point where two foils, or concave arches in the form of leaves, meet. See CINQUEFOIL.

CUTWATER
On a bridge, the extension of the pier in a wedge shape or angle to divide the current and preserve the bridge's structure from the destructive force of the river. Sometimes known as a starling.

DADO
The decorative covering of the lower part of an interior wall, sometimes topped with a dado rail, taking its name from classical architecture.

EMBRASURE
Opening in a parapet, battlement or wall, usually splayed and used for artillery.

FLUSHWORK
Decorative use of dressed flint and ASHLAR stone forming patterns.

FOGOU
Also known outside Cornwall as a souterrain. Undergound passage(s) and/or chambers, sometimes roofed over and used for refuge or storage in prehistory.

FOREBUILDING
In a castle, when the main entrance of the keep is at first floor level the stairway is contained within the forebuilding, sometimes with a room, or rooms, above.

FOREWORK
Outwork defences, guarding an entrance, usually earthworks.

FRIGIDARIUM
The cooling room of a Roman bath.

GARDEROBE
Privy.

GARTH
The area enclosed by the cloisters.

GUN PORT
Opening in a wall for artillery.

HAMMER BEAM ROOF

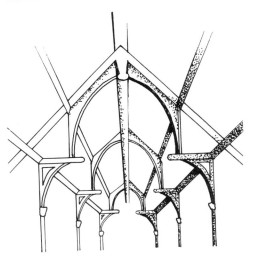

HENGE
Circular ceremonial earthwork surrounded by a ditch, with an inner or outer bank and one or two entrances. Some are edged with a circle of stones, others had a ring of timber posts.

HYPOCAUST
A room heated from below; the Roman method of central heating.

KING POST ROOF

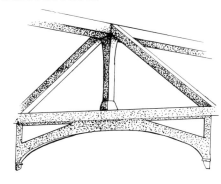

KNAPPED FLINT
Shaped, flaked flint forming cutting edge.

LAVATORIUM
A bowl or trough with running water where the monks washed their hands before meals. Usually built into the wall of the refectory, sometimes free standing in the cloister garth.

LAVER
In the Middle Ages, small recess built into wall for washbasin, sometimes with a drain.

LOBED SURROUND
In Romanesque architecture, semicircular shapes linked by CUSPS around an opening.

LOGGIA
An arcade or gallery having at least one of its sides open to the air.

MANGONEL
A medieval siege engine that threw projectiles. It operated on the principle of torsion, using twisted ropes.

MOTTE AND BAILEY
An artificial mound, fortification or early castle, originally carrying a timber structure. An area around the motte was enclosed by fortifications forming the BAILEY.

MULLION
A vertical bar dividing a window into lights.

NEWEL POST
The post at the head or foot of a length of stair supporting the handrail.

OBELISK
A tapering shaft of stone, square or rectangular in section, with a pyramidal top.

OGEE
In Gothic architecture, a double curve bending first one way and then the other.

Ogee

ORIEL
A bay window carried on corbels or brackets and projecting from a wall. An ORIEL BAY, a bay window of more than one storey which rises from ground floor level.

ORNE
Picturesque detailing emphasising the rusticity of a cottage or farm: popular late eighteenth to early nineteenth century.

PARALLEL RANGE
A double span roof.

PEDIMENT
In classical architecture a triangular shape or formalised gable, originating on the front of a temple, and also used over doors and windows, etc.

PILASTER
Rectangular column projecting slightly from wall; PILASTER BUTTRESS a buttress or support taking this form.

PISCINA
In a church, the basin for washing communion vessels set in the south wall of the chancel beside the altar.

POMPEIAN
In the manner of the ancient Roman style of wall decoration, named after the largest surviving collection of painted walls, to be seen at Pompei.

PORTE-COCHÈRE
A porch large enough for wheeled carriages to pass through.

PRECENTOR
Official in monastery who leads or directs the singing of a choir or congregation:

PRESBYTERY
The part of the church to the east of the choir, reserved for the clergy.

PULPITUM
In large medieval churches, the stone screen dividing the nave from the choir.

PUTLOG HOLES
Also known as putlock, the holes made in a wall to take the putlogs or horizontal timbers on which scaffolding boards were laid.

QUATREFOIL
Four leaf, see CINQUEFOIL.

REAR ARCH
In Gothic architecture the opening of an arched window on the interior as distinct from the exterior wall. The head of the opening is sometimes decorated.

REDOUBT
A detached earthwork fortification which is part of a large-scale system of fortifications.

REREDORTER
Latrine block situated at the back of a dormitory in a monastery or convent.

REREDOS
Ornamental screen behind and above an altar.

REVEALS
The sides of an opening, set at right angles to the vertical face of the wall opening.

ROOD SCREEN
A rood is a cross, and a rood screen is a screen dividing the nave from the chancel which was originally surmounted by a cross. (The crosses were nearly all destroyed at the Reformation.)

RUSTICATED
Exaggerated treatment of joints in masonry construction to give a greater feeling of strength and solidity.

SACRISTY
In a church, a room for keeping sacred vessels and vestments.

SARSENS
Large blocks or boulders of sandstone found in certain areas of Southern England and used in the construction of burial chambers and stone circles by prehistoric man.

SCISSOR BRACED ROOF

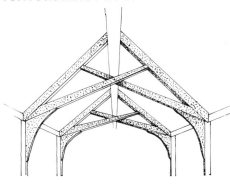

SCREENS PASSAGE
Cross passage between great hall and service rooms, separated from hall by a screen.

SEDILIA
Seats for the clergy, usually three in number, set into the south wall of the chancel.

SOLAR
An upper living room leading off hall of a medieval house, literally meaning sun room.

SPICERY
A room in which spices were kept in a large medieval house.

STRING-COURSE
Horizontal stone or brick course, or moulding, projecting from the surface of a wall.

TRACERY
Intersecting ribwork in the upper part of a window, being the decorative termination of the MULLIONS. Divided into two general types: PLATE tracery where decorative openings are cut through the solid wall at the head of the window, and the later BAR tracery, introduced *c.*1250 into England, where the mullions are continued as a decorative pattern. GEOMETRICAL tracery is a type of bar tracery characteristic of the period *c.*1250-1310 and composed mainly of circles and foiled circles.

TREFOIL
Three leaf, see CINQUEFOIL.

TUMULUS
A word for burial mound first used by the early antiquaries in the late seventeenth century and derived from the latin, *tumere*, to swell.

TYMPANUM
In classical architecture, the vertical recessed face of a PEDIMENT, often covered with sculpture; similarly in Gothic architecture the area over a doorway adorned with sculpture.

UNDERCROFT
A vaulted room, sometimes partly underground, with a more important room above.

VALLUM
The ditch on the south side of Hadrian's Wall.

VAULT

Barrel Vault

Quatripartite Vault

WAGON-ROOF
Closely set rafters with ARCH BRACES usually panelled or plastered and giving the effect of being inside a canvas-roofed wagon.

WARD
See BAILEY, the fortified courtyard of a castle.

WIND BRACE
In a roof, timbers set diagonally to strengthen the frame of rafters — either curved or straight and sometimes ornamented.

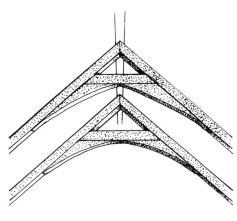

GAZETTEER

Opening hours vary considerably and it is advisable to telephone the monument, where a number is given, or ring English Heritage (01–734 6010) before setting off in order to avoid disappointment.

To assist the reader those archaeological sites that may be difficult to locate have been defined by their Ordnance Survey map number (OS) and National Grid Reference (NGR).

ABBOTSBURY ABBEY REMAINS
Abbotsbury, near Weymouth, Dorset

ABINGDON COUNTY HALL
The Market Place, Abingdon, Oxfordshire

ACTON BURNELL CASTLE
Acton Burnell, near Shrewsbury, Shropshire

ALDBOROUGH ROMAN TOWN
Aldborough, near Boroughbridge, North Yorkshire Tel: (09012) 2768

AMBLESIDE ROMAN FORT
Waterhead, Ambleside, Cumbria

APPULDURCOMBE HOUSE
Wroxall, near Ventor, Isle of Wight
Tel: (0983) 852484

ARBOR LOW
2m S of Monyash, 9 m SSE of Buxton, Derbyshire
OS Map 119; NGR SK 161 636

ARTHUR'S ROUND TABLE
Eamont Bridge, near Penrith, Cumbria
OS Map 90; NGR NY 523 284

ARTHUR'S STONE, DORSTONE
1m NNE of Dorstone, E of Hay-on-Wye, Hereford and Worcester
OS Map 148; NGR SO 319 431

ASHBY DE LA ZOUCH CASTLE
Ashby de la Zouch, Leicestershire
Tel: (0530) 413343

AUCKLAND CASTLE DEER HOUSE
Bishop Auckland Park, Durham

AUDLEY END HOUSE AND PARK
Near Saffron Walden, Essex Tel: (0799) 22399

AVEBURY MUSEUM
Avebury, near Marlborough, Wiltshire
Tel: (06723) 250

AVEBURY STONE CIRCLES
Avebury, near Marlborough, Wiltshire

AYDON CASTLE
Near Corbridge, Northumberland
Tel: (043471) 2450

BACONSTHORPE CASTLE
N of Baconsthorpe, near Holt, Norfolk
OS Map 133; NGR TG 122 382

BANKS EAST TURRET (52a)
E of Banks village, Brampton, Cumbria, Hadrian's Wall
OS Map 86; NGR NY 575 647

BANT'S CARN BURIAL CHAMBER AND ANCIENT VILLAGE
1m N of Hugh Town, St Mary's, Isles of Scilly
OS Map 203; NGR SV 911 124

BARNARD CASTLE
Barnard Castle, Durham

BARTON-UPON-HUMBER: ST PETER'S CHURCH
Barton-upon-Humber, Humberside

BATTLE ABBEY
High Street, Battle, near Hastings, East Sussex
Tel: (04246) 3792

BAYARD'S COVE FORT
Bayard's Cove, Dartmouth, Devon

BAYHAM ABBEY
Near Lamberhurst, East Sussex
Tel: (0892) 890381

BEESTON CASTLE
Beeston, near Nantwich, Cheshire

BELAS KNAP LONG BARROW
Between Winchcombe and Charlton Abbots, near Cheltenham, Gloucestershire
OS Map 163; NGR SP 021 254

BELSAY HALL, CASTLE AND GARDENS
Belsay, near Newcastle, Northumberland
Tel: (066181) 636

BENWELL ROMAN TEMPLE
Broomridge Avenue, Benwell, Newcastle, Hadrian's Wall

BENWELL VALLUM CROSSING
Denhill Park Avenue, Benwell, Newcastle, Hadrian's Wall

BERKHAMSTED CASTLE
Adjacent to Berkhamsted Station, near Hemel Hempsted, Hertfordshire

BERNEY ARMS WINDMILL
Accessible by boat or train only, near bank of River Yare, Berney Arms Station, near Great Yarmouth, Norfolk Tel: (0493) 700605
OS Map 134; NGR TG 465 051

BERRY POMEROY CASTLE
Off A385 E of Totnes, Devon

BERWICK-UPON-TWEED CASTLE
Adjacent to railway station, Berwick-upon-Tweed, Northumberland

BERWICK-UPON-TWEED RAMPARTS
Surrounding town centre, Berwick-upon-Tweed, Northumberland

BERWICK-UPON-TWEED: RAVENSDOWNE BARRACKS
The Parade, Church Street, Berwick-upon-Tweed, Northumberland
Tel: (0289) 304493

BINHAM PRIORY
Binham, near Wells-next-the-Sea, Norfolk

BIRDOSWALD FORT, WALL AND TURRET
W of Gilsland, Cumbria, Hadrian's Wall
OS Map 86; NGR NY 615 663

BISHOP'S PALACE, LINCOLN
S side of Lincoln Cathedral, Lincoln, Lincolnshire

BISHOP'S WALTHAM PALACE
Bishop's Waltham, near Winchester, Hampshire
Tel: (04893) 2460

BLACK CARTS TURRET (29a)
2m W of Chollerford, Northumberland,
Hadrian's wall
OS Map 87; NGR NY 884 712

BLACK MIDDENS BASTLE HOUSE
7m NW of Bellingham, Northumberland
OS Map 80; NGR NY 774 900

BLACKBURY CASTLE
SW of Southleigh, 5m NE of Sidmouth, Devon
OS Map 192; NGR SY 188 924

BLACKFRIARS, GLOUCESTER
Southgate Street, Gloucester Tel: (0452) 27688

BLAKENEY GUILDHALL
Blakeney, near Wells-next-the-Sea, Norfolk

BOLINGBROKE CASTLE
Old Bolingbroke, near Spilsby, Lincolnshire

BOLSOVER CASTLE
Bolsover, near Chesterfield, Derbyshire
Tel: (0246) 823349

BOSCOBEL HOUSE
Near Bishop's Wood, NW of Wolverhampton,
Shropshire Tel: (0902) 850244

BOWES CASTLE
Bowes, near Barnard Castle, Durham

BRADFORD-ON-AVON TITHE BARN
Barton Farm, Bradford-on-Avon, Wiltshire

BRAMBER CASTLE
Bramber, near Shoreham-by-Sea, West Sussex

BRATTON CAMP AND THE WHITE
HORSE
Near Westbury, Wiltshire
OS Map 184; NGR ST 900 516

BRINKBURN PRIORY
4½m SE of Rothbury, Northumberland
Tel: (066570) 628

BROUGH CASTLE
Brough, near Appleby, Cumbria

BROUGHAM CASTLE
Brougham, near Penrith, Cumbria
Tel: (0768) 62488

BROUGHAM: COUNTESS PILLAR
On A66 1m SE of Brougham, near Penrith,
Cumbria

BRUNTON TURRET (26b)
¼m S of Low Brunton, near Chollerford,
Northumberland, Hadrian's Wall
OS Map 87; NGR NY 928 696

BUILDWAS ABBEY
Near Iron Bridge, Shropshire Tel: (095245) 3274

BURGH CASTLE
W end of Breydon Water, 3m W of Great
Yarmouth, Norfolk
OS Map 134; NGR TG 475 046

BURTON AGNES MANOR HOUSE
Burton Agnes, near Bridlington, Humberside

BURY ST EDMUNDS ABBEY
Bury St Edmunds, Suffolk

BUSHMEAD PRIORY
Near Colmworth, 6m NNE of Bedford,
Bedfordshire Tel: (023062) 614
OS Map 153; NGR TL 115 607

BYLAND ABBEY
Near Wass, between Helmsley and Thirsk,
North Yorkshire Tel: (03476) 614

CAISTER ROMAN SITE
Caister-on-Sea, near Great Yarmouth, Norfolk

CALSHOT CASTLE
On spit 2m SW of Fawley, W side of
Southampton Water, Hampshire
Tel: (0703) 892023

CANTLOP BRIDGE
E of Condover, near Shrewsbury, Shropshire
OS Map 126; NGR SJ 517 062

CARISBROOKE CASTLE
Newport, Isle of Wight Tel: (0983) 522107

CARLISLE CASTLE
N side of Carlisle, Cumbria Tel: (0228) 31777

CARN EUNY ANCIENT VILLAGE
1¼m SW of Sancreed, near Penzance, Cornwall
OS Map 203; NGR SW 402 289

CARN GLOOSE (BALLOWALL BARROW)
1m W of St Just, near Penzance, Cornwall
OS Map 203; NGR SW 354 313

CARRAWBURGH: TEMPLE OF MITHRAS
3¾m W of Chollerford, Northumberland,
Hadrian's Wall
OS Map 87; NGR NY 869 713

CASTLE ACRE CASTLE AND BAILEY
GATE
CASTLE ACRE PRIORY
Castle Acre, near Swaffham, Norfolk
Tel: (07605) 394 (the Priory)

CASTLE RISING CASTLE
Castle Rising, near King's Lynn, Norfolk
Tel: (055387) 330

CASTLERIGG STONE CIRCLE
1½m E of Keswick, Cumbria
OS Map 90; NGR NY 293 236

CAWFIELDS ROMAN WALL AND
MILECASTLE (42)
1¼m N of Haltwhistle, Northumberland,
Hadrian's Wall
OS Map 87; NGR NY 716 667

CHATHAM DOCKYARD TIMBER
SEASONING SHEDS
Royal Naval Dockyard, Chatham, Kent
Tel: (0634) 812551

CHESTER CASTLE: AGRICOLA TOWER
AND CASTLE WALLS
Grosvenor Street, Chester, Cheshire

CHESTER ROMAN AMPHITHEATRE
Vicars Lane beyond Newgate, Chester, Cheshire

CHESTERHOLM (VINDOLANDA) FORT
AND ROMAN MILESTONE
1¼m SE of Twice Brewed, Northumberland,
Hadrian's Wall Tel: (04984) 277

CHESTERS BRIDGE ABUTMENT
On E bank of North Tyne River opposite
Chesters Fort, footpath from B6318 (½m), near
Chollerford Bridge, Northumberland, Hadrian's
Wall
OS Map 87; NGR NY 914 700

CHESTERS FORT AND MUSEUM
Near Chollerford, Northumberland, Hadrian's
Wall Tel: (043481) 379

CHICHELE COLLEGE
College Street, Higham Ferrers, near
Wellingborough, Northamptonshire

CHISBURY CHAPEL
Manor Farm, Chisbury, near Hungerford,
Wiltshire

CHISWICK HOUSE
Burlington Lane, London W4 Tel: (01) 995 0508

CHRISTCHURCH CASTLE AND NORMAN HOUSE
Near the Priory church, Christchurch, Dorset

CHYSAUSTER ANCIENT VILLAGE
2½m NW of Gulval, near Penzance, Cornwall
Tel: (0736) 61889
OS Map 203; NGR SW 473 350

CIRENCESTER AMPHITHEATRE
Next to bypass on W side of town, park in
Cirencester or in Cotswold Ave to S of
Amphitheatre by obelisk, Gloucestershire
OS Map 163; NGR SP 020 014

CLEEVE ABBEY
Washford, near Minehead, Somerset
Tel: (0984) 4377

CLIFFORD'S TOWER, YORK
Castle Street, York, North Yorkshire
Tel: (0904) 646940

CLIFTON HALL
By Clifton Hall Farm, Clifton, near Penrith,
Cumbria

CONISBROUGH CASTLE
Conisbrough, near Doncaster, South Yorkshire
Tel: (0709) 863329

CORBRIDGE ROMAN SITE
½m NW of Corbridge, near Hexham,
Northumberland, Hadrian's Wall
Tel: (043471) 2349

COW TOWER, NORWICH
NE of Bishopsgate, Norwich, Norfolk

CREAKE ABBEY
1m N of North Creake, near Fakenham, Norfolk

CROMWELL'S CASTLE
¾m NW of New Grimsby, Tresco, Isles of Scilly
OS Map 203: NGR SV 882 159

CROXDEN ABBEY
Croxden, near Uttoxeter, Staffordshire

DARTMOUTH CASTLE
1m SE of Dartmouth, near Torquay, Devon
Tel: (08043) 3588

DEAL CASTLE
Deal, Kent Tel: (0304) 372762

DEDDINGTON CASTLE
On E side of village by the sports field, 6m S of
Banbury, Oxfordshire

DENNY ABBEY
2½m from Waterbeach, N of Cambridge
Tel: (0223) 860489
OS Map 154; NGR TL 495 684

DENTON HALL TURRET (7b) AND WEST DENTON
On A69, 4m W of city centre, Newcastle, Tyne
and Wear, Hadrian's Wall
OS Map 88; NGR NZ 195 656

DONNINGTON CASTLE
Donnington, near Newbury, Berkshire

DOVER CASTLE
Dover, Kent Tel: (0304) 201628

DUNSTANBURGH CASTLE
On foot from either Craster or Embleton, near
Alnwick, Northumberland Tel: (066576) 231
OS Map 75; NGR NU 258 220

DUNSTER: BUTTER CROSS
400 yds NW of parish church, Dunster,
Somerset
OS Map 181: NGR SS 988 439

DUNSTER: GALLOX BRIDGE
S end of village, Dunster, Somerset
OS Map 181; NGR SS 990 432

DUNSTER: YARN MARKET
High Street, Dunster, near Minehead, Somerset

DUPATH WELL, CALLINGTON
1m E of Callington, near Liskeard, Cornwall
OS Map 201; NGR SX 374 693

DUXFORD CHAPEL
By Whittlesford Station, 8m S of Cambridge,
Cambridgeshire
OS Map 154; NGR TL 486 472

DYMCHURCH MARTELLO TOWER NO 24
On the seafront at Dymchurch, near Folkestone,
Kent Tel: (0303) 873684

EARL'S FARM DOWN BARROWS, AMESBURY
S side of A303, 1½ E of Amesbury, near
Salisbury, Wiltshire
OS Map 184; NGR SU 180 417

EASBY ABBEY
1m SE of Richmond, North Yorkshire

EDLINGHAM CASTLE
Edlingham (not to be confused with Eglingham),
SW of Alnwick, Northumberland

EDVIN LOACH OLD CHURCH
Edvin Loach, 4m N of Bromyard, near
Worcester, Hereford and Worcester
OS Map 149; NGR SO 663 585

EGGLESTONE ABBEY
1m S of Barnard Castle, Durham

ELEANOR CROSS, GEDDINGTON
Geddington, near Kettering, Northamptonshire

ELTHAM PALACE
Court Yard, Eltham High Street, Eltham,
London SE9 Tel: (01) 859 2112

ETAL CASTLE
Etal, 8m SW of Berwick, Northumberland

EYNSFORD CASTLE
Eynsford, near Orpington, Kent
Tel: (0322) 862536

FARLEIGH HUNGERFORD CASTLE
Farleigh Hungerford, 3½m W of Trowbridge,
Somerset Tel: (02214) 4026

FARNHAM CASTLE KEEP
½m N of Farnham town centre on A287
Tel: (0252) 713393

FAVERSHAM STONE CHAPEL
1¼m W of Faversham, near Sittingbourne, Kent
OS Map 178; NGR TQ 992 614

FIDDLEFORD MILL HOUSE
1m E of Sturminster Newton, near Shaftesbury,
Dorset Tel: (0258) 52597

FINCHALE PRIORY
3m NE of Durham Tel: (0385) 63828

FLITTON: THE DE GREY MAUSOLEUM
Attached to the Church of St John the Baptist,
Flitton, near Ampthill, Bedfordshire
Keyholder: address available at the church

FLOWERDOWN BARROWS
Littleton, 2½m NW of Winchester, Hampshire
OS Map 185; NGR SU 459 320

FORT BROCKHURST
Gunner's Way, Elson, Gosport, Hampshire
Tel: (0705) 581059

FRAMLINGHAM CASTLE
Framlingham, near Saxmundham, Suffolk
Tel: (0728) 723330

FURNESS ABBEY
1½m N of Barrow-in-Furness, Cumbria
Tel: (0229) 23420

GAINSBOROUGH OLD HALL
Parnell Street, Gainsborough, near Lincoln
Tel: (0427) 2669

GAINSTHORPE DESERTED MEDIEVAL
VILLAGE
On minor road W of A15, S of Hibaldstow, 5m
SW of Brigg, Humberside
OS Map 112; NGR SK 955 012

GARRISON WALLS
Encircling the headland W of Hugh Town, St
Mary's, Isles of Scilly
OS Map 203; NGR SV 898 104

GILSLAND VICARAGE ROMAN WALL
In former vicarage garden, Gilsland, near
Haltwhistle, Northumberland, Hadrian's Wall
OS Map 86; NGR NY 632 662

GLASTONBURY TRIBUNAL
High Street, Glastonbury, Somerset
Tel: (0458) 32949

GOODRICH CASTLE
5m S of Ross-on-Wye, Hereford and Worcester
Tel: (0600) 890538

GOODSHAW CHAPEL
Goodshaw, 2m N of Rawtenstall, near Burnley,
Lancashire
Keyholder: H. Rigby, 717 Burnley Road,
Crawshaw Booth, Rossendale, Lancs

THE GRANGE, NORTHINGTON
4m NW of New Alresford, near Winchester,
Hampshire
OS Map 185: NGR SU 562 362

GREAT YARMOUTH: GREYFRIARS'
CLOISTER
OLD MERCHANT'S HOUSE AND ROW
111 HOUSES
Guided tours from Row 111 House, Great
Yarmouth, Norfolk
Tel: (0493) 857900

GREYFRIARS, GLOUCESTER
Behind Eastgate Market, off Southgate Street,
Gloucester

GRIME'S GRAVES
Near Brandon, 7, NW of Thetford, Norfolk
Tel: (0842) 810656
OS Map 144; NGR TL 818898

GRIMSPOUND
W of Manaton, 6m SW of Moretonhampstead,
Devon
OS Map 191; NGR SX 701 809

GUISBOROUGH PRIORY
Guisborough, near Middlesbrough, Cleveland
Tel: (0287) 38301

HADLEIGH CASTLE
S of Hadleigh, near Southend-on-Sea, Essex

HAILES ABBEY
2m NE of Winchcombe, near Cheltenham,
Gloucestershire
Tel: (0242) 602398

HALLIGGYE FOGOU
E of Garras, 5m SE of Helston, Cornwall
OS Map 203; NGR SW 714 239

HARDKNOTT ROMAN FORT
Hardknott Pass, 9m NE of Ravenglass, Cumbria
OS Map 96; NGR NY 218 015

HARDWICK OLD HALL
6½m NW of Mansfield, 9½m SE of
Chesterfield, Derbyshire

HARE HILL
¾m NE of Lanercost, Cumbria, Hadrian's Wall
OS Map 86; NGR NY 562 646

HARROW'S SCAR MILECASTLE (49)
¼m E of Birdoswald Fort, 2¾m W of
Greenhead, Cumbria, Hadrian's Wall
OS Map 86; NGR NY 621 664

HARRY'S WALLS
¼m NE of Hugh Town, St Mary's, Isles of Scilly
OS Map 203; NGR SV 910 110

HAUGHMOND ABBEY
3m NE of Shrewsbury, Shropshire
Tel: (074377) 661

HEDDON-ON-THE-WALL
E of Heddon, near Newcastle, Tyne and Wear,
Hadrian's Wall
OS Map 88; NGR NZ 136 669

HELMSLEY CASTLE
Helmsley, North Yorkshire Tel: (0439) 70442

HETTY PEGLER'S TUMP (ULEY LONG
BARROW)
3½m NE of Dursley, 6m SW of Stroud,
Gloucestershire
OS Map 162; NGR SO 790 000

HORNE'S PLACE CHAPEL, APPLEDORE
1½m N of Appledore, 5m SE of Tenterden,
Kent

HOUGHTON HOUSE
1m NE of Ampthill, 8m S of Bedford,
Bedfordshire

HOUND TOR DESERTED MEDIEVAL
VILLAGE
1½m S of Manaton, near Moretonhampstead,
Devon
OS Map 191; NGR SX 748 796

HOUSESTEADS ROMAN FORT
2¾ NE of Bardon Mill, Northumberland,
Hadrian's Wall Tel: (04984) 363

HURLERS STONE CIRCLE
½m SW of Minions, N of Liskeard, Cornwall
OS Map 201; NGR SX 258 714

HURST CASTLE
On foot or by ferry to pebble spit S of Keyhaven,
near Lymington, Hampshire Tel: (05904) 2344

HYLTON CASTLE
3m NW of Sunderland, Tyne and Wear Tel:
(0783) 495048

INNISIDGEN LOWER AND UPPER
BURIAL CHAMBERS
1¾m NE of Hugh Town, St Mary's, Isles of
Scilly
OS Map 203; NGR SV 921 127

IRON BRIDGE
Iron Bridge, near Telford, Shropshire

ISLEHAM PRIORY CHURCH
Isleham, near Soham, 10m SE of Ely,
Cambridgeshire

JEWEL TOWER, WESTMINSTER
Abingdon Street, London SW1
Tel: (01) 222 2219

JEWRY WALL, LEICESTER
St Nicholas Street, Leicester, Leicestershire

JORDAN HILL ROMAN TEMPLE
2m NE of Weymouth, Dorset
OS Map 194; NGR SY 698 821

KENILWORTH CASTLE
Kenilworth, near Warwick, Warwickshire
Tel: (0926) 52078

KENWOOD
Hampstead Lane, London NW3
Tel: (01) 348 1286

KING CHARLES'S CASTLE
¾m NW of New Grimsby, Tresco, Isles of Scilly
OS Map 203; NGR SV 882 161

KING DONIERT'S STONE
1m NW of St Cleer, N of Liskeard, Cornwall
OS Map 201; NGR SX 236 688

KINGSTON RUSSELL STONE CIRCLE
W of Kingston Russell, 2m N of Abbotsbury,
near Weymouth, Dorset
OS Map 194; NGR SY 577 878

KINGSWOOD ABBEY GATEHOUSE
Kingswood, 1m SW of Wotton-under-Edge,
near Stroud, Gloucestershire

KIRBY HALL
Near Deene, 4m NE of Corby,
Northamptonshire Tel: (0536) 203230

KIRBY MUXLOE CASTLE
Kirby Muxloe, 4m W of Leicester, Leicestershire
Tel: (0533) 386886

KIRKHAM HOUSE, PAIGNTON
Kirkham Street, off Cecil Road, Paignton,
Devon Tel: (0803) 522775

KIRKHAM PRIORY
Kirkham, 5m SW of Malton, North Yorkshire
Tel: (065381) 768

KIT'S COTY HOUSE AND LITTLE KIT'S
COTY HOUSE
Near Aylesford, 2m N of Maidstone, Kent
OS Map 188; NGR TQ 745 608 & 745 604

KNIGHTS TEMPLAR CHURCH, DOVER
Western Heights, Dover, Kent

KNOWLTON CHURCH AND
EARTHWORKS
S of Wimborne St Giles, 3m SW of Cranborne,
Dorset
OS Map 195; NGR SU 024 100

LANDGUARD FORT, FELIXSTOWE
1m S of Felixstowe, near docks, Suffolk
Tel Area Office: (0223) 358911 ext 2245

LANERCOST PRIORY
S of Lanercost, 2m NE of Brampton, Cumbria
Tel: (06977) 3030

LANGLEY CHAPEL
1½m S of Acton Burnell, 9½m S of Shrewsbury,
Shropshire Tel Area Office: (0902) 765105

LAUNCESTON CASTLE
Launceston, Cornwall Tel: (0566) 2365

LEAHILL TURRET (51b)
2m W of Birdoswald Fort, Cumbria, Hadrian's
Wall
OS Map 86; NGR NY 585 653

LEISTON ABBEY
1m N of Leiston, E of Saxmundham, Suffolk

LEXDEN STRAIGHT ROAD AND
BLUEBOTTLE GROVE EARTHWORKS
Lexden Straight Road and Park Road, 2m W of
Colchester, Essex
OS Map 168; NGR TL 963 240

LILLESHALL ABBEY
Lilleshall, 5m N of Telford, Shropshire
Tel: (0952) 604431

LINDISFARNE PRIORY
Holy Island (reached at low tide across a
causeway), Northumberland Tel: (028989) 200

LONDON WALL, TOWER HILL
Near Tower Hill Underground Station, London
EC3

LONGTHORPE TOWER
Longthorpe, 2m W of Peterborough,
Cambridgeshire Tel: (0733) 268482

LONGTOWN CASTLE
Longtown, 4m WSW of Abbey Dore, SW of
Hereford, Hereford and Worester

LUDGERSHALL CASTLE AND CROSS
Ludgershall, 6m NW of Andover, Wiltshire

LULLINGSTONE ROMAN VILLA
½m SE of Eynsford, W of Orpington, Kent
Tel: (0322) 863467

LYDDINGTON BEDE HOUSE
Lyddington, 6m N of Corby, Leicestershire
Tel: (057282) 2438

LYDFORD CASTLE, BANKS AND FORT
In Lydford, off A386 S of Okeham
OS Map 191; NGR SX 510 848

MAIDEN CASTLE
2½m SW of Dorchester, Dorset
OS Map 194; NGR SY 670 885

MAISON DIEU, OSPRINGE
On A2 in Ospringe, ½m W of Faversham, Kent
Tel: (0795) 762604

MARBLE HILL HOUSE
Richmond Road, Twickenham, Middlesex
Tel: (01) 892 5115

MARMION TOWER
West Tanfield, N of Ripon, North Yorkshire

MATTERSEY PRIORY
1m E of Mattersey, 7m N of East Retford,
Nottinghamshire

MAYBURGH EARTHWORK
Eamont Bridge, 1m S of Penrith, Cumbria
OS Map 90; NGR NY 519 285

MEARE FISH HOUSE
Meare, near Glastonbury, Somerset

MERRIVALE PREHISTORIC SITE
1m E of Merrivale, 5m E of Tavistock, Devon
OS Map 191; NGR SX 553 746

MIDDLEHAM CASTLE
Middleham, 2m S of Leyburn, near Richmond,
North Yorkshire
Tel: (0969) 23899

MILTON CHANTRY, GRAVESEND
Fort Gardens, Gravesend, Kent
Tel: (0474) 321520

MINSTER LOVELL HALL AND DOVECOT
By Minster Lovell Church, 3m W of Witney,
Oxfordshire Tel: (0993) 75315

MISTLEY TOWERS
Mistley, 9m E of Colchester, Essex

MITCHELL'S FOLD STONE CIRCLE
NE of Priestweston, 16m SW of Shrewsbury,
Shropshire
OS Map 137; NGR SO 306 984

MONK BRETTON PRIORY
1m E of Barnsley town centre, South Yorkshire
Tel: (0226) 204089

MORETON CORBET CASTLE
Moreton Corbet, 7m NE of Shrewsbury,
Shropshire

MORTIMER'S CROSS WATER MILL
Mortimer's Cross, 7m NW of Leominster,
Hereford and Worcester

MOULTON PACKHORSE BRIDGE
Moulton, 4m E of Newmarket, Suffolk
OS Map 154; NGR TL 698 645

MOUNT BATTEN TOWER
RAF Mount Batten, Plymstock, Plymouth,
Devon

MOUNT GRACE PRIORY
S of Ingleby Arncliffe, 7m NE of Northallerton,
North Yorkshire Tel: (0609) 23249

MUCHELNEY ABBEY
Muchelney, 2m S of Langport, Somerset
Tel: (0458) 250664

NETHERAVON DOVECOT
Netheravon, 4½m N of Amesbury, near
Salisbury, Wiltshire

NETLEY ABBEY
Netley, facing Southampton Water, 7m SE of
Southampton, Hampshire Tel: (0703) 453076

NINE LADIES STONE CIRCLE
Stanton Moor, 5m SE of Bakewell, Derbyshire
OS Map 119; NGR SK 253 635

THE NINE STONES, WINTERBOURNE
ABBAS
½m W of Winterbourne Abbas, 4m W of
Dorchester, Dorset
OS Map 194; NGR SY 611 904

NORHAM CASTLE
Norham, 6½m SW of Berwick-upon-Tweed,
Northumberland Tel: (028982) 329

NORTH ELMHAM CATHEDRAL AND
EARTHWORKS
North Elmham, 6m N of East Dereham,
Norfolk

NORTH HINKSEY CONDUIT HOUSE
Harcourt Hill, North Hinksey, 2½m W of
Oxford, Oxfordshire
OS Map 164; NGR SP 494 054

NORTH LEIGH ROMAN VILLA
NW of North Leigh, 9m W of Oxford,
Oxfordshire Tel: (0993) 881830

NOTGROVE LONG BARROW
1½m NW of Notgrove, 10m E of Cheltenham,
Gloucestershire
OS Map 163; NGR SP 096 211

NUNNEY CASTLE
Nunney, 3½m SW of Frome, Somerset

NYMPSFIELD LONG BARROW
1m NW of Nympsfield, 4½m SW of Stroud,
Gloucestershire
OS Map 162; NGR SO 795 014

ODDA'S CHAPEL, DEERHURST
Abbots Court, Deerhurst, 3m SW of
Tewkesbury, Gloucestershire

OFFA'S DYKE
This section for walkers only, ½m SE of Tintern,
6m N of Chepstow, Gloucestershire
OS Map 162; NGR SO 545 005

OKEHAMPTON CASTLE
1m SW of Okehampton, Devon

OLD BISHOP'S PALACE, WOLVESEY
College Street, Winchester, Hampshire
Tel: (0962) 54766

OLD BLOCKHOUSE
Blockhouse Point, Old Grimsby harbour,
Tresco, Isles of Scilly
OS Map 203; NGR SV 898 155

OLD GORHAMBURY HOUSE
¼m W of Gorhambury House, access via private
drive to Gorhambury House from A414,
Bluehouse Hill, St Albans, Hertfordshire

OLD OSWESTRY EARTHWORKS
1m N of Oswestry, NW of Shrewsbury,
Shropshire
OS Map 26; NGR SJ 295 310

OLD SARUM
2m N of Salisbury, Wiltshire Tel: (0722) 335398

OLD SOAR MANOR, PLAXTOL
1m E of Plaxtol, N of Tonbridge, Kent

OLD WARDOUR CASTLE
2m SW of Tisbury, 15m W of Salisbury,
Wiltshire Tel: (0747) 870487

ORFORD CASTLE
Orford, 20m NE of Ipswich, Suffolk
Tel: (03944) 50472

OSBORNE HOUSE
1m SE of East Cowes, Isle of Wight
Tel: (0983) 200022

OVER BRIDGE
1m NW of Gloucester city centre at junction of
A40 and A419, Gloucestershire
OS Map 162; NGR SO 817 196

PENDENNIS CASTLE
Pendennis Head, 1m SE of Falmouth, Cornwall
Tel: (0326) 316594

PENRITH CASTLE
Opposite Penrith Station, Cumbria

PEVENSEY CASTLE
Pevensey, 4m NE of Eastbourne, East Sussex
Tel: (0323) 762604

PEVERIL CASTLE
S side of Castleton, 9m NE of Buxton,
Derbyshire Tel: (0433) 20613

PICKERING CASTLE
Pickering, 15m SW of Scarborough, North
Yorkshire Tel: (0751) 74989

PIEL CASTLE
Piel Island (access by ferry from Rhoa Island on
mainland), SE of Barrow-in-Furness, Cumbria
Tel: (0229) 26284

PIERCEBRIDGE ROMAN BRIDGE
Piercebridge, 4m W of Darlington, North
Yorkshire
OS Map 93; NGR NZ 214 154

PIKE HILL SIGNAL TOWER
E of Banks village, NE of Brampton, Cumbria,
Hadrian's Wall
OS Map 86; NGR NY 577 648

PIPER SIKE TURRET (51a)
2m W of Birdoswald Fort, NE of Brampton,
Cumbria, Hadrian's Wall
OS Map 86; NGR NY 588 654

PLANETREES ROMAN WALL
1m SE of Chollerford, N of Hexham,
Northumberland, Hadrian's Wall
OS Map 87; NGR NY 928 696

POLTROSS BURN MILECASTLE (48)
Immediately S of Gilsland village by railway
bridge, Northumberland, Hadrian's Wall
OS Map 86; NGR NY 634 662

POOR LOT BARROWS, WINTERBOURNE
ABBAS
2m W of Winterbourne Abbas, W of
Dorchester, Dorset
OS Map 194; NGR SY 590 906

PORTCHESTER CASTLE
S side of Portchester, near Portsmouth,
Hampshire Tel: (0705) 378291

PORTH HELLICK DOWN BURIAL
CHAMBER
1½m E of Hugh Town, St Mary's, Isles of Scilly
OS Map 203; NGR SV 929 108

PORTLAND CASTLE
By Royal Navy helicopter base, Portland
harbour, S of Weymouth, Dorset
Tel: (0305) 820539

PORTSMOUTH: GARRISON CHURCH
Grand Parade, S of High Street, Portsmouth,
Hampshire

PORTSMOUTH: KING JAMES'S GATE
Entrance United Services Recreation Ground
(officers), Park Road, Portsmouth, Hampshire

PORTSMOUTH: LANDPORT GATE
Entrance to United Services Recreation Ground
(men), St George's Road, Portsmouth,
Hampshire

PRIOR'S HALL BARN, WIDDINGTON
Widdington, 5m S of Saffron Walden, Essex
Tel: (0799) 41047

PRUDHOE CASTLE
Prudhoe, W of Newcastle, Northumberland
Tel: (0661) 33459

RANGER'S HOUSE
Chesterfield Walk, Blackheath, London SE10
Tel: (01) 853 0035

RAVENGLASS ROMAN BATH HOUSE
¼m E of Ravenglass, 14m SSE of Whitehaven,
Cumbria
OS Map 96; NGR NY 088 961

RECULVER TOWERS AND ROMAN FORT
Reculver, 3m E of Herne Bay, Kent
Tel: (02273) 66444

RESTORMEL CASTLE
Restormel, 1½m N of Lostwithiel, Cornwall
Tel: (020887) 2687

RICHBOROUGH CASTLE AND ROMAN
AMPHITHEATRE
1½m N of Sandwich, Kent Tel: (0304) 612013

RICHMOND CASTLE
Richmond, North Yorkshire Tel: (0748) 2493

RIEVAULX ABBEY
2¼m W of Helmsley, North Yorkshire
Tel: (04396) 228

ROCHE ABBEY
1½m S of Maltby, S of Doncaster, South
Yorkshire Tel: (0709) 812739

ROCHESTER CASTLE
Rochester, Kent Tel: (0634) 402276

RODMARTON CHAMBERED TOMB
(WINDMILL TUMP)
1m E of Rodmarton, 6m SW of Cirencester,
Gloucestershire
OS Map 163; NGR ST 933 973

ROMAN PHAROS, DOVER
Dover Castle, Dover, Kent

ROMAN WALL, ST ALBANS
Near Verulamium Museum, Blüehouse Hill, St
Albans, Hertfordshire

ROTHERWAS CHAPEL
Rotherwas Industrial Estate, Dinedor, 1½m SE
of Hereford, Hereford and Worcester
Tel Area Office: (0902) 765105

ROYAL CITADEL, PLYMOUTH
E end of Plymouth Hoe, Plymouth, Devon

RUFFORD ABBEY
Rufford Country Park, 2m S of Ollerton, NE of
Mansfield, Nottinghamshire Tel: (0623) 823148

RUSHTON TRIANGULAR LODGE
1m W of Rushton, 4m NNW of Kettering,
Northamptonshire Tel: (0536) 710761

RYCOTE CHAPEL
3m SW of Thame, E of Oxford, Oxfordshire
Tel: (08447) 346

ST AUGUSTINE'S ABBEY, CANTERBURY
¼m E of Cathedral Close, Canterbury, Kent
Tel: (0227) 67345

ST AUGUSTINE'S CROSS, EBBSFLEET
2m E of Minster, near Ramsgate, Kent
OS Map 179; NGR TR 340 641

ST BOTOLPH'S PRIORY, COLCHESTER
Near St Botolph's Station, Colchester, Essex

ST BREOCK DOWNS MONOLITH
On St Breock Downs, 3¾m SSW of
Wadebridge, Cornwall
OS Map 200; NGR SW 968 683

ST BRIAVELS CASTLE
St Briavels, 7m NNE of Chepstow,
Gloucestershire

ST CATHERINE'S CASTLE, FOWEY
¾m SW of Fowey, E of St Austell, Cornwall

ST CATHERINE'S CHAPEL,
ABBOTSBURY
By a footpath, ½m S of Abbotsbury, near
Weymouth, Dorset

ST CATHERINE'S ORATORY
On foot only, ¾, NW of Niton, W of Ventnor,
Isle of Wight

ST JAMES'S CHAPEL, LINDSEY
½m E of Rose Green, 8m E of Sudbury, Suffolk

ST JOHN'S ABBEY GATE, COLCHESTER
S side of central Colchester, Essex

ST JOHN'S COMMANDERY,
SWINGFIELD
Swingfield, 2m NE of Densole, NW of Dover,
Kent

ST LEONARD'S TOWER, WEST MALLING
SW of West Malling, 5m E of Maidstone, Kent

ST MARY'S CHURCH, KEMPLEY
Kempley, 6m NE of Ross-on-Wye,
Gloucestershire
Tel Area Office: (0272) 734472 ext 205

ST MARY'S CHURCH, STUDLEY ROYAL
Studley Royal Estate, 2½m W of Ripon, North
Yorkshire

ST MAWES CASTLE
St Mawes, near Falmouth, Cornwall
Tel: (0326) 270526

ST OLAVE'S PRIORY
St Olave's, 5½m SW of Great Yarmouth,
Norfolk

ST PAUL'S MONASTERY, JARROW
Jarrow, near Newcastle, Tyne and Wear

THE SANCTUARY, OVERTON HILL
Beside A4, ½m E of West Kennet, near Avebury,
Wiltshire
OS Map 173; NGR SU 118 679

SANDBACH CROSSES
Market Square, Sandbach, NE of Crewe,
Cheshire

SAWLEY ABBEY
Sawley, 3½m N of Clitheroe, Lancashire

SAXTEAD GREEN POST MILL
Saxtead Green, 2½m NW of Framlingham, Suffolk Tel: (0728) 82789

SCARBOROUGH CASTLE
Castle Road, Scarborough, North Yorkshire Tel: (0723) 372451

SEWINGSHIELDS WALL, TURRETS AND MILECASTLE (35)
1½m E of Housesteads Fort, Northumberland, Hadrian's Wall
OS Map 87; NGR NY 813 702

SHAP ABBEY
1½m W of Shap village, S of Penrith, Cumbria

SHERBORNE OLD CASTLE
½m E of Sherborne, Dorset Tel: (093581) 2730

SIBSEY TRADER WINDMILL
½m W of Sibsey, 5m N of Boston, Lincolnshire Tel: (0205) 750036

SILBURY HILL
1m W of West Kennet, near Avebury, Wiltshire
OS Map 173; NGR SU 100 685

SILCHESTER ROMAN CITY WALL
1m E of Silchester, 11m NW of Reading, Hampshire
OS Map 175; NGR SU 643 624

SIR BEVIL GRANVILLE'S MONUMENT, CHARLCOMBE
Landsdown Hill, 4m NW of Bath, Avon
OS Map 172; NGR ST 721 703

SKIPSEA CASTLE
W of Skipsea, 8m S of Bridlington, Humberside
OS Map 107; NGR TA 165 3551

SOUTHAMPTON: 58 FRENCH STREET
In French Street, between Castle Way and Town Quay, Southampton, Hampshire

SPOFFORTH CASTLE
Spofforth, 3½m SE of Harrogate, North Yorkshire

STANTON DREW STONE CIRCLES AND COVE
Circles: E of Stanton Drew; Cove: in garden of The Druid's Arms, Stanton Drew, 6m S of Bristol, Avon
OS Map 172; Circles ST 601 634; Cove ST 598 633

STANWICK IRON AGE FORTIFICATIONS
Stanwick, near Aldbrough, 5m W of Darlington, North Yorkshire
OS Map 92; NGR NZ 179 112

STEETON HALL GATEWAY
W of South Milford, 8m S of Tadcaster, North Yorkshire Tel Area Office: (0904) 58626

STOKESAY CASTLE
1m S of Craven Arms, 6m NNW of Ludlow, Shropshire Tel: (05882) 2544

STONEHENGE
2m W of Amesbury, N of Salisbury, Wiltshire Tel: (0980) 23108
OS Map 184; NGR SU 123 422

STONEY LITTLETON LONG BARROW
1m S of Wellow, 4m S of Bath, Avon
OS Map 172; NGR ST 735 573

STOTT PARK BOBBIN MILL
N of Newby Bridge at S end of Lake Windermere, Cumbria Tel: (0448) 31087

SUTTON SCARSDALE HALL
Sutton Scarsdale, between Chesterfield and Bolsover, Derbyshire

TATTERSHALL COLLEGE
Off Market Place, Tattershall, NW of Boston, Lincolnshire

TEMPLE CHURCH, BRISTOL
Off Victoria Street, Bristol, Avon

TEMPLE MANOR, STROOD
Knight Road, Strood, near Rochester, Kent Tel: (0634) 718743

THETFORD: CHURCH OF THE HOLY SEPULCHRE
W side of Thetford, off B1107, Norfolk

THETFORD PRIORY
W side of Thetford, near station, Norfolk

THETFORD WARREN LODGE
2m W of Thetford, off B1107, Norfolk

THORNTON ABBEY
6m SE of Barton-upon-Humber, Humberside Tel: (0469) 40357
OS Map 113; NGR TA 115 190

TILBURY FORT
½m E of Tilbury, Essex Tel: (03752) 78489

TINTAGEL CASTLE
By footpath to Tintagel Head, 12m NNE of Wadebridge, Cornwall Tel: (0840) 770328

TITCHFIELD ABBEY
½m N of Titchfield, between Southampton and Portsmouth, Hampshire Tel: (0329) 43016

TOTNES CASTLE
Totnes, W of Paignton, Devon Tel: (0803) 864406

TREGIFFIAN BARROW
2m SE of St Buryan, near Newlyn, Cornwall
OS Map 203: NGR SW 430 245

TRETHEVY STONE QUOIT
1m NE of St Cleer, N of Liskeard, Cornwall
OS Map 201; NGR SX 259 688

TYNEMOUTH CASTLE AND PRIORY
Tynemouth, Tyne and Wear Tel: (0632) 571090

UFFINGTON CASTLE, WHITE HORSE AND DRAGON HILL
Between Swindon and Wantage, Oxfordshire
OS Map 174; NGR SU 301 866

UPNOR CASTLE
Upnor, NE of Rochester, Kent Tel: (0634) 718742

UPPER PLYM VALLEY
4m E of Yelverton, N of Plymouth, Devon Tel Area Office: (0272) 734472 ext 205
OS Map 202

WALL ROMAN SITE
Wall, S of Lichfield, Staffordshire Tel: (0543) 480768

WALLTOWN CRAGS WALL AND TURRET (45a)
1m NE of Greenhead, Northumberland, Hadrian's Wall
OS Map 87; NGR NY 674 664

WALMER CASTLE
S of Walmer, near Dover, Kent Tel: (0304) 364288

WALTHAM ABBEY GATEHOUSE AND BRIDGE
Waltham Abbey, near Enfield, Essex

WARKWORTH CASTLE AND HERMITAGE
Access to Hermitage by boat, or on foot only, Warkworth, 7½m S of Alnwick, Northumberland Tel: (0665) 711423

WARTON OLD RECTORY
Warton, 1m N of Carnforth, N of Lancaster,
Lancashire

WAVERLEY ABBEY
2m SE of Farnham, Surrey

WAYLAND'S SMITHY
S of Compton Beauchamp, between Swindon
and Wantage, Oxfordshire
OS Map 174; NGR SU 281 854

WEETING CASTLE
Weeting, 2m N of Brandon, NNW of Thetford,
Norfolk

WENLOCK PRIORY
Much Wenlock, 11m SE of Shrewsbury,
Shropshire Tel: (0952) 727466

WEST KENNET AVENUE
Avebury, near Marlborough, Wiltshire
OS Map 173; NGR SU 105 695

WEST KENNET LONG BARROW
¾m SW of West Kennet, near Avebury,
Wiltshire
OS Map 173; NGR SU 104 677

WESTMINSTER ABBEY CHAPTER HOUSE
AND PYX CHAMBER
Dean's Yard, Westminster, London SW1
Tel: (01) 222 5897

WINDMILL HILL
1½m NW of Avebury, near Marlborough,
Wiltshire
OS Map 173; NGR SU 086 714

WINSHIELDS WALL AND MILECASTLE
(40)
W of Steel Rigg car park, Northumberland,
Hadrian's Wall
OS Map 87; NGR NY 745 676

WITCOMBE ROMAN VILLA
W of Great Witcombe, 5m SE of Gloucester,
Gloucestershire
OS Map 163; NGR SO 899 144

WITLEY COURT
Great Witley, 10m NW of Worcester, Hereford
and Worcester

WOODHENGE
1½m N of Amesbury, N of Salisbury, Wiltshire
OS Map 184; NGR SU 151 434

WREST PARK HOUSE AND GARDENS
¾ E and Silsoe, near Ampthill, Bedfordshire
Tel: (0525) 60718

WROXETER ROMAN CITY
Wroxeter, 5m E of Shrewsbury, Shropshire
Tel: (074375) 330

YARMOUTH CASTLE
Yarmouth, Isle of Wight Tel: (0983) 760678

WETHERAL PRIORY GATEHOUSE
Wetheral, 6m E of Carlisle, Cumbria

WHALLEY ABBEY GATEHOUSE
Whalley, 6m NE of Blackburn, Lancashire

WHARRAM PERCY CHURCH AND
DESERTED MEDIEVAL VILLAGE
½m S of Wharram le Street, 6m SE of Malton,
North Yorkshire Tel Area Office: (0904) 58626
OS Map 100; NGR SE 859 645

WHEELDALE ROMAN ROAD
S of Goathland, 7m S of Whitby, North
Yorkshire
OS Map 94; NGR SE 805 975

WHITBY ABBEY
Whitby, North Yorkshire Tel: (0947) 603568

WHITE LADIES PRIORY
1m SW of Boscobel House, 8m NW of
Wolverhampton, Shropshire

WILLOWFORD BRIDGE ABUTMENT
Willowford Farm, ¾m W of Gilsland, Cumbria,
Hadrian's Wall
OS Map 86; NGR NY 629 664

WINCHESTER PALACE
Corner of Clink Street and Storey Street,
Southwark, London SE1

INDEX